T0346936

LÜTZEN

GREAT BATTLES

LÜTZEN

PETER H. WILSON

OXFORD
UNIVERSITY PRESS

OXFORD
UNIVERSITY PRESS

Great Clarendon Street, Oxford, OX2 6DP,
United Kingdom

Oxford University Press is a department of the University of Oxford.
It furthers the University's objective of excellence in research, scholarship,
and education by publishing worldwide. Oxford is a registered trade mark of
Oxford University Press in the UK and in certain other countries

Published in the United States of America by Oxford University Press
198 Madison Avenue, New York, NY 10016, United States of America

British Library Cataloguing in Publication Data
Data available

Library of Congress Control Number: 2017941115

ISBN 978–0–19–964254–0

Printed in Great Britain by
Clays Ltd, St Ives plc

For Margaret Micrander

FOREWORD

For those who practise war in the twenty-first century the idea of a 'great battle' can seem no more than the echo of a remote past. The names on regimental colours or the events commemorated at mess dinners bear little relationship to patrolling in dusty villages or waging 'wars amongst the people'. Contemporary military doctrine downplays the idea of victory, arguing that wars end by negotiation not by the smashing of an enemy army or navy. Indeed it erodes the very division between war and peace, and with it the aspiration to fight a culminating 'great battle'.

And yet to take battle out of war is to redefine war, possibly to the point where some would argue that it ceases to be war. Carl von Clausewitz, who experienced two 'great battles' at first hand—Jena in 1806 and Borodino in 1812—wrote in *On War* that major battle is 'concentrated war', and 'the centre of gravity of the entire campaign'. Clausewitz's remarks related to the theory of strategy. He recognized that in practice armies might avoid battles, but even then the efficacy of their actions relied on the latent threat of fighting. Winston Churchill saw the importance of battles in different terms, not for their place within war but for their impact on historical and national narratives. His forebear, the Duke of Marlborough, commanded in four major battles and named his palace after the most famous of them, Blenheim, fought in 1704. Battles, Churchill wrote in his biography of Marlborough, are 'the principal milestones in secular history'. For him 'Great battles, won or lost, change the entire course of events, create new standards of values, new moods, new atmospheres, in armies and nations, to which all must conform'.

Clausewitz's experience of war was shaped by Napoleon. Like Marlborough, the French emperor sought to bring his enemies to battle. However, each lived within a century of the other, and they fought their wars in the same continent and even on occasion on adjacent ground. Winston Churchill's own experience of war, which spanned the late nineteenth-century colonial conflicts of the British Empire as well as two world wars, became increasingly distanced from the sorts of battle he and Clausewitz described. In 1898 Churchill rode in a cavalry charge in a battle which crushed the Madhist forces of the Sudan in a single day. Four years later the British commander at Omdurman, Lord Kitchener, brought the South African War to a conclusion after a two-year guerrilla conflict in which no climactic battle occurred. Both Churchill and Kitchener served as British cabinet ministers in the First World War, a conflict in which battles lasted weeks, and even months, and which, despite their scale and duration, did not produce clear-cut outcomes. The 'Battle' of Verdun ran for all but one month of 1916 and that of the Somme for five months. The potentially decisive naval action at Jutland spanned a more traditional twenty-four-hour timetable but was not conclusive and was not replicated during the war. In the Second World War, the major struggle in waters adjacent to Europe, the 'Battle' of the Atlantic, was fought from 1940 to early 1944.

Clausewitz would have called these twentieth-century 'battles' campaigns, or even seen them as wars in their own right. The determination to seek battle and to venerate its effects may therefore be culturally determined, the product of time and place, rather than an inherent attribute of war. The ancient historian Victor Davis Hanson has argued that seeking battle is a 'western way of war' derived from classical Greece. Seemingly supportive of his argument are the writings of Sun Tzu, who flourished in warring states in China between two and five centuries before the birth of Christ, and who pointed out that the most effective way of waging war was to avoid the risks and dangers of actual fighting. Hanson has provoked strong criticism: those who argue that wars can be won without battles are not only to be found in Asia. Eighteenth-century European commanders, deploying armies in close-order formations in order to deliver concentrated fires, realized that the destructive consequences of battle for their own troops could be self-defeating. After the First World War, Basil Liddell Hart developed a theory of strategy which he called 'the indirect approach', and suggested that manoeuvre might substitute for hard fighting, even if its success still relied on the inherent threat of battle.

The winners of battles have been celebrated as heroes, and nations have used their triumphs to establish their founding myths. It is precisely for these reasons that their legacies have outlived their direct political consequences. Commemorated in painting, verse, and music, marked by monumental memorials, and used as the way points for the periodization of history, they have enjoyed cultural afterlives. These are evident in many capitals, in place names and statues, not least in Paris and London. The French tourist who finds himself in a London taxi travelling from Trafalgar Square to Waterloo Station should reflect on his or her own domestic peregrinations from the Rue de Rivoli to the Gare d'Austerlitz. Today's Mongolia venerates the memory of Genghis Khan while Greece and Macedonia scrap over the rights to Alexander the Great.

This series of books on 'great battles' tips its hat to both Clausewitz and Churchill. Each of its volumes situates the battle which it discusses in the context of the war in which it occurred, but each then goes on to discuss its legacy, its historical interpretation and reinterpretation, its place in national memory and commemoration, and its manifest-ations in art and culture. These are not easy books to write. The victors were more often celebrated than the defeated; the effect of loss on the battlefield could be cultural oblivion. However, that point is not universally true: the British have done more over time to mark their defeats at Gallipoli in 1915 and Dunkirk in 1940 than their conquerors on both occasions. For the history of war to thrive and be productive it needs to embrace the view from 'the other side of the hill', to use the Duke of Wellington's words. The battle the British call Omdurman is for the Sudanese the battle of Kerreri; the Germans called Waterloo 'la

Belle Alliance' and Jutland Skagerrak. Indeed the naming of battles could itself be a sign not only of geographical precision or imprecision (Kerreri is more accurate but as a hill rather than a town is harder to find on a small-scale map), but also of cultural choice. In 1914 the German general staff opted to name their defeat of the Russians in East Prussia not Allenstein (as geography suggested) but Tannenberg, in order to claim revenge for the defeat of the Teutonic Knights in 1410.

Military history, more than many other forms of history, is bound up with national stories. All too frequently it fails to be comparative, to recognize that war is a 'clash of wills' (to quote Clausewitz once more), and so omits to address both parties to the fight. Cultural difference and, even more, linguistic ignorance can prevent the historian considering a battle in the round; so too can the availability of sources. Levels of literacy matter here, but so does cultural survival. Often these pressures can be congruent but they can also be divergent. Britain enjoys much higher levels of literacy than Afghanistan, but in 2002 the memory of the two countries' three wars flourished in the latter, thanks to an oral tradition, much more robustly than in the former, for whom literacy had created distance. And the historian who addresses cultural legacy is likely to face a much more challenging task the further in the past the battle occurred. The opportunity for invention and reinvention is simply greater the longer the lapse of time since the key event.

All historians of war must, nonetheless, never forget that, however rich and splendid the cultural legacy of a great battle, it was won and lost by fighting, by killing and being killed. The battle of Waterloo has left as abundant a footprint as any, but the general who harvested most of its glory reflected on it in terms which have general applicability, and carry across time in their capacity to capture a universal truth. Wellington wrote to Lady Shelley in its immediate aftermath: 'I hope to God I have fought my last battle. It is a bad thing to be always fighting. While in the thick of it I am much too occupied to feel anything; but it is wretched just after. It is quite impossible to think of glory. Both mind and feelings are exhausted. I am wretched even at the moment of victory, and I always say that, next to a battle lost, the greatest misery is a battle gained.' Readers of this series should never forget the immediate suffering caused by battle, as well as the courage required to engage in it: the physical courage of the soldier, sailor, or warrior, and the moral courage of the commander, ready to hazard all on its uncertain outcomes.

HEW STRACHAN

ACKNOWLEDGEMENTS

Historians are never really 'lone scholars', and I am pleased to acknowledge the assistance of a great many good people who have helped me in the research, writing, and production of this book. Margaret Micrander kindly devoted many hours to translating Swedish material, giving me access to rich resources well beyond my own rudimentary reading knowledge of that language. The staff of the Stadtarchiv Lützen were particularly welcoming and helpful, notably Maik Reichel and Frau Quente. Whilst in Lützen, Philipp Rösner kindly drove me out to the monument and chapel, greatly speeding my walk around the battlefield. I am also grateful for the hospitality of Siegrid Westphal and Joachim Arenth who gave me a chance to visit more of Thuringia. That part of my research was facilitated by a grant from the Faculty of Arts and Social Sciences at the University of Hull where I then worked. Anna Maria Forssberg of the Swedish Army Museum provided helpful advice during the initial stages of my research. I am grateful to Rick Schneid, Steve Murdoch, Adam Marks, and Ryan Crimmins who all provided invaluable copies of documents or further references.

PETER H. WILSON

CONTENTS

LIST OF ILLUSTRATIONS

LIST OF MAPS

ABBREVIATIONS

BA	H. Hallwich (ed.), *Briefe und Akten zur Geschichte Wallensteins* (1630–4) (4 vols, Vienna, 1912)
Col.	Colonel
GAV	Gustav-Adolf-Verein
HA	Hatzfeldt-Wildenberg Archive, Schloss Schönstein
Lt.Col.	Lieutenant Colonel
Maj.Gen.	Major General
SAL	Stadt Archiv Lützen

1

Introduction

The battle of Lützen between the imperial and Swedish armies was fought about 19 km southwest of Leipzig in Saxony, Germany, on Tuesday 16 November 1632. It was neither the largest nor the bloodiest battle of the Thirty Years War (1618–48), Europe's most destructive conflict prior to the twentieth-century world wars, but it is certainly the best remembered today. This book addresses why that is the case and, in doing so, seeks to reconstruct the battle as far as is possible, to locate it within its wider historical context, and to explore its place in military history, together with its cultural and political legacy.

The picture that will emerge departs in several ways from the received image of both Lützen and the Thirty Years War. The human past is complex, and ambiguous stories are hard to remember. It is both more convenient and often more expedient for subsequent generations to fashion simpler narratives more in tune with their current concerns, than to remember and accept uncomfortable truths. Those viewing events from a distance, such as English speakers watching the Thirty Years War rage across Europe, may see things more clearly than the participants, but also may have less desire to engage with complexities which do not concern them or their descendants so directly. Simplified narratives often begin as genuine attempts at concise and lucid explanations, but can become increasingly detached from actual evidence as they get subsumed within stories of other developments, such as the emergence of Europe's sovereign state system.

The Thirty Years War has been remembered primarily as a bloody religious war which began in the Holy Roman Empire before allegedly spiralling out of control and engulfing most of Europe. Supposedly, it finally burnt itself out through mutual exhaustion, paving the way for the Peace of Westphalia which is widely regarded as the birth of a new secular international order. English-speaking historians have generally followed the lead established by contemporary British observers who saw the war as a struggle between an evil Austrian Habsburg emperor seeking to impose Catholicism and valiant Protestant Germans fighting for their religious 'freedom'. Aided by the 'mercenary' general, Albrecht Wenzel Eusebius von Wallenstein, the Habsburgs finally had complete victory in their grasp when the German Protestants were 'saved' by the Swedish king, Gustavus Adolphus, who invaded the Empire in June 1630. Over the next two years, Gustavus won a string of spectacular victories which convinced later generations of military historians not only that he was one of the world's greatest generals, but that Sweden had 'revolutionized' war making.

Lützen became central to this received image, because it was where the Swedish Protestant 'hero-king' 'met his death in the hour of victory'.[1] However, unlike Yorktown (1781), Waterloo (1815), or Königgrätz (1866), Lützen did not end a conflict or even mark a significant turning point in the Thirty Years War, which continued for another sixteen years. It did not repel an invasion like Marathon (490 BCE), Trafalgar (1805), or the Battle of Britain (1940). It was extremely hard-fought, with over a quarter of the combatants being killed or seriously wounded during the nine hours of fighting, but the bloodletting did not constitute a heroic 'last stand' like Thermopylai (480 BCE), Little Big Horn (1876), Isandlwana (1879), or Dien Bien Phu (1954). Nor was Lützen 'decisive' in the sense of a clear-cut victory with immediate tangible strategic and political results, unlike Naseby (1645) or Blenheim (1704). Given these comparisons, it is fair to ask why so much significance has been attached to it and why it is still commemorated annually today.

The battle in 1632 was not the only one fought at Lützen. Napoleon scored a costly tactical victory over a combined Prussian and Russian army on 2 May 1813 just 4 km south of the scene of the earlier action.

Both are commemorated in large dioramas in the town's museum, with the Napoleonic battle represented by 5,500 miniature figures, or around 1,900 more than the one depicting the earlier engagement. While each has an important place in local heritage, only the first has secured a prominent place in history, while the second remains a footnote to the campaign which ended Napoleon's rule in Germany at the Battle of the Nations in Leipzig five months later.

The contrast between these two battles provides an opportunity to reflect on what makes a great historical 'event'. Neither ended a war or produced a major shift in international relations, yet the first battle of Lützen found an immediate echo in image and print, and became the object of political and historical disputes. Though its outcome has always remained contested, it is generally remembered as a great Swedish or, more broadly, 'Protestant' triumph thought worthy of official public commemoration and a firm place in military history. To study Lützen's legacy is to explore how such events are constantly rewritten as elements of propaganda, religious and national identity, and professional military culture. More specifically, the battle exemplifies how the Thirty Years War is remembered and how it has been written into wider military and European history.

Its impact is heightened by the presence of the seventeenth-century's two most famous generals, Wallenstein and Gustavus Adolphus, and above all by the latter's death. Swedish propaganda swiftly fostered the lasting image of the king's sacrifice for the Protestant cause against the spectre of Catholic Habsburg 'universal monarchy'. This heightened the confessional element in Swedish rhetoric, contributing to the general interpretation of the Thirty Years War as the last and most destructive of Europe's 'religious wars'. While confession played a part in Sweden's motives, most Germans had regarded its intervention in the Holy Roman Empire two years before as a foreign invasion. The image of selfless sacrifice was polished over the next sixteen years to legitimate Sweden's substantial territorial acquisitions in Germany that were confirmed by the Peace of Westphalia. The confessional dimension continued into the nineteenth century, becoming overlaid by the struggle between Catholic Austria and Protestant Prussia for mastery of Germany.

The fact that Lützen was and has remained a predominantly Lutheran town assisted the development of a culture of public remembrance. After several near misses whilst campaigning in Catholic Poland, Gustavus narrowly escaped again whilst attacking Ingolstadt in Bavaria in April 1632 when his horse was killed beneath him.[2] His death on Catholic soil would have inhibited the kind of commemoration later associated with Lützen. He would not have been forgotten, but his memory would have become detached from the actual location of his death. It is this physical connection to the battlefield that first attracted wider attention during the eighteenth century and led to religious services at Lützen held annually since 1832 on 6 November in line with the old Julian calendar used by European Protestants until around 1700.

Changes in the way Gustavus' death has been remembered allow us to see how society has interpreted the notion of 'sacrifice' since the seventeenth century. The king's death has remained largely in its early modern form as an individual sacrifice of a hero-king and Protestant martyr, in contrast to the twentieth-century concept of collective sacrifice associated with the mass slaughter of the two world wars. Yet, Gustavus' continued prominence as a recognizable historical figure has contributed to the stronger memory of Lützen, in contrast to most other battles of the Thirty Years War (except, perhaps, White Mountain in 1620). Gustavus thus serves as a symbolic link to what is now clearly perceived as a distant pre-modern past.

Lützen's place in military history has even wider resonance. Gustavus is widely credited as the 'father' of the standing army; even of 'modern warfare'. His martial qualities were already emphasized by Swedish wartime propaganda, but what secured his reputation was the seal of approval by Napoleon and later generals. His campaigns became a core element of the curricula in nineteenth-century staff colleges, as well as in standard accounts of the rise of 'Western' warfare, not least through the influential 'military revolution' thesis. The battle marked

4

the climactic end of what seemed a lightning campaign of conquest since Gustavus' landing in northern Germany in June 1630 and which appeared to demonstrate the merits of the strategy and tactics of decision over those of attrition practised by Wallenstein.

Chapter 2 explores the deeper historical context for the battle by explaining the outbreak of the Thirty Years War and outlining its course until Sweden's intervention in 1630. Understanding what the war was about provides the necessary background for the discussion of the battle's legacy later in the book. Chapter 3 explains why the battle was fought by examining Gustavus' campaigns across 1630–2, as well as the wider network of alliances the Swedish king was trying to construct. Any attempt to reconstruct the battle itself is hindered by the hagiography of Gustavus as military innovator and Protestant saviour, as well as by the simple fact that it was fought in fog as well as in gunsmoke. Scarcely any of the contemporary accounts agree. Nonetheless, as Chapter 4 will show, such a reconstruction is worth attempting, because it is often the points of disagreement which have proved important for how Lützen is remembered. Chapter 5 assesses the battle's meaning for military history, beginning with its immediate aftermath before examining its place in debates about wider developments in warfare and military institutions. The discussion will build on the material presented across Chapters 2 to 4 to argue that the way Lützen came to be remembered greatly distorted perceptions of Gustavus' actual significance as a general and as a military innovator. Chapter 6 explains how and why Lützen became a site of a particular form of Protestant and national remembrance culture, and charts how this has persisted to the present.

2

Context

The Thirty Years War

Causes

The battle of Lützen occurred roughly midway through the prolonged and destructive Thirty Years War. The causes, meaning, and even the dating of this conflict have been interpreted in many ways which have affected how Lützen has been remembered. For most contemporaries, the war was a distinct conflict beginning in May 1618 and ending in the Peace of Westphalia of October 1648. Other, later writers have often subsumed it within wider, longer-running struggles, especially those between France and the two branches of the Habsburg dynasty ruling Austria and Spain, or simply a symptom of a greater 'General Crisis' caused variously by climatic or economic change affecting Europe or even the entire globe. Regardless of their specific approach, most interpretations present the war as initially about religious or political issues but which subsequently spiralled out of control, descending into 'meaningless violence' before ending in mutual exhaustion.[1] This is certainly how the war was remembered in its immediate aftermath and has been central to the way Lützen has been commemorated with Gustavus Adolphus' death supposedly marking the end of the end of the age of principle and coherent strategy. However, this memory is false and misleading. Though it may seem a diversion, these misunderstandings need to be corrected before we can examine the battle itself.

The Thirty Years War was indeed a distinct conflict, though it was related through issues and the range of participants to other European conflicts, notably Spain's long struggle against the Dutch Revolt (1568–1648), the Franco-Spanish rivalry which spilled into open war 1635–59, and a series of wars between Denmark, Sweden, Poland, and Russia for supremacy over the Baltic. All these struggles had their own causes and trajectories. The origins of the Thirty Years War lay in a dispute amongst the ruling elite of the Holy Roman Empire, Europe's largest state. The exact extent of imperial jurisdiction remained unclear, reflecting the Empire's origins as an idealized, universal Christian political and religious order, but the core lands encompassed not only German-speaking Central Europe, but the five provinces of the kingdom of Bohemia which included Silesia, now in Poland. Switzerland, the Netherlands, and most of northern Italy were also associated with the Empire, though their exact relationship remained disputed. The position of emperor was in the gift of the seven most senior princes, known as 'electors', though in practice only the Austrian Habsburgs were viable candidates. Ruling Austria and Bohemia directly as hereditary possessions, the Habsburgs also held a third of Hungary beyond imperial frontiers to the east. This gave them both the means to sustain the imperial role largely independently of material assistance from the other German princes and imperial cities, and the incentive to discharge that task responsibly, because their own possessions lay directly on the front line with the Ottoman Empire, the Muslim superpower which menaced Christian Europe into the eighteenth century.

Power and status were distributed unequally between the emperor, electors, princes, lesser lords, and imperial cities which collectively constituted the 'imperial Estates' responsible for maintaining public order, upholding justice, and generally governing the Empire and its 23 million or so inhabitants. Like those of other European states, the imperial constitution had evolved as an accretion of charters, commentaries, recorded precedents, and performed rituals, all of which in turn expressed the underlying hierarchical corporate socio-political order. At the most basic level, the Empire was an amalgam of numerous individual communities and lordships bound together within a complex legal web of rights and jurisdictions. Imperial institutions emerged relatively rapidly across the fifteenth and sixteenth centuries with the greater use of writing to fix and demarcate these legal arrangements, and to resolve conflicts between them. The vastness of the Empire combined with the varied regional patterns of dense or sparse settlement had long encouraged rule by consensus rather than centralized command.[2] However, the process of fixing rights and status in written law and formal institutions was incomplete when the Protestant Reformation shattered the medieval unity of religion and law after 1517.

The theological issues posed by the Reformation were politically explosive because of the centrality of religion to morality and life in general. Plurality was profoundly unsettling in an age where truth could only be conceived as singular. Nonetheless, differences of faith alone were insufficient to cause war. The Thirty Years War was waged by regular armies organized and legitimated according to the prevailing laws of war. Official pronouncements and propaganda avoided Holy War rhetoric, and there were no attempts to arm the faithful or encourage sectarian violence. On the contrary, all belligerents emphasized secular control over both war and peace making. The often shocking level of violence after 1618 had complex causes and cannot be explained simply as the consequence of sectarianism.[3]

The Empire's elite were divided confessionally, but the groupings were incomplete and unstable, despite the formation of two overtly sectarian alliance systems in 1608–9. The Protestant Union, established in 1608, was really a vehicle for the ambitions of the Palatine branch of the extensive Wittelsbachs, the Empire's second family after the Habsburgs. The Palatine Wittelsbachs converted to Calvinism in 1560 and were, according to most contemporaries, excluded from the compromise Peace of Augsburg negotiated five years earlier. This peace gave equal rights of ecclesiastical supervision to Catholic and Lutheran imperial Estates, allowing each to oversee the church and religious life within their political jurisdictions. It was deliberately ambiguous, reflecting the Empire's political culture which valued peace above constitutional precision. The treaty text did not define Catholicism or Lutheranism, allowing those who subsequently converted to Calvinism to claim they were entitled to the same legal safeguards on the grounds they were merely continuing Luther's work. This certainly created tension, but actually slowed any slide to war by inhibiting the formation of a solid Protestant front. Lutherans were more alarmed than Catholics by Calvinism's spread since conversions to the new faith were largely from their own ranks, while the political controversies this process generated threatened to undermine the legal guarantees only recently secured in the Peace of Augsburg. Consequently, Saxony, the most powerful Lutheran imperial Estate, led the majority of its co-religionists in boycotting the Union, which remained a collection of minor principalities and cities under an increasingly secretive Palatine leadership.[4]

The rival Bavarian branch of the Wittelsbachs established the Catholic League in 1609 in an attempt to supplant the Palatinate in the upper echelon of the Empire's princely elite. The League attracted a large proportion of those imperial Estates which had remained Catholic, notably the numerous, though individually small, ecclesiastical principalities which collectively constituted what was known as the imperial church. Comprising two-fifths of all imperial Estates, these archbishoprics, bishoprics, abbeys, and priories all had their own territories and political jurisdictions, as well as spiritual oversight of religious affairs throughout those parts of the Empire which remained Catholic. The 1555 Augsburg Peace formally reserved these church lands for Catholic princes, but the ambiguities of that treaty allowed Protestant influence to grow through the conversion of the cathedral and abbey canons who elected each territory's ecclesiastical prince. Many ecclesiastical princes saw League membership as a way of stemming the spread of Protestantism in their territories. However, the Austrian Habsburgs refused to back the League, despite remaining Catholic, because they recognized that their imperial role depended on defusing tensions within the Empire.

The Bohemian Revolt

There was no direct line from the formation of the rival alliances to the Bohemian Revolt a decade later. War was not inevitable and, in some respects, tensions eased after 1612 and the Habsburgs managed to force Bavaria to disband the League in 1617. Nor were imperial politics dictated by external developments, such as the imminent expiry of the Twelve Year Truce signed by Spain with the Protestant Dutch rebels in 1609. Bohemian events also had their own dynamic, as well as being connected in complex ways to wider imperial and European affairs.[5] The famous Defenestration of Prague on 23 May 1618 saw a small group of disgruntled Bohemian aristocrats demonstrate their rejection of Habsburg authority by ejecting three imperial officials from the castle window. The subsequent revolt was neither a national nor a popular religious rising, though it certainly had some features of both.[6]

The revolt took virtually everyone by surprise. Thereafter, what became the Thirty Years War stemmed from the successive failure to contain this and subsequent crises. None of the belligerents thought in terms of total victory. Military operations were always a means to pressure the other party to make peace on favourable terms. All parties legitimated their actions by reference to the imperial constitution which, though contested, remained the common legal framework and was cited as justification by foreign powers as well as the rival factions within the Empire. The conflict was, essentially, a civil war over the interpretation of the imperial constitution since this legitimated the possession and exercise of status, secular jurisdictions, and religious rights.

No one was equipped to fight a protracted struggle and all had to seek the assistance of allies, including from outside the Empire. Such assistance always came at a price, complicating the process of formulating strategy and agreeing peace terms, not least because many allies were promised rewards which first had to be conquered from opponents. The Bohemian aristocrats appealed to Frederick V, Elector Palatine and head of the Protestant Union, to whom they offered their kingdom's crown having already revised the country's constitution to ensure they retained real power. Frederick's acceptance of this poisoned chalice in autumn 1619 spread the war from Bohemia to the Lower Rhine where his core possessions were.[7] Most of his Union allies refused to follow him, and the organization dissolved itself in May 1621, having never formally been a belligerent. The Habsburgs, headed from 1619 by Emperor Ferdinand II, responded by calling on military and financial assistance from their Spanish cousins and the papacy, though the latter refused further support after 1623. More substantial assistance came from Bavaria which was allowed to reestablish the League in October 1619. Bavarian and Spanish forces were instrumental in defeating Frederick V's forces at White Mountain outside Prague in November 1620. However, this victory was also facilitated by the assistance of Saxony in return for a promise that Lutheran princes could keep their rights and possessions provided they did not assist Ferdinand's enemies.

Unlike Lützen, White Mountain was a comprehensive victory which gave the Habsburgs complete control of Bohemia.[8] Ferdinand was now free to implement his interpretation of the conflict as unlawful rebellion. To him, his opponents had forfeited their rights by taking up arms against him. Following their defeat, he was free to confiscate their titles and property and distribute these to compensate those who had served him loyally through the crisis. This process began in 1621 and saw the largest transfer of landed property in Central Europe prior to the Communist era after 1945 as around 1,000 leading families lost their land and were driven into exile. Having transferred Habsburg provinces to Bavarian and Saxon control as an interim measure, Ferdinand eventually agreed to give the prestigious Palatine electoral title and associated lands to Bavaria's Duke Maximilian I in 1623.

The war could have ended then, and indeed Spain withdrew its troops and most of the Empire remained at peace into 1625. However, Ferdinand's expropriation of his opponents created a cause which was soon espoused by other powers pursuing a variety of often partially contradictory agendas. One was Britain's Stuart monarchy which was related by marriage to Frederick V and wished to see him restored to his original Palatine lands. Another was Denmark which saw Ferdinand's redistribution of lands and titles as threatening its own influence in northern Germany.[9] Many in the Empire hoped to avoid further war, not least Ferdinand who, contrary to the received opinion in Anglophone historiography, was naturally cautious and feared God would punish hubris.[10] The newly minted elector Maximilian I believed that opening operations in northern Germany risked merging the Empire's conflict with Spain's struggle against the Dutch which he regarded as entirely separate. He also doubted that the League could sustain new operations and pressured Ferdinand to increase the small imperial army.

Wallenstein

The result was the appointment of Albrecht von Wallenstein, a relatively junior general, to raise and command a new imperial army additional to the small forces already operating in Hungary, Bohemia, Alsace, and north Italy.[11] This army was raised around a core of units which had already served against Frederick V, but the financial basis reflected the acceptance that the emperor's own resources were insufficient to pay his troops, while the conflict against internal enemies inhibited the use of the Empire's formal tax structure. Those taxes that were available were now reserved for capital expenditure like weaponry and munitions, with the army's pay and supplies being met from 'contributions'. This term covered a wide range of taxes and exactions levied under the threat of violence, rather than negotiated through formal representative institutions. Wallenstein did not invent this system, but he did practise it on an unprecedented scale. The intention was to make it both more measured and systematic by forcing neutral or enemy territories to redirect their existing taxes, often at much higher rates, to maintain parts of the imperial army. This did involve the dispersal of forces to ensure continued payment, but it was

Illustration 1: The classic image of the brooding Wallenstein, engraving after a painting by Van Dyck

relatively limited at this stage in the war. The real problem was that the system diverted taxes direct to Wallenstein's senior commanders and their quartermasters, bypassing the imperial treasury and military administration which might have provided some accountability. In addition to opening opportunities for abuse and graft, contributions lacked any clear sanction through imperial law, and so gave grounds to the charges of Ferdinand's enemies that his rule was tyrannical.

Wallenstein did not intend this system to be permanent. It was an expedient to enlarge the imperial army rapidly to block the intervention of King Christian IV of Denmark, Europe's richest monarch, who was able to raise a substantial army from his lucrative toll revenues. Wallenstein aimed to win without risking battle by confining Christians in northern Germany until he ran out of funds. This strategy of attrition was in stark contrast to that of Jean Tserclaes de Tilly, the League commander, who consistently sought to defeat his opponents in battle. There were other, less obvious differences. Tilly remained in constant correspondence with his political master, Maximilian of Bavaria, who frequently provided detailed instructions.[12] Wallenstein sought and received autonomy, arguing that he had to respond to rapidly changing circumstances. This caused him to act very differently from contemporary figures like Richelieu, Olivares, or Buckingham who all exerted political influence through controlling access to their monarchs at the royal courts of France, Spain, and England, respectively.[13] While Wallenstein could influence decisions through the flow of military information to the emperor, his absence from the imperial court prevented him from cultivating other patrons or supporters. Meanwhile, his personal ambitions were to advance his status by obtaining lands and higher titles. This curtailed his autonomy, since he could not flout the rules of the socio-political order without devaluing the very things he desired. He had to remain deferent to the emperor who alone could legitimate the rewards he sought and the military operations that secured them. Ferdinand granted him a succession of lands in lieu of payment, before enfeoffing him in 1628 with the duchy of Mecklenburg which had been confiscated from its original owner who had backed Denmark. Ultimately, Wallenstein was unable to resolve the paradox of his own achievements: he had become an imperial prince because he was a successful general, yet serving as a general prevented him from enjoying his new status by keeping him constantly in the field.[14]

From 1625 Wallenstein and Tilly operated in uneasy cooperation against Christian IV and his motley assortment of minor north German princes and unreliable French, English, and Dutch backers. By 1628 the Danes had lost their mainland possessions and had sought shelter on their islands. Thinking that the war in the Empire was over, Spain expected Ferdinand to support its plans to defeat the Dutch by creating a new imperial navy and to block French influence by acquiescing to Spanish interference in Mantua, one of the Italian principalities under imperial jurisdiction. Meanwhile, facing a Swedish invasion, the king of Poland also expected help in return for the assistance he had sent Ferdinand during 1618–20. A large part of the imperial army was sent south to Italy, as much to uphold imperial jurisdiction as to assist Spain directly. Another 15,000 men went to Poland where they contributed to the defeat of Gustavus Adolphus at Stuhm in 1629. Maximilian of Bavaria, the other Catholic electors in Cologne and Trier, and Wallenstein all opposed these moves which they feared risked involving the Empire in new conflicts before peace had been fully secured at home.

Ferdinand did follow Wallenstein's advice and granted Denmark generous terms at the Peace of Lübeck in June 1629, restoring all its territory in return for a free hand to settle affairs throughout the Empire. Unfortunately, his attempt to do this through the Edict of Restitution in March 1629 created new problems. The Edict was intended to end the controversy over religious rights in the Empire by imposing a narrowly Catholic interpretation of the terms of the Peace of Augsburg, primarily by summarily ordering the return of church lands allegedly illegally usurped by Protestants since 1555. Many moderate Lutherans like the Saxon elector were not completely opposed to this, but were alarmed that Ferdinand attempted this through a unilateral edict rather than a negotiated settlement. Even Catholics, like Maximilian, believed the emperor had exceeded his powers. Wallenstein opposed the edict, but was widely blamed, because his troops were used to implement it, making it appear simply a device to sustain the inflated imperial army through the confiscation of further lands from the Protestants. Though hostilities had largely ceased by March 1629, the situation in the Empire remained tense when Gustavus Adolphus reignited the war by landing on Usedom Island off the Pomeranian coast on 6 July 1630.

3

The Campaigns of 1630–2

Swedish Intervention and Motives

The reasons behind Sweden's intervention not only form the deeper context for Lützen, but became entwined with remembrance of the battle. Gustavus Adolphus began a major war without a clear 'exit strategy'; a fault shared by many in history. His goals changed over time, clearly expanding in line with his successes across 1631–2.[1] The destruction of many of his papers by fire in 1697 added to the difficulty of disentangling his motives which were often deliberately concealed in his official statements. Intervention was rationalized as the defence of Protestant and 'German' liberties, by which he meant the more radical of the various Protestant interpretations of the imperial constitution. The secular elements dominated propaganda intended for external consumption, whereas religious motives were more prominent in that intended for Swedes which presented the conflict in simplified terms as a struggle between good and evil; a story eagerly conveyed independently by Protestant observers elsewhere, notably in Britain, who saw what they wanted in Sweden's actions.[2]

In practical terms, Gustavus initially intended to set the political clock back to 1618 by restoring the exiled Austrians, Bohemians, and dispossessed German princes like the Elector Palatine and the Duke of Mecklenburg. This objective would directly serve Swedish security interests by rolling back Habsburg gains since 1620 and ensuring that the emperor could not assist Poland or Denmark against Sweden in the future. Less clearly articulated, but no less significant, was the

Map 1: General political and military situation in the Empire, 1630–2

desire of Gustavus and many of his noblemen to be recognized as equals within wider European politics. However, there was no plan to make war simply to satisfy any material aspirations the nobles may have had. War was costly in noble blood. Sweden had a small elite of perhaps 400 adult males, and the conflicts with Poland since 1621 had already taken a heavy human toll. It was certainly hoped that war in Germany would pay for itself, and that the seizure of the north German Baltic ports would help finance Sweden's international influence. Sweden already replaced Denmark in 1628 as protector of the Pomeranian port of Stralsund which Wallenstein had unsuccessfully besieged with the intention of using it as a naval base against Denmark. Stralsund's council was coerced into 'inviting' longer-term Swedish protection, and the city was the only German community to openly request Swedish assistance prior to Gustavus' invasion.[3]

Swedish intervention was unwelcome to Saxony and Brandenburg, the most prominent Protestant imperial Estates which were in the midst of negotiations with their moderate Catholic counterparts to induce Ferdinand to modify or suspend the Edict of Restitution. While there is no evidence that Ferdinand did not take the Swedish invasion seriously, his refusal to compromise on the Edict lost his best chance to rally broader German support.[4] Nonetheless, his decision is understandable. Sweden's military record had been mixed, its Polish war had ended in stalemate and Gustavus had only extracted himself thanks to French diplomatic assistance in negotiating a truce in September 1629. From the perspective of 1630, there seemed no pressing reason for Ferdinand to abandon a decade of political and religious gains when he still had the most powerful army the Empire had ever seen.

However, an immediate military response was delayed by Ferdinand's desire to remain within the Empire's consensual political culture by meeting the electors at their congress in Regensburg which opened just three days before Gustavus landed. The discussions were intended to complete Ferdinand's settlement of the Empire's problems on his own terms, but the changed circumstances forced him to compromise with the electors who saw Wallenstein's army as a threat to the constitutional order. Wallenstein was dismissed and eventually replaced by Tilly who was to head a force of 60,000 men, one-third of whom were to be the still autonomous army of the League. These arrangements took till 9 November 1630 to finalize, during which the morale of both the imperial and League armies continued to deteriorate. Though the planned troop reductions were not implemented, Tilly inherited only 53,000 imperialists, of whom only 9,000 were in Pomerania. The 30,000 or so League troops were scattered across northwest Germany, while another 55,000 imperialists were in north Italy where they had contracted the plague.

Gustavus landed with 13,600 men while a further 5,000 were already nearby in Stralsund, giving him local superiority. Further reinforcements pushed his field strength to 29,000 by September, while another 40,000 or so garrisoned Sweden and its Baltic empire against possible Danish or Polish attacks. Crucially, Sweden's powerful navy allowed him to choose his landing site which was consolidated during July 1630 through the capture of the remaining Pomeranian islands.[5] The Swedes were resupplied by sea, whereas the imperialists were unable to find sufficient supplies in Pomerania which had been exhausted by three years of Wallenstein's contributions.

Most accounts concentrate on Gustavus' skill in breaking out from his bridgehead against seemingly impossible odds. In fact, the strategic situation remained stalemated for over a year. Sweden was a poor country incapable of financing a major war. French assistance covered only a fraction of the real costs. The same dearth of supplies hindering Tilly's countermeasures also made it difficult for Gustavus to move far from the coast. More fundamentally, Gustavus urgently needed German support to augment his army and legitimate his presence as more than a foreign invader. Yet, without a clear victory, few imperial Estates were prepared to declare openly for him, even if they wanted to. Despite being Gustavus' brother-in-law, the elector of Brandenburg immediately realized that the Swedish presence in Pomerania threatened his own hopes of inheriting that duchy from its childless duke.

However, Gustavus could not advance deeper into Germany unless he was sure that Brandenburg and Saxony would not back the emperor.

Ferdinand's refusal to compromise compelled the Saxon elector Johann Georg and his Brandenburg colleague to convene a new Protestant alliance in Leipzig in February 1631. Intended as a neutral third party, the alliance agreed to raise 40,000 troops to add weight to their demands that Ferdinand modify the Edict of Restitution. The new organization further imperilled the imperial army's precarious finances, because members of the Leipzig Convention refused to pay taxes or contributions to Tilly who felt obliged to respect their neutrality for fear of pushing them into the arms of Sweden. In the meantime, Tilly was forced to scatter his forces, partly to ease the supply situation, but also to watch the Leipzig members, notably Hessen-Kassel which was (rightly) suspected of inclining towards Sweden. He was further hampered because he lacked the autonomy previously enjoyed by Wallenstein. Though he now commanded both the imperial and League armies, the two remained administratively and politically separate, obliging Tilly to seek instructions from Ferdinand and Maximilian.[6] Maximilian's reluctance to see League units venture into northeast Germany forced Tilly to refrain from his usual strategy of seeking battle.

Gustavus attempted to break out of Pomerania in January 1631, switching his forces back and forth between the Oder river to the east and Mecklenburg in the west, trying to outwit Tilly and score a success sufficient to convince the Leipzig Convention to join him. This compelled him to take risks, notably storming the heavily defended town of Frankfurt on the Oder on 13 April without a preliminary siege. None of this disrupted Tilly who had joined the League detachment under General Pappenheim to besiege Magdeburg, an important city on the river Elbe. Like Stralsund, Magdeburg has entered history as a symbol of Protestant defiance to Catholic-imperial tyranny, not least because it had already opposed Emperor Charles V in the mid-sixteenth century. However, also like Stralsund the local situation was far more complex, reflecting the deeper controversies in imperial politics.[7] There were many in the city who preferred an accommodation with the emperor, something which Wallenstein had already offered since 1627 and Tilly repeated in 1631. Others, for a variety of reasons, declared openly for Gustavus on 1 August 1630, making Magdeburg the first place to do so after his landing in Pomerania. The loss of Magdeburg would represent a serious setback, most likely deterring the Leipzig Convention from backing Sweden. Yet, Gustavus refused to risk moving that far south without firm support from Brandenburg and Saxony. Fearing the city would surrender, he sent a loyal officer, Colonel Dietrich von Falkenberg, to stiffen the defence. Falkenberg continually promised the Magdeburgers that help was on its way, inducing them to reject Tilly's repeated offers to accept surrender. Around 22,000 imperial and League troops launched an assault early on 20 May 1631, swiftly overcoming the depleted defenders. In the process, the city caught fire and the ensuing conflagration and sack saw the deaths of around four-fifths of the 25,000 inhabitants in what was the worst slaughter in an already brutal war.

Magdeburg's destruction was a strategic and public relations disaster of the first order, forcing the normally reticent Tilly to publish an official account to refute charges he had personally ordered the atrocity. The catastrophe allowed pro-Swedish pamphleteers to deflect criticism of Falkenberg's role and Gustavus' failure to relieve the city. The Swedish king now seized the moral high ground, citing Magdeburg as a consequence of the failure of German Protestants to join him. There was not a moment to waste, because Ferdinand had finally lost patience with the Leipzig Convention which he openly denounced on 14 May. At that point, Egon von Fürstenberg arrived with over 20,000 imperialists from Mantua and was able to execute the emperor's orders to disarm the Convention's south German members by August. Meanwhile, the League congress agreed new funding to recruit its army back to full strength and add a further 9,000 on top.[8] At last it looked as if Tilly would have the forces he needed to throw the Swedes back into the Baltic.

Gustavus forced Brandenburg literally at gun point to allow him access through its territory on 20 June, but still hesitated to confront

Tilly without firm Saxon support and so deployed on that electorate's northern border to pressure it into an alliance. Tilly meanwhile camped to the west, hoping the elector would declare for the emperor instead. However, the arrival of Fürstenberg and the imperial contingent from Italy exacerbated Tilly's already precarious supply situation. Unable to remain any longer in the devastated area around Magdeburg, Tilly pushed some units into Saxony on 5 September. A week later, Johann Georg finally declared for Sweden. The alliance was unlike any other signed by Gustavus who always insisted on absolute control of his allies' territories and military assets, as well as expecting them to help finance Sweden's army. It was a measure of Saxony's political importance that Gustavus formally accepted Johann Georg as an equal. In practice, he knew that Saxon friendship was only a tactical device to pressure Ferdinand into concessions over the Edict and that if the emperor ever granted these, Saxony would most likely defect. However, Saxony was the heartland of the Protestant Reformation and the most prominent of all Protestant imperial Estates. Its adherence to Sweden was essential to legitimate Gustavus' presence in the Empire.

More immediately, Johann Georg brought 16,000 troops, the largest of the German armies after that of the League. These soldiers joined Gustavus' 23,000 men to confront Tilly's 37,000 at Breitenfeld, just northwest of Leipzig on 17 September.[9] The ensuing battle was one of the largest of the Thirty Years War and involved twice as many combatants as Lützen. Despite being outnumbered, Tilly employed his customary offensive tactics, whereas Gustavus initially fought a defensive battle. Fürstenberg on the imperial right routed the Saxon army opposite, exposing the Swedish centre under Gustav Horn who reacted quickly, repositioning his men at right angles to meet the imperial right hook. As a result, Tilly's army became overextended, especially as Pappenheim on the left had failed to defeat the Swedish right. Gustavus timed his counterattack perfectly, breaking the imperial centre and causing Tilly's army to disintegrate. In all, Tilly lost 7,000 dead and 9,000 prisoners compared to a combined Swedish–Saxon loss of 5,000.

Unlike Lützen, Breitenfeld immediately transformed the political and strategic situation. There was no need for Swedish propagandists to exaggerate what was an utterly convincing victory, the impact of which was magnified by the loss of nerve among the imperial and League leadership. Other than detaching Pappenheim with a small force to protect Westphalia, Tilly abandoned northern Germany and retreated south. The war spread rapidly, becoming general across most of the Empire, whereas previous fighting had been restricted to a few regions at a time. Gustavus divided his forces, sending trusted commanders with small Swedish detachments in all directions to combine with the minor German princes, counts, and cities which now declared openly for him. The expansion of the war fuelled his ambitions which, though never spelled out coherently, now focused on subverting the imperial constitution as a means of extending Sweden's Baltic empire into central and southern Germany. It is doubtful that he ever wanted to seize the imperial title himself, since this was too closely associated with Catholicism, but he did force allies and conquered territories to renounce feudal subordination to the emperor and accept an equivalent relationship to the Swedish crown.[10]

A sign of Gustavus' growing ambitions is his decision to ignore previous promises to France not to attack the territories of the Catholic League, arguing that the presence of League units at Breitenfeld meant these were now clearly enemies.[11] Ten days after Breitenfeld he plunged southwest through the mountainous and wooded terrain of Thuringia to strike deep into the Catholic heartland of Franconia, capturing Würzburg on 15 October, the first of many church lands seized over the following few months. If Breitenfeld convinced Protestant Germans that Gustavus was a viable protector, Würzburg added the lure of rich rewards. Mirroring Habsburg practice after White Mountain, Gustavus rewarded his loyal officers and German collaborators by 'donating' church lands and other properties confiscated from aristocrats serving in the imperial and League forces. This policy proved far more important in attracting and retaining support than the limited French subsidies or even the many thousands of Britons who joined the Swedish army, either as volunteers or in the official contingents sent by the Stuarts in the vain hope Gustavus would restore the Palatinate to Frederick V. The 'Swedish' army in the Empire rose from 45,000 men at the end of 1630 to 100,000 by March 1632, largely through the provision of new regiments directly by German collaborators, in addition to a further 30,000 men in the Saxon, Brandenburg, and Hessen-Kassel forces still serving under their own generals. However, the donations created a new set of winners and losers to join those from the Habsburg policies of the 1620s, further complicating the process of settling the war peacefully.

There were also adverse strategic consequences. The dispersal of Swedish forces across the Empire was driven by the need to retain allies rather than any grand design to converge on key targets like Vienna. German support was almost always conditional on Gustavus' ability to advance local objectives. The rulers of Hessen-Kassel, Baden-Durlach, Württemberg, Brunswick, and numerous other allies resented his attempts to control them and instead sought to conquer neighbouring Catholic lands or settle long-standing scores. The war rapidly assumed a regionalized character as the various nominally 'Swedish' commanders pursued their own agendas against detachments of the League and imperial armies. Gustavus was forced to detach trusted generals and reliable Swedish or Finnish regiments not merely to stiffen these regional armies, but to ensure some compliance with his own directives. Other units had to be posted to secure the lines of communication back to the Pomeranian bridgehead which was now earmarked as a permanent Swedish acquisition. Consequently, the royal army under Gustavus' direct command rarely exceeded more than 24,000 men, roughly the same as Tilly's field army during the 1620s. Yet, the presence of comparable forces on both sides in several regions simultaneously greatly increased the burden of warfare which in turn was exacerbated by the plague spread by the imperial units returning from Mantua.

Wallenstein's Reappointment

The aftermath of Breitenfeld strained relations between Ferdinand and Maximilian. The elector seriously considered placing the League directly under French protection, but had abandoned this idea by February 1632 when he realized that France could not restrain Sweden. The capture of Bamberg, the second most important Franconian bishopric after Würzburg, clearly demonstrated that Gustavus would not follow French directives to spare League territories. Moreover, Maximilian recognized that he risked losing his new electoral title and lands if he abandoned Ferdinand. His decision to stick by the emperor had immediate consequences. Tilly surprised the Swedes at Bamberg on 9 March, forcing them back in disorder.

Despite this success, Tilly's days as supreme commander were numbered. Ferdinand had already starting taking Wallenstein's military advice in January 1631, and there had been persistent rumours of his imminent reinstatement since the loss of Frankfurt on the Oder that April. The general finally agreed to return for three months on 15 December and immediately set about reorganizing the main section of the imperial army which had retreated into Bohemia after Breitenfeld. His return renewed confidence. Numerous former officers applied for commissions in the new or rebuilt regiments and by April 1632 Wallenstein mustered 50,000 men, whereas Tilly had 26,000 League troops in Bavaria and Pappenheim and another 8,000 in Westphalia and Magdeburg.[12]

Tilly's brief counterattack at Bamberg convinced Gustavus to ignore French concerns and to invade Bavaria. In a series of brilliant manoeuvres, he crossed the river Lech forming Bavaria's western frontier on 15 April 1632. Tilly was mortally wounded, obliging Maximilian to assume personal command of the remaining League forces which retreated into Ingolstadt Fortress. Tilly's death conveniently cleared the last obstacle to Wallenstein's full reinstatement which had been finalized in an agreement concluded at Göllersdorf near Vienna on 13 April.[13] The exact terms are not fully known, because the original copy was most likely destroyed by Habsburg officials after Wallenstein's assassination in 1634. The agreement certainly gave him far wider autonomy than he had enjoyed during his first generalship in 1625–30, including a free hand to decide strategy and to confiscate the properties of the emperor's opponents to fund operations.

Meanwhile, Pappenheim had been made League commander in northwest Germany in December 1631. He cultivated Wallenstein's style of independent command, acting on his own initiative to protect the clutch of Westphalian church lands held by Maximilian's brother, Elector Ferdinand of Cologne. Pappenheim faced the forces of Hessen-Kassel and the Guelph family ruling the two Brunswick duchies of Lüneburg and Wolfenbüttel who all joined Sweden towards the end of 1631 in the hope of conquering the Westphalian bishoprics. Gustavus had despatched reinforcements giving his allies a five-to-one numerical superiority over Pappenheim, but the king found it hard to control his partners, not least because he insisted on doing this by courier. Johan Banér, the most senior Swedish general in the region, would lead Sweden's armies successfully in 1635–41, but at this stage of his career he lacked the authority and experience needed to subordinate the proud German princes to a single will. In a series of brilliant, rapid moves after January 1632, Pappenheim dodged his poorly coordinated opponents as he withdrew troops from isolated fortresses like Magdeburg and Stade in order to reinforce other garrisons or capture new posts on the numerous rivers which cut across northwest Germany. By October, Pappenheim had secured a strategic corridor running east from Hameln through Calenberg, Hildesheim to Wolfenbüttel. With this he both divided the Hessians to the south from the Guelph troops to the north, and freed himself to range from his base in Westphalia eastwards to help Wallenstein's imperial army. Moreover, contrary to the usual trajectory of armies during the war which became progressively weaker over the spring and summer campaign season, Pappenheim tripled his field forces to 16,000, especially through new regiments raised from Walloons from the Spanish Netherlands.[14]

Gustavus' 1632 Campaign

Gustavus' problems with his northwest German allies were replicated throughout Germany. He was a victim of his own success during autumn 1631. The scale of the imperial-League collapse opened a vacuum sucking the Swedes and their new allies in all directions, further regionalizing the war and hindering coordination. The rapidity of the Swedish advance left many of their conquests incomplete. For example, imperial garrisons in the small Franconian towns of Forchheim and Kronach remained to harass communications and tie down the troops of Sweden's local allies. Even in those areas free of enemy troops, the Swedes still met resistance from the local population. The Swedes promised respect for existing arrangements, including Catholic religious rights, and signs of Gustavus' good intentions, such as his attendance at Catholic services in Erfurt and Munich, were widely publicized by propagandists. Yet, toleration was contingent on circumstances, not least the lack of qualified administrators and Protestant clergy to replace local Catholics. Many Catholic officials fled, or refused to cooperate, exacerbating the problems of revenue collection at the point when Swedish demands rose sharply in line with the expanding size of their forces. The decade of imperial-League successes had stoked resentment, especially among exiles prominent among the German and Bohemian officers in the Swedish army. The church lands were treated as conquests. Supply arrangements were no more efficient than those of the imperial and League armies and Gustavus' famous disciplinary code was ignored by his own officers who took what they wanted.[15] Bad treatment extended to allies. Gustavus made fine speeches on his entry into the important Protestant city of Nuremberg on 31 March 1632, but immediately obliged it to surrender its war material from its arsenal and allow its infantry regiment to be incorporated into his own army.[16]

These conditions blunted Gustavus' spring offensive which soon ran out of steam once he broke across the Lech into Bavaria. Maximilian refused to negotiate, and instead abandoned Munich having sent his archive, relics, and much of his treasury to safety in the Alps. Gustavus could range freely across southern Bavaria, but was cut off from the northern half and Franconia beyond, because Bavarian and imperial forces held Ingolstadt, Regensburg, and Passau along the Danube. He was forced to abandon a planned advance into Austria for fear of being separated from his allies in southwest Germany. Undecided what to do, he split his main army, leaving half to hold the gains in southern Bavaria, while retracing his steps to move northwards again in the hope of collecting reinforcements. This proved illusory, since most of his allies and collaborators were busy seeking their own conquests, or were tied down in front of enemy garrisons like those in Forchheim and Kronach.

The Saxons, Gustavus' most important allies, had invaded Bohemia on 4 November 1631, reaching Prague ten days later where they restored the exiles but otherwise behaved badly, alienating the local population.[17] Gustavus was reluctant to reinforce the small Swedish corps with the Saxons for fear his troops would be lost should Johann Georg defect to the emperor. He had forbidden his allies to negotiate separately, but suspected that the Saxon elector was engaged in this through his commander, Armin, who had served previously under Wallenstein.[18] Arnim stopped aiding the exiles and deliberately spared Wallenstein's Bohemian properties from destruction. Wallenstein reciprocated by ensuring Arnim received the pay still owing from his imperial service.

As with all of Wallenstein's secret negotiations, there were doubts over his sincerity, not least because he launched an offensive in May 1632 once he had collected 40,000 men in Moravia around the nucleus of imperial units which survived the previous campaign. In contrast to Pappenheim who had been forced to recruit entirely new regiments, Wallenstein was able to rebuild existing ones, ensuring that the raw recruits were stiffened by a cadre of veterans. He swiftly chased the Saxons out of Bohemia and across the mountains into their electorate. However, he still hoped to persuade them to abandon Gustavus, and so refrained from further attacks. Instead, he left blocking forces to hold Bohemia and Silesia, and marched along the south side of the mountains to Eger (Cheb), the westernmost Bohemian town from where he could threaten Swedish positions in Franconia or reinforce the League army in northern Bavaria. Raiding parties fanned out to unsettle the Swedes; one captured some professors from Nuremberg's famous Protestant university at Altdorf, just east of the city, who had to be rescued by Swedish cavalry.[19]

Alte Veste

The threat to Nuremberg mounted as Maximilian took advantage of Gustavus' indecision and, swallowing his distaste, agreed to cooperate with Wallenstein by moving the bulk of the League field army north to join the imperialists at Waldsassen, just west of Eger on 28 June. It was the first time the elector and the generalissimo had met and both made an effort to get along. Maximilian was careful to address Wallenstein by his princely title as Duke of Mecklenburg and loaned him money for provisions.[20] Together the two had 50,000 men. If they took Nuremberg, they would close the main route between Gustavus and both Saxony and the Swedish bridgehead further north in Pomerania.

Gustavus reacted, but not fast enough, racing north only to find that Maximilian and Wallenstein had already combined, obliging him to retire to Nuremberg where he completed a massive entrenchment around the city in just ten days. Wallenstein and Maximilian arrived outside on 17 July. Though Gustavus had only 18,500 men, they deemed his position too strong to attack, and so moved south around the city to Zirndorf, 10 km to the southwest, where they built their own fortified camp on a hill, secured by the ruined castle of Alte Veste at the northern end.[21] The Regnitz river separated the two armies which called in further detachments in the hope of gaining numerical superiority over the other. Wallenstein lacked the manpower to trap Gustavus completely, but enjoyed significant advantages. His forces drew supplies from Austria and Bohemia, whereas the Swedes were largely shut inside their entrenchments where the situation was exacerbated by the presence of 100,000 refugees from the surrounding countryside. Wallenstein also had five times as many dragoons and light cavalry, and so was better able to interdict supply convoys than the Swedes could disrupt his own. Gustavus' men were soon on half rations.

Informed by Swedish deserters of the dire conditions in Nuremberg, Wallenstein hoped Gustavus would be forced to do something rash. The imperialists captured the last significant Swedish post outside Nuremberg on 5 August, cutting off all major routes northwards to Saxony and Pomerania. However, time was also running out for Wallenstein. It was now high summer and conditions in the imperial camp were becoming unbearable. The 50,000 troops, 25,000 camp followers, and 15,000 cavalry and draught horses produced three tons of excrement daily. Disease was rife and worsened by a horse infection which spread across the entire region north of the Danube. A bold Swedish sortie destroyed a valuable supply convoy of over 1,000 wagons on 9 August. Parts of the imperial-League army were no longer fully operational.

Meanwhile, Wallenstein came under pressure from the emperor to do something about the Saxons. Intimidated by Gustavus, Johann Georg had broken off secret negotiations with Wallenstein on 28 June. As the imperial army then moved west into Franconia, Johann Georg felt sufficiently safe to order Arnim and the main Saxon army of 12,000 men to invade Silesia to the east. As with all Saxon operations, this move was intended to force Ferdinand to offer the concessions Johann Georg felt necessary to secure peace in the Empire. The Swedes had done nothing to allay the elector's fears about their true intentions. On the contrary, Gustavus had now revealed that he intended to keep Pomerania as 'satisfaction' for assisting the cause of 'German liberty'. It was clear the Swedish king intended to displace both the Saxon and Palatine electors as political leader of German

Protestants who were to be marshalled into a *corpus evangelicorum*, or Protestant alliance under Sweden's 'absolute directory'.[22] Johann Georg wanted to avoid this by persuading Ferdinand to restore Lutheran rights and possessions to their state in 1618. Calvinists were to be excluded, which would mean that Bavaria and the emperor could keep many of their gains, especially those at the Palatinate's expense. Additionally, the elector wanted a ban on all partisan alliances to prevent the formation of a new Protestant Union which had proved so divisive in 1608, as well as forcing Bavaria to dissolve the League. Many of these demands were directly in the emperor's own interests, yet Ferdinand was not yet ready to agree, while Johann Georg did not feel safe enough to switch sides until Gustavus had been convincingly defeated in battle. Therefore, Arnim pressed on into Silesia, this time not sparing Wallenstein's personal property. Saxon operations were successful, with Arnim defeating the imperial corps in Silesia at Steinau early in September.[23] News of the Saxon offensive already pushed Wallenstein into detaching 8,000 men under his trusted subordinate, the former Danish general Heinrich Holk, on 15 August to march northeast through Thuringia into southwestern Saxony. Holk in turn sent his Croatian light cavalry under Colonel Marcus Corpes ahead to ravage the Saxon countryside to increase the pressure on Johann Georg to defect on the emperor's terms.[24]

Holk's departure weakened Wallenstein's main army just as detachments from across Germany finally arrived to reinforce Gustavus, including 2,000 Saxons sent by Johann Georg as a sign of his good faith. These reinforcements poured through the gap northwest of Nuremberg left by Holk as he entered Thuringia. By 27 August, Gustavus mustered 45,000 men and 175 guns, the largest army he ever commanded directly, at last giving him a rough parity with the forces of Wallenstein and Maximilian in the Zirndorf camp.[25] Gustavus was disappointed that Wallenstein had not sallied out of his camp to intercept the Swedish reinforcements. However, Wallenstein knew that he still held the advantage since conditions in Nuremberg were only worsened by the arrival of the new troops. His calculation paid off, as Gustavus decided the only way he could force battle was to assault the imperial entrenchments directly. The Swedes seized the small town of Fürth just northwest of Nuremberg to secure a crossing over the Regnitz on 31 August. An artillery bombardment of Wallenstein's camp across the river the following day produced no result. Gustavus finally moved 25,000 men across to a position opposite Alte Veste at the north end of the Zirndorf camp. These attacked early on 3 September, but their efforts were hindered by poor coordination and stiff resistance from the imperial and League troops who were defending the most heavily fortified sector of their position. Gustavus gave up after losing 2,500 killed and wounded compared to around 900 casualties suffered by his enemies. Heavy rain that night ended any prospect of renewing the unequal struggle.

The king hung about for another two weeks to avoid the appearance of having suffered a major reverse. However, his men knew they had been defeated, and 11,000 of them deserted by mid-September. Around 10,000 more had died of disease during the two month stand-off. A further sign of Sweden's deteriorating position was that Gustavus acted to please his German allies by sending peace proposals to Wallenstein. These were wholly unrealistic, expecting the emperor to cede Habsburg territory to satisfy Bavaria and Saxony, whilst allowing Sweden to keep Pomerania and its other German allies to annex the church lands. Wallenstein was to receive the bishopric of Würzburg; a proposal clearly intended as a bribe. The generalissimo refused to be drawn, knowing he still had his opponent on the back foot.[26] Having celebrated the first anniversary of his victory at Breitenfeld on 17 September, Gustavus left a garrison in Nuremberg and marched 35 km westwards to Windsheim where he waited another nine days in vain for Wallenstein to attack him.

The Invasion of Saxony

Wallenstein was praised by the imperial court for his victory at Alte Veste, but the emperor's advisors recognized that it was now too late

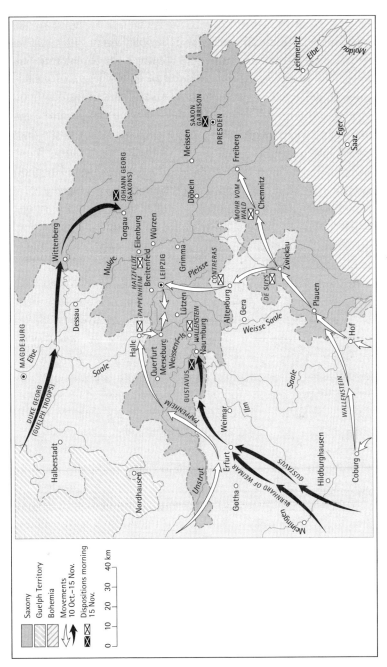

Map 2: Strategic situation, October–November 1632

in the year to accomplish much else. The mood was pessimistic, since it was expected that Gustavus would recover his strength during the winter. The court viewed the continuation of the war into another year with dread, yet Ferdinand still refused to compromise over the Edict of Restitution.[27] Imperial strategy thus remained the same, containing Sweden whilst pressuring Saxony to defect. Wallenstein burned his unhealthy camp on 21 September and headed north through Forchheim to reach Coburg on 8 October. He retained the strategic initiative. Coburg was a key crossroads from where he could cross Thuringia into Saxony whilst still threatening Sweden's garrisons in Franconia, several of which his forces now captured. Meanwhile, Matthias Gallas was despatched ahead with another 10,000 men to reinforce Holk's troops in southwestern Saxony.[28]

Gustavus believed this latest detachment so weakened Wallenstein's main army that it no longer posed an immediate threat. He divided his own forces, sending Bernhard of Weimar north to secure Thuringia and the routes to Saxony with 7,500 men, including the five Saxon cavalry regiments which had served throughout the Alte Veste campaign.[29] Meanwhile, he marched with the rest southwest through Bavaria heading for Swabia where he planned to do exactly as the imperial court feared: rest and rebuild his army during the winter. In fact, this played into Wallenstein's hands, since the generalissimo was now free to move northeast into Saxony to recuperate at the Saxons' expense and add to the pressure on Johann Georg to defect. Maximilian was not prepared to leave Bavaria exposed and insisted on returning south with the League army which now numbered just 6,000 effectives.[30] In view of the threat posed to Bavaria by Gustavus' move south, Wallenstein agreed to lend Maximilian 10,000 imperialists under General Aldringen. In return, Maximilian agreed that Pappenheim's army, largely composed of League units, would pass under Wallenstein's overall command as the generalissimo headed north.[31]

Maximilian and Aldringen headed south on 14 October. Wallenstein set off the following day from Coburg through Thuringia with 18,000 men to join Gallas and Holk in western Saxony. Johann Georg had only 2,000 troops to defend his electorate, because the bulk of the Saxon army under Arnim was still in Silesia. Holk had already captured Chemnitz on 11 October, followed by the rich silver mining town of Freiberg three days later and then Meissen a week after that, directly threatening the capital Dresden. His Croatian cavalry burned five small towns and thirty villages, spreading panic, until orders arrived to switch to a more orderly exploitation of Saxon resources to ensure the army could spend the entire winter in Saxony.[32]

Wallenstein reached Zwickau, about 35 km west of Chemnitz, on 24 October. On Holk's advice, he decided against attacking Dresden, but instead to seize Leipzig, a city of about 15,000 inhabitants which was northeast Germany's largest commercial centre.[33] The city surrendered on 2 November, just three days after the imperialists arrived. Only 18 soldiers and 207 militiamen held out in the Pleissenberg castle under Hans Vopelius. The city council had no jurisdiction over Pleissenberg which belonged directly to the elector, but they feared the consequences of angering Wallenstein so they gave Holk a list of the militiamen. Holk threatened to conscript their families as military labourers unless the castle surrendered. Having fired a cannonball at the city hall in disgust, the militiamen forced Vopelius to surrender on 3 November. The castle was promptly occupied by 700 men under Major Melchior Mosen, but Leipzig itself was left unmolested in line with Wallenstein's desire for better relations with the inhabitants during the winter. Johann Georg was furious the city had fallen so easily and had Vopelius executed. Meanwhile, a detachment under Hatzfeldt took Halle around 30 km northwest of Leipzig. Though a small Swedish garrison held out in the Moritzburg castle, Halle's capture opened a route for Pappenheim to reach Saxony.[34]

Wallenstein had conquered western Saxony, but his situation remained difficult. He had been in contact with Holk and Gallas throughout October, but could never be sure his couriers were getting through. Communication with Pappenheim was even more difficult, as he was currently at Hildesheim in Westphalia, around

200 km from Leipzig. Moreover, Pappenheim had enjoyed his year of independent command since Breitenfeld and was reluctant to obey the directive from Maximilian to join Wallenstein. There were considerable practical obstacles as well. Men would have to be detached from his field force to hold his strategic corridor across Westphalia and northwest Germany, while his route across northern Thuringia was occupied by Bernhard of Weimar's troops plus another 3,000–4,000 under the Guelph duke Georg of Brunswick-Lüneburg who was moving to reinforce the Saxons. It was not until 1 November that Wallenstein received confirmation that Pappenheim was actually coming.[35]

Even with this good news, Wallenstein still faced the problem that the Swedes held the key fortified crossing points over the Elbe at Magdeburg, Torgau, and Wittenberg preventing him from occupying eastern Saxony, or besieging Dresden since that city straddled the river. In retrospect, the decision to attack Leipzig first was a mistake, since it delayed Holk's advance towards the Elbe. Wallenstein was forced to recall Holk on 5 November when he learned that Duke Georg had reinforced the Saxon post at Torgau which was now too strong to be taken quickly.[36]

Holk's return at least compensated for the departure on 6 November of Gallas with 8,300 men and thirty guns for Bohemia. Wallenstein had grown concerned at the situation in Silesia where he did not trust the local imperial commanders to cope with Arnim. The decision to despatch Gallas safely through Bohemia to Silesia made sense at the time: Gallas could reinforce the imperialists and drive Arnim back northwest into Saxony. Liberating Silesia would also play well at the imperial court, while Wallenstein believed he would still have enough men to hold western Saxony, especially with Pappenheim's imminent arrival. In fact, Silesia was no longer in immediate danger. Though Arnim refused to bring his whole army back to defend Saxony, he did bow to Johann Georg's pleas and march west with 6,100, leaving 8,400 in Silesia. Gallas' troops would be sorely missed at Lützen, whereas the outcome of that battle allowed Arnim to return to Silesia.

Gustavus' March to Saxony

Gustavus had stopped his southward march on 13 October when he realized that Wallenstein was not following him, and took the fateful decision to return northwards to save Saxony. Orders were despatched to his north German allies to reinforce the Saxons in the meantime—it was these instructions that had brought Duke Georg to Torgau. The king set out from the Danube on 18 October covering 630 km in 17 days, a punishing pace that killed 4,000 of his army's horses.[37] On his way he passed Maximilian and Aldringen heading in the opposite direction, but decided against attacking them for fear this would push them back on Wallenstein and so increase the odds against him. Instead, he hurried on, hoping to trap Wallenstein between himself and his allies posted along the Elbe. Having already collected the 4,000 men he had left in Nuremberg, he halted for a six-day rest at Erfurt on 2 November where he was joined by Bernhard's corps.

News of Gustavus' march prompted Pappenheim to hasten his own. He managed to slip passed Erfurt unmolested to join Wallenstein at Wurzen, just east of Leipzig on 7 November with 8,000 men. By now Wallenstein also knew that Gustavus was approaching and so marched his main force west hoping to seize Naumburg near the junction of the Saale and Unstrut rivers in order to prevent the Swedes from leaving Thuringia. Meanwhile, Hatzfeldt was ordered east from Halle to reinforce the units left watching the Saxons in Torgau. This would cover Leipzig and secure the rear of the imperial army as it moved southwest. Shortage of troops had prevented a strong defensive cordon along the Saale and there were only thirty musketeers in Naumburg when the Swedish advance guard arrived on 9 November, just hours before two imperial regiments intended to garrison the town. With Naumburg secured, Gustavus entered the following day at the head of his 19,000 men to a rapturous welcome from the inhabitants, and pushed on towards Leipzig. Gustavus was unaware that Wallenstein and Pappenheim were fast approaching and as soon as he heard they were already in Weissenfels 15 km to the northeast 'he ordered a retreat as fast as possible' to Naumburg when he proceeded to entrench as he had done at Nuremberg that summer.[38]

The Road to Lützen

Wallenstein was also surprised by the rapidity of his opponent's advance. Hearing of the loss of Naumburg, he halted at Weissenfels on 12 November where he also entrenched. The bulk of his 28,000 strong army camped between there and Lützen, further up the highway towards Leipzig on whose market they depended for supplies. Already two days earlier he realized his mistake in detaching Gallas and sent orders for him to return. Gallas received these instructions the next day, but bad weather slowed his march and he only reached Chemnitz on 20 November, well after it was too late.[39] The stand-off resembled that at Nuremberg during the summer, but after Alte Veste both were fully aware of the dangers of assaulting a fortified camp. Gustavus was concerned that he was short of cavalry and ordered Duke Georg to send his 2,000 horsemen from Torgau. Such a move was risky, given that the entire imperial army lay between Georg and Gustavus, but it was vetoed anyway by Johann Georg who refused to weaken his already small forces. Duke Georg was not allowed to set off until 16 November, by when the situation had changed dramatically.[40] Meanwhile, Gustavus consulted his officers on 14 November, proposing to seek battle and allegedly claiming he was ready to die for the cause.[41] He demurred, however, when several officers objected that the imperial army was twice as strong, and it was agreed to wait for Duke Georg to arrive.

Meanwhile, ill with gout and in no mood to risk battle, Wallenstein also consulted his senior officers. Hans W. Schmidt's painting of this event shows dark-clad officers in heated debate in the Bagpipe Inn in Weissenfels.[42] In fact, Wallenstein's command style was austere and he avoided face-to-face meetings where possible. He asked Pappenheim and Holk to canvas opinion and report back.[43] The exact timing of this process is one of the many minor controversies surrounding Lützen, but it most likely occurred on the same day as Gustavus' council of war. The decision to retreat was not one to go into winter quarters, as widely reported in later accounts, since wintering in Saxony had been Wallenstein's intention since October. Rather, having decided not to risk attacking Gustavus' camp, there were good reasons to pull back from Weissenfels. The weather was now very cold, making it imperative to put the troops into better shelter. Weissenfels was too far from Leipzig for the army to counter any surprise move by the Saxon and Lüneburg forces in Torgau. Pappenheim was anxious to return to Westphalia where his enemies had nibbled away at the fortified positions protecting his strategic corridor. It was mistakenly believed that the Swedish army had been sufficiently weakened by its recent forced march that it would not pose an immediate threat if the imperialists camped around Leipzig.

Yet, Wallenstein recognized that Gustavus would follow him northeastwards if he pulled back towards Leipzig, so he made plans to reassemble his forces if necessary, whilst also repositioning Hatzfeldt and his 2,500 men so as to better pin the Saxons and Lüneburgers in Torgau. In a more significant move, he sent Pappenheim to Halle which had been abandoned when Hatzfeldt was switched east against Torgau a week before. This detachment seriously weakened the main body of imperialists, but was understandable given that Halle lay squarely on the main route by which the Torgau group might reach Gustavus; indeed, the king had ordered Duke Georg to bring his cavalry this way to Naumburg. Halle also commanded the roads to Magdeburg and Halberstadt which offered good locations to extend the area of imperial winter quarters, as well as the road back to Westphalia. Pappenheim was instructed to spread out from Halle across the entire Merseburg region to draw supplies to sustain his men across the winter. Once the area was secure, he could go with a small cavalry escort back to Westphalia to resume command of the garrisons he had left there.

Having most likely already sent their heavy artillery and baggage back during the night, the imperialists drew up in battle order on the heights above Weissenfels at 7 a.m. on Monday 15 November. This was not in the hope that Gustavus would attack them, but simply to give more time for the guns and wagons to clear the highway behind them.[44] After two hours, the main body set off towards Lützen, roughly halfway between Weissenfels and Leipzig, covered by a screen of dragoons and Croatian light cavalry. Pappenheim soon turned north via Merseburg to Halle where he arrived at 4 p.m.[45] Colonels de Suys and Contreras led another smaller column of 1,100 infantry directly eastwards to Pegau, intending to secure the routes to Bohemia through Altenberg and Zwickau. These departures reduced the main column to around 13,000 men under Wallenstein and Holk. They halted at Lützen shortly after midday, proposing to wait there until the detachments had reached their destinations.

News that Wallenstein proposed detaching Pappenheim already reached Gustavus on 14 November. The information was revealed in a letter intended for the officer commanding the imperial outpost at Querfurt, but which had been carried by its Saxon courier to Gustavus instead.[46] It is unlikely that Gustavus acted on this alone. On the contrary, he seems uncertain whether Wallenstein had weakened his army, and only gradually concluded that he had done so as further confirmation was brought 'by some local peasants and gentlemen' across the morning.[47] Having been woken three hours before dawn, the Swedes advanced cautiously from Naumburg in full battle order, a deployment that slowed their pace to about 2 kph. It was not until well into the morning that Gustavus decided 'to go after the Wallensteiner' immediately rather than wait any longer for Duke Georg's cavalry to arrive.[48]

The Swedish advance guard halted at 12.30 when it saw imperialists lining the northeast bank of the Rippach stream, about 7 km in front of Lützen. Commanded by Rudolfo Colloredo, this force numbered 1,200 dragoons, Croatians, and musketeers at the most, but they had the advantage of higher ground which prevented the Swedes on the opposite bank from being able to gauge their true numbers.[49] The stream was 7–8 m wide, and up to 2 m deep with a muddy bottom, thus forming a serious obstacle. Gustavus proceeded methodically, deploying his artillery to bombard the other bank, while sending cavalry to cross at a ford about 1.5 km to the west. With the Swedes threatening his flank, Colloredo pulled back around 3.30 having lost 40–100 killed and 21 prisoners.

The crossing had been carried out with textbook efficiency, but it was also like using a sledgehammer to crack a nut, costing the Swedes valuable time, and it was now too late in the day to catch up with Wallenstein. Worse, Gustavus had lost the element of surprise. Nonetheless, Swedish morale was high and it was widely believed 'that if there had only been one more hour of daylight, they would undoubtedly have disordered and routed the entire enemy army'.[50] Along with the prisoners, the Swedes had taken two standards, including one from the Croatians showing the goddess Fortuna, naked, balancing on a ball. This image was typical of imperial standards, but its capture was widely reported subsequently in pro-Swedish accounts as a good omen.[51]

Such optimism was misplaced. Wallenstein had already received word from Colloredo around 2 p.m. and ordered three cannon shots to be fired as a pre-arranged signal for the army to reassemble. An aide galloped towards Halle to fetch Pappenheim. The letter was marked *cito citissme* (in greatest haste), yet the generalissimo often used that expression and it was not a sign of panic. The units left by Pappenheim in Merseburg as he headed north to Halle already reached Lützen that evening, though it is extremely unlikely that de Suys and Contreras came up from Pegau 15 km away.[52] Likewise, Hatzfeldt remained east of Leipzig to watch Torgau.

That evening, Wallenstein consulted his astrologer Gianbattista Senno. His long-standing interest in astrology was considered by many to be theologically suspect, because it implied that the stars, not God, governed human actions, and it was later seized upon by his detractors to discredit him.[53] It is perhaps an indication of his low spirits. He was certainly suffering acutely from gout and Holk later claimed this was the reason why he had decided to stay in Lützen rather than retreat further that day.[54] Only 50, he was prematurely aged. His first principality, Friedland, had been devastated earlier that year by the Saxons, while his second, Mecklenburg, now seemed irretrievably lost. His only son had died four years earlier, and his doctor's prognosis for his own health was bleak. Yet, it is extremely unlikely that he needed Senno to convince him to fight. It was clear Gustavus would attack him the next day, but would do so largely on Wallenstein's terms, allowing the imperial general to fight his preferred tactic of a defensive battle.

4

The Battle

The Battlefield

L ützen had developed around a toll post on the Frankfurt–Leipzig highway, originally on land belonging to the bishopric of Merseburg which was secularized and incorporated into the Electorate of Saxony in the sixteenth century. The town comprised 300 houses surrounded by an old stone wall, girded by gardens and orchards, in turn bordered by mud walls as high as a man. The thirteenth-century castle at the southwest corner had been expanded during the 1530s into a fortified four-storey palace around a high tower, with four smaller corner towers, surrounded by its own double wet ditch. The castle immediately overlooked the bridge over the Mühlgraben stream running northwards to the Saale river and which would form the western boundary of the coming battle. The St Vitus church tower, just northeast of the castle, provided a view over the entire area which appeared almost entirely flat, but in fact rose gently from the highway towards Meuchen village, about 2 km to the southeast.[1] The only higher ground was a slight mound immediately north of the highway, about 300 m northwest of Lützen, which has become known as Windmill Hill thanks to four wooden mills on top.[2] Some accounts refer to a further Gallows Hill about 700 m to the north, but the ground actually slopes further away and this alleged feature played no part in the action.[3]

Other than the town, the main geographical markers were the two watercourses and the highway. The Mühlgraben was not itself a major obstacle, but became marshy as it approached Lützen: indeed, the

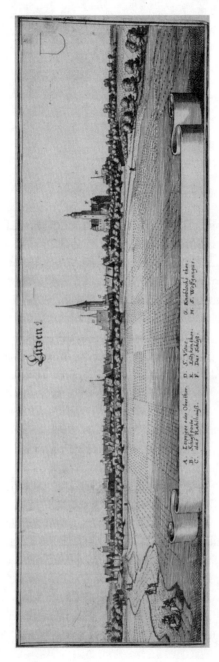

Illustration 2: Lützen c.1650

Illustration 3: Lützen Castle

Illustration 4: The Lützen windmills photographed around 1900

mud walls around the town were flood defences rather than fortifications. The area north of the highway and west of Lützen was completely waterlogged and impassable, meaning that Wallenstein could be sure the Swedes would have to cross the stream south of the town. The other watercourse was the Flossgraben canal dug in 1578 to float firewood from the Elster to the Saale rivers. It began as a branch of the Mühlgraben around 1.5 km south of Lützen and flowed northeast for around 3 km, before bending north in a series of zigzags to cross the highway around 2,700 m northeast of the town. The Flossgraben was broad, with steep banks and thick vegetation, making it impassable except for two bridges carrying country roads running southeast from Lützen past Meuchen, as well as a third bridge at the highway as it exited the battlefield to the northeast.

The Imperial Deployment

Having consulted Holk, Wallenstein decided not to contest a crossing of the Mühlgraben, most likely because he knew Gustavus was skilled in pinning his opponents with a frontal assault whilst sending cavalry across elsewhere to outflank them; as he had done successfully at the Lech in April and the previous day at Rippach. Instead, Wallenstein wanted to draw Gustavus into the relatively cramped ground immediately southeast of Lützen and force him to assault the imperial army which would be drawn up along the highway. The task of crossing the Mühlgraben would also delay the start of the battle and give time for the rest of Pappenheim's units to arrive from Halle.

Contemporary Swedish accounts estimated the imperial army at 30,000–48,000 men; figures which are accepted by many later writers favouring the Swedes.[4] In fact, Wallenstein had around 13,900 men, with a further 5,300 expected with Pappenheim. The prevailing pro-Swedish bias in subsequent accounts has given a confused impression of how these troops were deployed. The lack of a vantage point was compounded by the smoke accompanying the battle so that, to the Swedes, the imperial army appeared as a single line along the highway.[5] Some later plans presented this, while others made up for the lack of detail by showing the imperial infantry deployed in wholly anachronistic large squares, called tercios, copied from old tactical manuals.[6] The square tercio formation was never used during the Thirty Years War, even by Tilly whom later commentators have unfairly considered the most conservative of the commanders. Instead, the League and imperial infantry deployed in large rectangles of sixteen to twenty-six ranks deep during the 1620s, with the first few ranks being entirely musketeers to provide a continuous front of firepower. The remaining ranks in the centre were pikemen flanked by the rest of the musketeers. Variations were available for specific circumstances. For example, the pikemen would move to the front if the unit intended to charge, while the musketeers could retire behind or to the centre of the formation if it was attacked by cavalry. Such formations derived much of their strength from their massive size: theoretically up to 3,000 men each, but usually only half that. The numbers gave confidence, while officers and sergeants were posted on the edges of the unit as additional motivation and to keep the ranks aligned. Such units could absorb considerable punishment whilst remaining effective, but were vulnerable to artillery fire or to a combined attack as at Breitenfeld where Gustavus had used his cavalry to pin Tilly's infantry by threatening to charge, meanwhile pulverizing them with artillery and musket fire until they lost coherence.

Breitenfeld influenced the new tactical instructions issued by Wallenstein when he rebuilt the imperial army at the beginning of 1632. The infantry now deployed in units of around 1,000 men called 'battalions' or 'brigades', with larger regiments forming one each, while smaller ones were combined to give the right size. Each battalion deployed in ten ranks, though some may have been as thin as seven at Lützen in order to lengthen the frontage and bring more muskets to bear simultaneously on the enemy.[7] The musketeers still formed around two-thirds of the unit and drew up either side of the pikemen, whose role remained both protecting them against enemy cavalry and charging wavering enemy infantry. The significance of tactical changes was much debated at the time and subsequently, and is often used to explain the outcome of battles and military developments generally, as we shall see in Chapter 5. However, troop quality was at least as important, and Wallenstein was fortunate that most of his infantry were veteran formations, four of which had seen continuous service since 1618, with the rest since 1630 bar one (Jung Breuner) raised at the start of 1632.

Most battle plans also depict the imperial cavalry incorrectly. The League and imperial armies had long abandoned the old Spanish practice of small, independent companies, and instead massed their cavalry in 'squadrons' of up to 500 men deployed, from 1632, six ranks deep. The most formidable were the cuirassiers, comprising just over a quarter of the total cavalry. They wore thick boots and gloves, metal back and breast plates, helmets with a nose guard, additional armour on their arms and thighs, all over a thick leather coat. The armour was blackened against rust, and the practice of riding dark-coloured horses added to the grim impression which was intended to intimidate opponents into breaking before contacted in a charge. Most of the cuirassiers present were veterans, and only Regiment Lohe had been raised earlier that year and was still weak and probably lacked full equipment. The cuirassiers previously used the tactic known as the 'caracole', involving riding in successive ranks to fire pistols at an opponent, before returning to reload and repeat the process. This still had some value against static infantry, but had been abandoned against enemy cavalry in favour of firing at maximum pistol range (30–50 m) and closing with drawn swords. While using 'cold steel', this tactic nonetheless fell far short of the wild charges seen in historical war films, since accelerating only around 40 metres from the enemy meant the maximum speed that could be reached was only a trot. Though slower than a full gallop, this had the advantage that the unit kept its intimidating formation of a solid wall riding boot to boot.

Nearly half of the imperial cavalry were arquebusiers, who were armed with a carbine (previously called an arquebus), plus two pistols and a sword like the cuirassiers. A carbine outranged pistols, but required both hands to fire, rendering it difficult to use while mounted. The longer range also encouraged arquebusiers to fight by shooting, rather than charging the enemy which was psychologically more demanding. However, arquebusiers wore less armour, and were correspondingly lighter than cuirassiers, and so could be mounted on smaller horses; all factors making them cheaper to raise.

The received view among military historians is that the imperial and League cavalry were tactically inferior to the Swedes, because of their apparent reliance on firepower rather than charging with drawn swords. In fact, the bulk of the Swedish cavalry were equipped as arquebusiers and combined firepower and shock tactics. The Swedes generally reinforced their front line of cavalry with detachments of musketeers posted in the gaps between the squadrons. The musketeers fired a 'salvo' or volley in unison with the stationary cavalry who discharged their carbines, before the horsemen trotted forward to fire their pistols prior to surging forward across the remaining 50 m or so against the enemy. The relatively short distance meant that the Swedish cavalry probably only reached a full gallop of about 14 to 19 kmh in the final metres. The full transition to pure shock tactics, involving galloping across 100 m to hit the enemy at full speed, was only implemented during Charles XII's reign in 1697–1718.[8] The real problem with the imperial arquebusiers at Lützen was not their equipment or training, but the fact that all, except the Piccolomini Regiment, were relatively raw recruits from earlier that year.

Dragoons, Croatian light horsemen, and Polish Cossacks formed the rest of Wallenstein's and Pappenheim's cavalry. They wore no armour and were intended for scouting, raiding, and screening the army as it advanced or retreated. In battle, the Croatians and Poles were often used to sweep round enemy lines to cause panic by attacking the baggage, or to swirl around enemy units disordering them by firing pistols or carbines, before riding off before they could be counterattacked. They would perform all these roles effectively on 16 November.

The imperial deployment had been planned on 13 or 14 November while the army was at Weissenfels. The surviving sketch accordingly shows units which were no longer present two days later. Pappenheim had a copy of the plan, and it is likely so did other senior officers so that they would know where to place their units should the army have to reassemble. Having helped devise it, Holk was able to adapt its application during the night of 15–16 November to take account of the units actually available.[9] The imperial infantry were placed in the centre with five battalions in the first line, two more in the second supported by two squadrons of heavy cavalry, with a reserve third line of one weak battalion and two cavalry squadrons. The rest of the cuirassiers and arquebusiers were echeloned backwards at a 45° angle on each flank. The 900 Croatians already present at the start of the battle were posted forward from the main position to observe the Swedes, and later fell back with a larger group deploying where the highway crossed the Flossgraben, and the rest in the small gap between Lützen and Windmill Hill.

Around 700 musketeers were 'commanded', meaning drawn from their parent regiments for special service. About half of these were placed in Lützen and its surrounding gardens which formed a bulwark protecting the imperial right. It is unlikely that the remainder were posted between the cavalry squadrons in the Swedish manner.[10] Contemporary accounts indicate they lined the ditches either side of the highway, and this fact has been developed by later historians to explain why the Swedes found it so difficult to dislodge the imperialists. Deepening the ditches on both sides of the highway would have entailed shifting 4,000 m^3 of earth; a task which would not have been impossible, but was still highly unlikely to have been completed within a single night by an army that was still assembling and deploying.[11] Recent archaeology indicates that, contrary to later accounts, the highway was a sunken road flanked by two shallow ditches, neither of which shows signs of having been deepened into a trench. Holk's report makes no mention of this having been done. Moreover, it would have made little sense, since deeper ditches would have hindered the imperial cavalry from counterattacking. In any case, the highway on the imperial left bent southwards in a wide arc, meaning

any musketeers posted there would have been dangerously far forward from the rest of the army. The road and ditches would have
provided some cover for musketeers, but were certainly not in a
position to be defended at all costs.

The most likely position of the remaining musketeers, as well as
the 100 dragoons who fought dismounted, was close to the two
artillery batteries Wallenstein planted to defend either end of his
first line of infantry. He had between 19 and 21 heavy guns, of which
13–17 were placed on Windmill Hill, while the other 6–7 were
around 1 km away at the left end of the line. Some of the dragoons
occupied the miller's house which was in front of the mills and had
been loopholed for defence. The two batteries were potent thanks to
improvements in gunpowder across the preceding two centuries
which had seen a 60 per cent increase in energy production, meaning that a smaller charge gave a greater propellant effect. Combined
with better gun-founding techniques, this made even large cannon
lighter and consequently more manoeuvrable. Muzzle velocity generally exceeded 300 m/second and could reach half as much again;
sufficient to break the sound barrier. By comparison, a modern
9 mm semi automatic has a velocity of 360 m/second.[12] Maximum
effective range depended on calibre, but was between 500 and 800
metres for solid shot which bounced in ever decreasing bounds, but
was lethal when rolling along the ground when it could take the
foot off any soldier foolish enough to try and stop it. The ricochet
effect would, however, have been shortened by the waterlogged
conditions at Lützen.

Some accounts suggest there was a further three- or four-gun
battery in the imperial centre.[13] If there were further guns, they were
probably two to four small groups of lighter, so-called regimental
guns firing a 3 pdr roundshot with an effective range of around 250
metres. Pre-prepared cartridges, combining the ball and the explosive
charge to propel it, were used to speed loading and so increase the rate
of fire. Like heavy guns, regimental pieces could also fire bags or
canisters of musket balls, scrap metal or small stones which effectively

converted them into massive shot guns to mow down enemy troops at close range. Regimental guns are generally reckoned as a Swedish invention, notably the famous 'leather guns' which used a combination of thin metal tube wrapped in leather to lighten overall weight, enabling them to be pushed along as the infantry advanced. Leather guns were soon abandoned in the mid-1620s because their barrels quickly wore out, rendering them dangerous to use, and they were replaced by specially cast bronze barrels mounted on light carriages.[14] Wallenstein had instructed each infantry regiment to have two, and those in Gallas' corps in Bohemia certainly had them.[15] Many secondary sources claim there were none at Lützen, though two regimental guns reportedly captured by the Swedes in the battle were later seen passing through Staßfurt.[16] Either way, neither side's regimental guns had an appreciable impact on the course of the battle, unlike the two imperial heavy batteries.

From these dispositions it is clear Wallenstein intended a defence in depth with the infantry to blunt Gustavus' expected frontal assault. The deployment of the cavalry was intended to prevent the infantry from being outflanked, as well as to provide close support for local counterattacks, rather than to be used in a massive blow. The two heavy batteries served to anchor each end of the infantry line and were ideally placed to catch the advancing Swedes in crossfire. The proximity of the main body to Lützen made best use of the terrain, since the town and marshy Mühlgraben prevented the army being outflanked to the right. Any Swedish attack in this area would be funnelled into the small gap between Lützen and the Windmill Hill battery where it could be counterattacked by the cavalry echeloned to the rear. The real weakness lay on the left where insufficient troops meant that there was a 500 m gap between the smaller seven-gun battery and the Croatians at the Flossgraben bridge. This gap could have been closed by extending the main body further left, but that would have thinned the imperial centre and left it vulnerable to the Swedes breaking through. The space on the left was supposed to be filled by Pappenheim's men as they arrived from Halle. In the meantime, Wallenstein placed two large blocks well to the rear composed of baggage attendants and other non-combatants who held sticks and sheets to resemble pikes and flags. Their presence indicates that Wallenstein was well aware of the weakness of his left and did not, as some have claimed, simply expect Gustavus to attack his right wing.[17]

Reports that Wallenstein remained in his crimson sedan chair stem from a hostile French pamphlet which also misrepresents his gout as the advanced stages of syphilis. In fact, at dawn he mounted a grey horse lent him, ironically, by Colonel Butler, one of his principal assassins two years later. Silk had been wrapped around the stirrups to ease the pain of gout, and he only wore a thick leather coat rather than armour for the same reason.[18] He rode along the waiting lines of troops, speaking quietly and giving out the watch word 'Jesus Maria'. This pre-arranged, suitably Catholic formulation could be called out in the smoke of battle to distinguish friend from foe.[19] Having inspected the artillery positions, he took station on the right with a large entourage of the aristocrats who typically accompanied the imperial army, including his brother-in-law Count Otto Friedrich von Harrach, Johann Schenk zu Schweinsberg abbot of Fulda, and Emperor Ferdinand II's two Florentine teenage nephews, Matteo and Francesco de' Medici. Holk meanwhile took charge on the left.

The Swedish Deployment

Gustavus had around 18,700 effectives, giving him a four-to-three superiority over the imperial forces present at the start of the battle.[20] Only 3,425 were native Swedes and Finns, but the majority of the others were German veterans who had served since 1630, plus around 600 Scots.[21] The least tested units were those raised by Duke Wilhelm of Weimar who only joined Gustavus in autumn 1631, as well as the 1,880 electoral Saxons and 882 Hessians representing Gustavus' principal German allies. Duke Wilhelm had recently left the army in disgust after Gustavus refused to enfeoff him with conquered Catholic church lands in Thuringia.[22] His place was taken by his youngest brother,

Bernhard, who had no prospect of ruling Weimar himself and enthusiastically backed Sweden in the hope of personal advancement.

The Swedes awoke two hours before dawn at their camp some way between Rippach and Lützen, but found the day foggy.[23] The weather would play an important part in the coming events. One pro-Swedish report claims it was already misty the previous evening and blames this for Gustavus' failure to catch Wallenstein.[24] However, the Englishman Colonel Fleetwood reported a bright morning until 10 a.m., while another account claims the entire Leipzig region was sunny except for Lützen which remained so foggy 'that one could not see more than a pistol shot the whole time'.[25] So much about the battle is as murky as these conflicting weather reports. It seems likely, though, that the dawn fog did not clear until between 7 and 8 a.m., but that it was never sufficiently thick as to disrupt Swedish plans. What writers recorded as 'fog' later in the day was in fact thick smoke from gunfire and the fact that the imperialists set Lützen ablaze as the battle began.

Without eating breakfast, Gustavus mounted his horse, Streiff, and rode in front of his assembled troops, speaking to them in Swedish and German.[26] The king then said a short prayer, either whilst still mounted, or kneeling by his horse. Morning prayers were customary in the Swedish army, so it is not clear whether the king's involvement was part of this, or a separate act. The speeches and prayers were widely reported in all pro-Swedish accounts and remain a central feature in later discussions of the battle.[27] They have become part of the Gustavus Adolphus legend, serving to demonstrate the king's piety, as well as the morality and justice of his cause. However, even these seemingly firm fixtures slip into the historiographical fog, as some accounts place them later, once the army had crossed the Flossgraben, or that these later prayers and speeches were a second event after the normal morning prayers before the force left its camp. Similarly, Gustavus is said to have dictated the battle hymn *Verzage nicht, du häuflein klein* (O little flock, fear not the foe) to his chaplain Fabricius on the eve of the battle. The two earliest printed editions say

III.

GUSTAV ADOLPH
betet vor der Schlacht bei Lützen.

Illustration 5: 'Gustavus Adolphus praying before the battle of Lützen', early nineteenth-century print

the king sang it at Lützen, but it was more likely written by the Thuringian pastor Michael Altenberg after Breitenfeld.[28]

There is no contemporary evidence that Gustavus had a clear plan or even knew exactly where Wallenstein was or how he had deployed. Having advanced directly along the highway, the leading Swedish units stopped just west of Lützen as they came under fire from the musketeers posted there around 8 a.m. Having reconnoitred, Gustavus clearly judged a frontal assault against Lützen to be too costly, while the marshy ground to the north prevented any crossing of the Mühlgraben from there. Accordingly, he did as Wallenstein had predicted and marched southeast to cross the stream some way south of the town around 8.30. The exact spot is not known, but was almost certainly south of the point where the Flossgraben branched eastwards from the Mühlgraben. Any attempt further north would have exposed his army to a counterattack from the imperial right wing

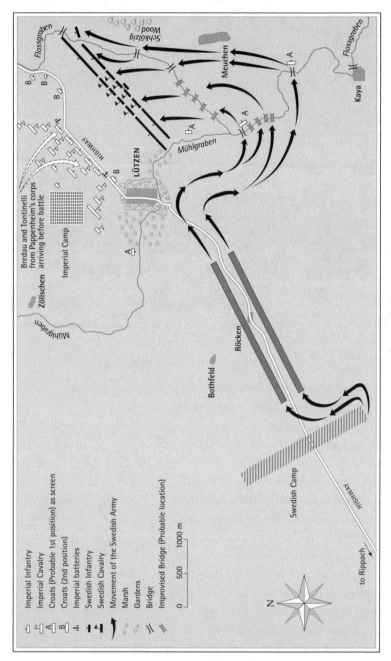

Map 3: Lützen: the Swedish approach

Legend:
- Imperial Infantry
- Imperial Cavalry
- Croats (Probable 1st position) as screen
- Croats (2nd position)
- Imperial batteries
- Swedish Infantry
- Swedish Cavalry
- Movement of the Swedish Army
- Marsh
- Gardens
- Bridge
- Improvised Bridge (Probable location)

0   500   1000 m

Map labels:
- Flossgraben
- Schkölzig Wood
- Meuchen
- Kaya
- Flossgraben
- Mühlgraben
- HIGHWAY
- LÜTZEN
- Bredau and Tontinelli from Pappenheim's corps arriving before battle
- Zöllschen
- Imperial Camp
- Mühlgraben
- Bothfeld
- Röcken
- Swedish Camp
- HIGHWAY
- to Rippach
- N

around Lützen. It is likely that the Swedes moved in an arc to cross the Flossgraben at the bridges near Meuchen, quickly driving off the Croatians who had moved along the other side of the canal to watch them.[29] Additional bridges were improvised from timber lying near the canal to speed the crossing.

Like the imperialists, the Swedes used a pre-arranged deployment already employed three times: at Naumburg, during the initial advance to Rippach on 15 November, and in the camp overnight. This shortened the time required, because each unit already knew its place. However, it took little account of the actual terrain which was too cramped for the number of men. As they crossed the canal, the Swedes pushed their forward units northwards to make room for the others to follow over the bridges behind them, gradually forming two parallel lines of about 300 m. The infantry formed the centre under Knyphausen, an experienced German general, and the cavalry were on the wings under Bernhard (left) and Gustavus (right). This pattern was already becoming conventional in Europe and would remain the norm for the next 150 years.

Later accounts almost universally praise the Swedish deployment as a model of progressive tactics in contrast to the supposedly conservative imperialists. The Swedish infantry were grouped into 'brigades', formed, like the imperial battalions, by combining smaller regiments where necessary to give a standard number of (theoretically) 1,200 men each. The brigade developed during the 1620s when each was subdivided into four 'squadrons', each approximately one-third pikemen and two-thirds musketeers. Two squadrons stood in a thin line, six ranks deep for the musketeers and three to four for the pikemen. Another squadron formed a block placed forward of the line, with the fourth stationed in reserve behind. This deployment was hardly a direct step towards the true linear tactics of the later seventeenth and eighteenth centuries when infantry relied on maximizing firepower. Rather, it was a defensive formation developed to confront the more fluid tactics of the Poles who were Sweden's principal enemies after 1621. The four-squadron brigade was depicted in printed

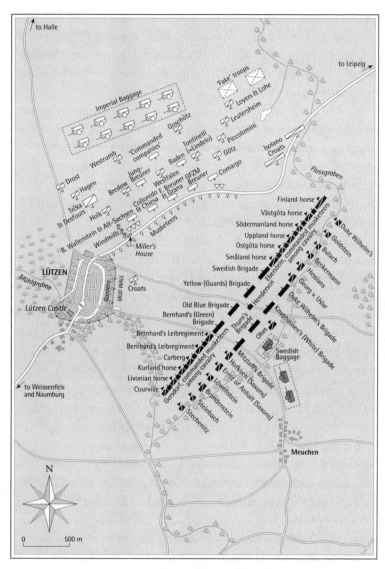

Map 4: Lützen: initial deployment

tactical manuals disseminated widely through Europe and was seemingly employed by the Royalists at Edgehill 1642, the opening battle of the English civil wars.[30] In fact, Swedish brigades only deployed in three squadrons after 1630, abandoning the fourth reserve squadron in favour of bolstering the others. However, the continued presence of the forward block wasted manpower by denying a fifth of the musketeers a clear line of fire. Rather than representing a progressive innovation, the Swedish brigade was a tactical dead end, and by 1634 the Swedes were deploying like the imperialists in a single line of pikemen flanked by musketeers. The only difference was that their lines were somewhat longer and thinner at six ranks, compared to the six to ten of their opponents.

At Lützen, each of the two infantry lines had four brigades, with the Swedish and Yellow brigades, both considered elite, posted on the right of the first line. The German allied and mercenary units were on the left, traditionally the less honourable position, but also an indication that Gustavus intended his main attack to be made by the most trusted regiments on the right. This is confirmed by the massing of the Swedish and Finnish cavalry on the right under the king's personal command, while Bernhard had the less effective German regiments on the left. The large Småland and Finnish cavalry regiments deployed in two squadrons of 200 troopers each, whereas the others were weaker and formed one squadron each, or were combined as a single unit like the four Hessian regiments. These variations meant that the reality of Swedish deployment was less neat or uniform than depicted on near contemporary engravings and plans. Five commanded musketeer detachments were posted between the squadrons in the first line of both cavalry wings in accordance with the Swedish practice of combining firepower and shock.[31]

Gustavus had a decided advantage in artillery, with twenty heavy guns and thirty-nine to forty regimental pieces. Some of the latter were assigned to the commanded musketeers, with the rest distributed among the eight infantry brigades. Unlike the imperial artillery, the heavy guns were not massed and probably only reached their firing positions once the battle was underway. Even if they were in place once the first line had fully deployed, their field of fire would have been obscured as soon as the infantry began their advance.

The exact length of the Swedish deployment cannot be known for certain, but was probably at least 200 m longer than the 2,500 calculated 300 years later by officers of the country's general staff.[32] The line of the Flossgraben meant there was insufficient space for the Swedes to deploy parallel to the imperialists lining the highway. Instead, the Swedish right stood about 2 km north of the left, meaning it started the battle much closer to the enemy. This probably also influenced Gustavus' decision to attack from this direction first, but it meant that the assault arrived in stages, because each unit to the left was that much further from the enemy. Additionally, it is highly likely that the second line lacked enough space, meaning that the three cavalry squadrons on the extreme right under Colonel Zorn von Bulach had to deploy on the other (eastern) side of the canal.[33] Worse, the terrain hindered the Swedes from using their longer line and numerical superiority to outflank the shorter imperial line. Instead, the terrain would funnel them into the smaller space between Lützen and the Flossgraben bridge.[34] Bernhard on the left had an especially difficult task, because the marshy ground near Lützen forced his units to the right, further cramping the overall space available.

It is difficult to avoid the conclusion that the Swedish command was imprisoned in its own tactical model and adopted a deployment that conformed to the theory, but took too little account of the actual terrain. Bernhard had too many cavalry and insufficient infantry and artillery for his task of taking the most heavily defended part of the imperial position, while Gustavus lacked enough cavalry to fully exploit any breakthrough he might make against the weaker imperial left. The entire strength was evenly distributed in an overly long deployment, with only one cavalry regiment in reserve behind the second line, and just 228 musketeers under Colonel Henderson behind the first.

The Battle Opens

The Swedish deployment north of the canal was completed around 10.30 a.m. Some Swedish accounts say the mist descended again, hindering the attack for another hour, but published imperial reports note the battle beginning at 10 a.m.[35] The real reason for the delay was the 90 minutes or so it took the Swedes to cross the canal and deploy on the other side. All the while, Gustavus' men could see the imperialists near Lützen and hear the tramp of marching feet, suggesting not all of Wallenstein's army was yet in position. Most accounts have Gustavus initiating battle by firing all the guns of one of his heavy batteries simultaneously as a signal to move forward, but it is more likely that the imperial Windmill battery already bombarded the Swedes as they deployed, firing 'incessantly, but without doing much damage'.[36] The second battery opened up as well as the Swedish right wing came within range. The Swedes appear to have had only three heavy guns available to reply at this stage, primarily hitting the imperial cavalry near Lützen, since these stood on higher ground and were more visible.

It is likely that the Swedish right moved first, perhaps with the left-centre and left standing off to allow their artillery to fire, or because these elements of the army were still arriving. This would explain why Gustavus already reached the bend of the highway south of the Flossgraben bridge around 11 a.m. The most likely sequence is that Colonel Thorsten Stålhandske (literally 'iron hand') was sent ahead with the Finnish Cavalry Regiment and its supporting musketeers on the extreme right over the highway to attack the Croatians screening the bridge. Archaeological evidence suggests two or possibly three clashes on this part of the battlefield. In one, the Croatians appeared to have fired their carbines at long range, before retreating to avoid contact with the Finnish horsemen. Another suggests a Croatian unit being caught and then chased until its faster horses carried it beyond the pistol range of the pursuing Swedes. In both cases, the Swedish-commanded musketeers provided support, probably by firing an initial salvo before the cavalry charged.[37] Whatever the precise sequence, it is clear the Croatians were driven off to the north, and the Swedish first line pushed into the gap between the imperial left and the Flossgraben. The two blocks composed of baggage attendants fled at this point, while the nearby wagons were moved westwards to a safer position nearer Lützen. Colonel Bulach's three squadrons advanced along the east bank of the canal to secure the other side of the bridge, while the other three squadrons of the second line rode directly forward to support their comrades in the first line.

Swedish accounts blame the depth of the ditches along the highway for delaying the Småland Regiment at the left end of Gustavus' first line. It is more likely that it was held back by the fire of the imperial seven-gun battery, and only crossed the highway around 11.30 as the Swedish Brigade arrived, soon followed on its left by the Yellow, or Guards Brigade. These two elite infantry units quickly seized the imperial cannon, forcing the gunners to flee behind the left-most imperial battalion (Comargo). Gustavus now (11.45 a.m.) crossed the highway with the two squadrons of the Småland Regiment and that of the Östagöta Cavalry on their immediate right while the other cavalry pushed north hoping to turn the imperial flank. Fire from the commanded musketeers and their regimental guns drove back the Götz cuirassiers, allowing men from the Swedish Brigade to turn around the captured imperial cannon and fire them at the infantry behind. The Old Blue Brigade, another veteran unit and next in the first line, now came up on the left of the Yellow Brigade.

By this time, the Swedish left was already in action, having reached the outskirts of Lützen around 11.30. The imperialists had impeded their advance by setting the town on fire in two or three places shortly after 11 a.m.[38] Wallenstein allegedly had the inhabitants locked in the castle cellar so they could not extinguish their blazing homes. The smoke drifted south and east into the faces of Bernhard's men who also suffered from the fire of the Windmill battery. It is likely that the Swedes planned merely to screen Lützen while making their main effort against the 150 m gap between the town and Windmill Hill. Having chased off the few Croatians nearby, Bernhard sent his commanded musketeers to engage their imperial counterparts ensconced in the gardens. Meanwhile, his cavalry pushed into the gap, while the Green Brigade on the far left of the Swedish centre advanced directly against the Windmill battery. The Croatians had fled through the gap, disordering the raw arquebusier regiments posted further back. Regiment Hagen raced to the rear in panic, and though they rallied, the troopers refused to return and instead drew up behind the large combined squadron of the Trčka and Desfours regiments.

The Swedish Attack Fails

The imperial infantry stood firm, while the Green Brigade was insufficient for an immediate attack on Windmill Hill. Bernhard's attack stalled, and the action in this sector was reduced for now to a mutual cannonade, adding to the dense smoke emanating from Lützen. Wallenstein felt sufficiently secure to send five companies of cavalry to reinforce Holk on the left. The identity of this unit and the exact timing of its despatch remain one of the many matters of speculation, but it was most likely the Bredow cuirassier regiment since this was certainly later engaged on the left. Some modern accounts[39] have various units shuttling to the left and back again throughout the day; something which is extremely unlikely given that the distance was over 1 km and that pulling a unit out of line could easily alarm neighbouring troops and spread panic. This apparently minor point provides a significant insight into the limited opportunities available to the commanders on either side to alter dispositions once the battle started.

The situation now resembled that at Breitenfeld over a year earlier, but with the roles reversed. Like Gustavus in 1631, Wallenstein was threatened on the left, where the Swedish advance north of the highway was turning his flank. However, he did not need to reposition his centre as Horn had done at Breitenfeld, because his initial deployment already placed units echeloned back from his front line. Meanwhile, by continuing to press north of the highway in an effort to outflank the imperialists, Gustavus, like Tilly in 1631, was overstretching his army, creating a gap in the centre between the Old Blue Brigade and the Green Brigade now much further to the left and stalled in front of Windmill Hill.

Units on the imperial left began counterattacking around midday. Unlike Gustavus' brilliant counterstroke at Breitenfeld, these efforts were probably initiatives of Holk and the imperial regimental commanders, rather than coordinated by Wallenstein. The Comargo battalion, a veteran League unit, moved forward, supported by the Götz cuirassiers, and later supplemented by the Piccolomini arquebusiers and the Baden battalion from the second line. Their combined efforts to recover the battery led to a protracted struggle against the Swedish Brigade. That unit had probably already suffered casualties from the battery during the advance. It was now hit by the Piccolomini regiment which swung round to attack its exposed right flank. It has been plausibly suggested that the imperial cavalry deliberately targeted the Swedish pikemen by firing their pistols from a safe distance, rather than charging home. Most of the Swedish units lacked their full complement of pikemen, and the additional casualties they now suffered further reduced the capacity of the remainder to protect the musketeers, thus further confirming the continued effectiveness of the supposedly obsolete caracole tactics.[40]

The Swedish Brigade eventually fell back having lost half its strength. Next to go was the Yellow Brigade to its left which had been halted by musketry from the Breuner battalion. Imperial accounts record that the opposing infantry 'approached each other so closely that they could also fight with pikes', but that musketry proved the deciding factor with the 'best Swedish units being shot dead'.[41] Again, this outcome demonstrates that Swedish tactics and equipment were not inherently superior. Fifteen minutes after the Yellow Brigade gave way at 1.15, the Old Blue Brigade was also in full retreat having lost two-thirds of its strength, including its two senior officers, Colonel Winckel and Lieutenant Colonel Caspar Wolf, falling severely wounded. Major Hans von Münchhausen of the Baden battalion was later decorated for bravery after he presented fifteen flags to Wallenstein which had been taken from Winckel's unit. The virtual destruction of these three Swedish units removed the inner core of their infantry, killing men of seven to eight years' service.

Gustavus' Death

During this epic struggle in the centre of the battlefield, two important events occurred further east: Gustavus' death and Pappenheim's arrival and death. The exact sequence is not clear, with either happening before the other, or both simultaneously, depending on the surviving accounts. On balance, the king's death probably occurred first, though its timing, manner, and significance all remain controversial. One influential claim is that Bernhard felt his attack had failed and sent urgent requests to Gustavus around midday for assistance. Gustavus supposedly felt able to dash to his left, because Pappenheim had not yet arrived and things appeared to be going well on his right at that point with the Swedish cavalry still pushing north of the highway. This claim was advanced by Josef Seidler, a Bohemian German who emigrated west after the Second World War and who made it his life's mission to reinterpret the battle. His account of this episode hinges on a single source: Galeazzo Gualdo Priorato, an Italian count who had served on both sides during the Thirty Years War and later become the Habsburgs' court historiographer. This led Seidler to claim Gustavus died over 1 km west of the site commemorated later, in turn prompting him to argue that Bernhard's subsequent attacks were intended to recover the royal corpse rather than win the battle.[42]

This entire version is inherently implausible. Given his later gung-ho conduct, it is extremely unlikely that Bernhard would have been discouraged so easily, especially as he had not yet drawn on the more immediate support offered by the Swedish second line. Even if he was despondent, insufficient time had yet elapsed for him to send a

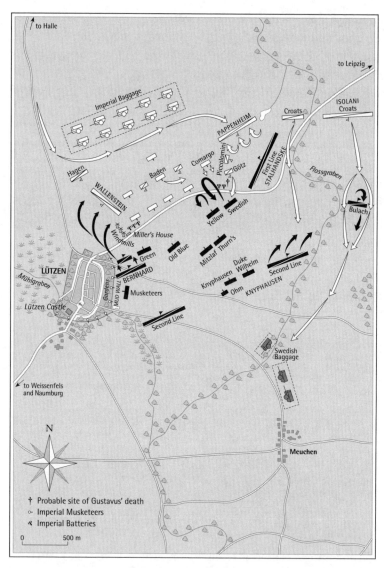

Map 5: Lützen: middle phase

messenger who would have needed to ride across the entire battlefield and then find the king amidst the smoke and confusion on the left. Finally, it is unlikely that Gustavus would have simply handed command to Stålhandske at the point when his attempt to outflank the imperial left—the blow intended from the outset to win the battle— was not yet complete.

Another narrative has the king engaged on a more local mission to rescue either the Swedish or Old Blue Brigades from the imperial counterattack.[43] This is more plausible, since this event was within his immediate vision, unlike Bernhard's situation shrouded in smoke far to the left. Colonel Fredrik Stenbock of the Småland Regiment had been incapacitated by a musket shot to the foot, while Major Lennart Nilsson Bååt of the Östagöta horsemen had been killed. Thus, it is also explicable why Gustavus should place himself at the head of the Smålanders to lead the charge. Most secondary accounts follow this version which still ascribes a purpose to the king's death. However, it

Illustration 6: Death of Gustavus Adolphus, engraving by Merian

is equally possible that the king and his entourage became detached from the main Swedish line in the smoke and confusion as they advanced across the highway and simply blundered into imperial units counterattacking the Swedish infantry.[44]

The most likely time for the start of this sequence was shortly after midday, because all accounts indicate that only the Småland regiment was immediately available to accompany the king as the others had advanced further north to turn the imperial flank.[45] With his customary impetuosity, the king 'went to farre on'.[46] Gustavus was shortsighted, yet refused to wear glasses. The thick smoke further hindered visibility. Either he charged ahead and was shot, or was wounded and stopped with his entourage while the Smålanders pressed on beyond him. The initial wound was caused by a musket ball, most likely fired by a corporal of the Breuner battalion, which hit his left arm below the elbow, driving part of the bone through the sleeve of his leather coat. The ball continued through into the neck of Streiff, his horse. Unable to hold the reins with his left hand, Gustavus risked losing control of his wounded horse. He dropped his sword to use his right hand instead.

He then turned to Duke Franz Albrecht von Sachsen-Lauenburg who headed his entourage and asked to be helped to safety. The duke emerges as the Judas of the king's martyrdom. He is indeed hard to like. Sachsen-Lauenburg was a small duchy on the lower Elbe; a remnant of a once extensive territory. Like Weimar, the ruling family had too many sons to accommodate, prompting Franz Albrecht and his brothers to seek advancement through recruiting troops after 1618. The duke first served the elector Palatine until captured in 1620. Pardoned by Ferdinand II, he repaid the emperor's generosity by joining Wallenstein's army in 1625, rising to major general's rank six years later. As a Lutheran prince, he seemed an ideal intermediary for the generalissimo's secret negotiations with Saxony after January 1632, but he was angered when Wallenstein chose more skilful generals for operational command. He resigned from imperial service and appeared as a volunteer at the Swedish camp at Nuremberg that summer. Even amongst the numerous rough characters of the Thirty Years War, Franz Albrecht stood out for his brutal extortion of civilians. As recently as 14 November, he forced Johann Georg Maul, a town official in Naumburg, to serve him a thirty-two-course banquet costing the equivalent to the annual income of an ordinary burgher. The next morning at breakfast, he thanked his host by almost coming to blows with Maul's wife.[47]

There were many such individuals in the Swedish army, so the duke's presence at the king's side did not cause comment until much later. Contemporary accounts present the duke as supporting the king by riding alongside, leading the group in an attempt to return to the main Swedish line. Bloodstains on Franz Albrecht's coat supported this version of events. However, they now blundered into a party of imperial cuirassiers from the Götz Regiment, allegedly led by Lieutenant Colonel Moritz von Falkenberg, a Catholic relation of the officer who misled the Magdeburgers the previous year. Falkenberg is supposed to have recognized the king and fired his pistol, hitting Gustavus in the back. This shot went through his right shoulder blade to enter his lung. Falkenberg was shot in turn, perhaps by the duke, but the other cuirassiers pressed close. Anders Jönssen, the king's groom, was killed. Franz Albrecht was obliged to defend himself as a pistol shot burned his face, and he let go of Gustavus who fell from his horse.

The eighteen-year-old page, August Leubelfing, offered his own horse to the king, but was then mortally wounded. Later hostile accounts claimed the duke panicked and spurred his horse away, shouting that the king was dead. Others claim he could do nothing, because Gustavus' foot was still caught in a stirrup and the king was dragged away into the smoke by the injured Streiff. The rest of the entourage had by now left, though exactly who was there is unclear, because several individuals subsequently claimed to be present, though of course in ways which excused them of any blame.[48]

It did not help Franz Albrecht's reputation that he already joined the Saxon army on 4 December 1632 and was immediately entrusted with the ongoing covert peace talks with Wallenstein. Within two years, he was complaining about the appearance of pamphlets openly accusing him as an accomplice in Gustavus' 'murder'.[49] He was captured by the imperialists in murky circumstances during Wallenstein's attempt to defect to the Saxons in February 1634. Having converted to Catholicism, he became a general in the imperial army and was captured by the Swedes in 1642, but died of wounds before they could put him on trial for his part in Gustavus' death. Later writers including Pufendorf and Schiller elaborated the story, alleging that he had worn a green sash as a pre-arranged signal to help the imperialists identify Gustavus' entourage. What this story really reveals is the contemporary sense of an unlawful killing by 'arch-murderers'.[50] Lurking beneath this was the anguish that perhaps, after all, the king had not died heroically leading his troops in a battle-winning charge, but pointlessly while he blundered about in the smoke.

The injured king was now found lying abandoned by another party of three troopers from Piccolomini's regiment led by Major Pier Martinelli who shot him again in the head and stomach. One of the party then allegedly asked the dying Gustavus who he was and on hearing the answer rushed off to find Octavio Piccolomini, the regiment's commander.[51] Piccolomini is another unsympathetic figure. He rose to prominence as the commander of Wallenstein's bodyguard, securing the colonelcy of his own regiment in 1626, but would later be a key player in the plot to persuade Ferdinand II to sanction the generalissimo's assassination.[52] Conveniently, Piccolomini's unwavering loyalty to the Habsburgs also served his own advancement. He subsequently claimed he had wanted to move Gustavus to safety, but either abandoned it as too dangerous, or because he doubted it was indeed the king. He later boasted in a letter that although Martinelli fired the fatal shot, 'I was the cause of his [Gustavus'] death, because I held the position and destroyed two of his best regiments'.[53]

The soldiers plundered the corpse, with Martinelli taking the king's gold chain, while the troopers took his watch, silver spurs, jacket, hat, and boots, leaving him only in his blood-stained shirt and stockings. Martinelli was later killed, which probably explains why others are credited with taking the chain. Likewise, a trumpeter from Holk's regiment later acquired the spurs and some other items.[54] Most contemporary accounts place the king's death around 1 p.m., suggesting he had blundered about in the smoke for over half an hour while his infantry were slowly battered by the imperial counterattack. Seeking meaning from his demise, many authors claim that the king's final charge forced the Götz and Piccolomini regiments to retire, relieving the pressure on the Swedish infantry and allowing them to retire over the highway.[55] Given the likely timing of both Gustavus' death and his infantry's retreat, this is improbable, because the battered three brigades fell back well over half an hour after the Smålanders charged. The imperialists in any case obeyed their pre-battle instructions and did not pursue the Swedes once they had retaken the battery and the highway. Their halt thus had nothing to do with the king's death which made little difference to the broader course of the battle.

Pappenheim's Attack and Death

Gustavus died around the time Pappenheim launched a fresh counterattack against the Swedish cavalry on the right wing. As with much else, considerable controversy surrounds Pappenheim's arrival. He had captured Halle at 4 p.m. on 15 November, forcing the small Swedish garrison to retire again to the Moritzburg castle. Wallenstein's recall letter arrived some hours later. Discrepancies in contemporary accounts of the timing probably derive from the time it took for the new orders to be passed to the different units of Pappenheim's command which had spread out amongst the neighbouring villages for the night.[56] The cavalry set off immediately, but the infantry left around three hours later at 2 a.m., or possibly later. Pro-Swedish accounts attribute the delay to the soldiers' desire to plunder Halle, but this seems unlikely.[57] No matter when the signal was given, it would have taken time for the troops to be roused and organized for the march. Even the direct route to Lützen was 33 km and would have required at least six hours for the cavalry to cover, making it very unlikely that

Pappenheim's men appeared much before midday.[58] Many reports heighten the drama by placing Pappenheim's arrival just as parts of the imperial left wing fled in the face of Gustavus' attack across the highway. In fact, none of the imperial units had been broken by this point, except those composed of the baggage attendants, for even the Croatians had rallied after their defeat by the bridge. Though the seven-gun battery had been lost, the Swedish infantry had been halted and were possibly already threatened by the local counterattacks described above.

Hastening along the Halle road, Pappenheim's cavalry would have first appeared immediately north of Lützen on the imperial right, before turning east to move along the rear of the centre; something which may also explain the reports that Wallenstein had detached cavalry from his own wing to reinforce Holk during the battle. It would have taken time to deploy from column of march into battle order, probably lengthened a little by the need to give the horses at least a brief rest after the march. Pappenheim probably took the opportunity to consult Holk and to plan their counterstroke. Having agreed arrangements, Holk handed over command to Pappenheim and set out across the battlefield to join Wallenstein on the right.

Pappenheim began his counter attack around 1 p.m.[59] Contrary to many secondary accounts, his numerical superiority was slight, while nearly two-thirds of his horsemen were Croatians and other light cavalry.[60] With these, he launched a two-pronged attack, advancing with his heavy cavalry directly against the Swedish right wing, while sending his light cavalry south along both sides of the Flossgraben around the enemy flank. Pappenheim led from the front, riding near Lieutenant Colonel Albrecht von Hofkirchen who commanded the Sparr cuirassiers.

With Gustavus having disappeared into the smoke, command on the right devolved to Stålhandske who, seeing Pappenheim approaching, abandoned the attempt to outflank the imperial army, and instead fell back to reorder his cavalry in a line just north of the highway. The Swedes appear to have followed their standard tactic of receiving the oncoming imperialists with the fire of their commanded musketeers and regimental guns, before their own cavalry countercharged. The impact of the Swedish salvo was heightened by the fact it was received by relatively raw units who were tired after their march to the battle-field. The Sparr Regiment faltered, while Bönninghausen's troopers broke before the Swedes began their own charge.

Worse, Pappenheim was one of the first to be hit by what is described as a 'wire ball' which ripped off his right hip.[61] The Swedes used wire to bind the cartridges used by their regimental pieces, so it is possible that it was this waste material that fused together during firing.[62] Pappenheim was soon engulfed by the Swedish countercharge. Conrad Ehinger, Pappenheim's trumpeter, called out to Hofkirchen 'for God's sake' to help him rescue the injured general, but the colonel refused. Ehinger shot a Swede who had taken Pappenheim prisoner and began to move him to safety. Pappenheim tried to break free and return to the battle 'and with his eyes full of tears, cried out "Oh brothers, God have mercy! Is there no one left who will fight loyally for the emperor?"'[63] Ehinger eventually got Pappenheim to his coach and drove off to Leipzig, arriving between 3 and 7 a.m., depending on accounts. Realizing he was dying, Pappenheim kissed his ring and gave it to Ehinger to pass to his wife and child whom he entrusted to Wallenstein 'like a father'. He died of blood loss, either on the way or three hours after arriving at Leipzig. The uncertainty surrounding the timing gains significance with the controversy as to whether Pappenheim died consoled by the news of Gustavus' death. Such issues indicate contemporaries' and later generations' desire to personalize events with, for instance, the entirely fabricated story that Pappenheim had encountered Gustavus in the smoke and each had mortally wounded the other.[64]

Pappenheim's injury further discouraged his troopers. Already in retreat, the Bönninghausen regiment paused to plunder the imperial baggage to the rear. Some accounts place an explosion of the imperial reserve powder wagons at this point, adding to the confusion.[65] Certainly, most of the remaining baggage attendants cut the traces of the wagons and rode off on the horses, including those belonging to the imperial heavy guns, thus immobilizing them. Captain-Lieutenant Luigi Broglia then led five of Bönninghausen's companies in full flight towards Halle, passing Colonel Reinach with Pappenheim's infantry around 2 p.m. Broglia called out that Pappenheim was dead, the battle lost, and Wallenstein already fleeing to Leipzig. Reinach refused to be deterred and continued down the road to Lützen. Colonel Bönninghausen eventually managed to rally another two of his companies and return to the battle two hours later. The rest of his regiment simply dispersed. The Lohe Regiment also fled after its commander was killed, while the Goschütz Arquebusiers standing in the reserve third line were carried away in the confusion. The Sparr Cuirassiers retained cohesion, but were led to the rear by Hofkirchen who ignored direct orders from Piccolomini and Götz to return to the battle, and instead took up position safely behind the imperial right wing.

The infantry on the extreme left of the imperial centre were unaware of Pappenheim's mortal wound and cried out 'where can the Pappenheimer be, that he doesn't come with his cavalry to help us!'[66] The subsequent conclusion that the infantry were saved by a return of the mist concealing the cavalry's flight appears to derive from Swedish efforts to attribute meaning to Gustavus' death: his attack had won the battle, but its impact was lost in the fog.[67] In fact, the Bredow Cuirassiers and Lamboy Arquebusiers met the Swedish countercharge head on: Lieutenant Colonel Tavigny of the Lamboy Regiment was later decorated for bravery. Piccolomini's and Götz's regiments meanwhile threw the Småland and Östagöta cavalry back over the highway. Piccolomini led seven charges, having five horses shot from under him and being hit by six musket balls which failed to pierce his armour. These efforts coincided with the success of the imperial infantry in recovering the seven-gun battery and forcing the three leading Swedish brigades to retreat.

Meanwhile, Pappenheim's light cavalry also met with success. The bulk of them swung east over the Flossgraben and then south past the

Schkölzig wood, while a smaller party advanced directly along the canal's west bank. Colonel Bulach's three squadrons east of the canal were surprised as the Croatians swirled around them, firing their carbines. The Sachsen-Weimar regiment on the extreme right panicked and fled.[68] Without stopping, the Croatians and Cossacks pressed on to attack the Swedish army's small park of 100 wagons which had drawn up between Meuchen and the canal that morning. Some powder wagons were blown up, while the baggage personnel fled to Naumburg. Eventually, Bulach reformed his three squadrons and, assisted by the other three units of the right wing's second line, chased the Croatians north of the highway, probably around 2 p.m. The attack certainly had more than mere 'nuisance value'.[69] It contributed directly to the defeat of the Swedish right wing and centre-right by tying down over 1,000 heavy cavalry and preventing them from aiding the first line as it buckled under the combined weight of the imperial infantry and cavalry counterattacking along the highway.[70]

Renewed Assault on Lützen

Almost certainly still unaware of Gustavus' death, Bernhard had launched another attack against Wallenstein's right wing around 1 p.m. Brigades Thurn and Mitzlaff on the left of the Swedish centre's second line moved forward to support the stalled Green Brigade, along with four of the six cavalry squadrons in the second line of the Swedish right. The remaining two initially stayed in reserve. The last two infantry brigades (Bose and Knyphausen) also moved up in support.[71] Two developments assisted this new attack. First, the Swedish-commanded musketeers finally took the gardens outside Lützen, easing the problem of trying to punch through the narrow gap between the town and Windmill Hill. Second, and paradoxically, the retreat across the highway of the three battered brigades to the right meant these no longer obscured the field of fire of the twenty Swedish heavy guns. These now concentrated their fire on the Windmill battery, forcing the outnumbered imperial guns to withdraw temporarily behind the miller's house. With the way ahead clear, Bernhard's cavalry attacked, driving back the cavalry of the imperial right, and exposing the flank of their infantry stationed behind the Windmill battery. The Green Brigade then surged across the highway, capturing the battery and turning the guns around against the imperialists. Encouraged by these successes, the battered Swedish right also advanced, recapturing the seven-gun battery.

In this critical situation, Wallenstein's 'presence and lively words so animated' the imperial infantry that they rallied and counterattacked.[72] More directly, Wallenstein attached himself to Holk's cuirassier regiment and led this, followed by the Trčka and Desfours troopers, against Bernhard's cavalry. Riding to within four paces of the generalissimo, the Hessian captain Bodo von Bodenhausen fired his pistol, but missed. A musket ball also grazed Wallenstein's left hip, though without breaking his skin. Holk arrived from the left to find his commander at risk of being surrounded, and personally led a successful rescue mission. Adam Trčka had the sole of one of his boots shot off, but remained at the head of his regiment. His lieutenant colonel, Rauchhaupt, was later rewarded for bravery. Others were less fortunate. Berthold Waldstein, one of Wallenstein's distant cousins, died after his foot was shot off, while General Colloredo was wounded in the head.[73] The fighting continued another half hour until Bernhard's men were driven back, relinquishing the Windmill battery to the victorious imperialists. The Swedish centre-right, already tired from their earlier struggle, was also soon repulsed back across the highway sometime between 2 and 3 p.m.

As they retreated, the Swedes 'hastily spiked' the seven-gun battery by driving nails into the touch holes on the barrels to prevent the imperialists from reusing the cannon. However, 'seeing that no enemy soldiers were attempting to retrieve them, Knyphausen ordered the nails taken off... and ordered continuous fire on the enemy'.[74] The fire halted the imperial infantry north of the highway. Their left had been weakened by the earlier flight of half of Pappenheim's heavy cavalry, while the Croatians and Cossacks had returned from their raid to their starting position near the Flossgraben bridge. Some of them may have continued north to plunder what was left of the imperial baggage. By now, Wallenstein had learned of Pappenheim's mortal injuries. Mentally and physically exhausted, the generalissimo relied heavily on Holk's assistance.

However, the Swedes were also tiring. The Yellow and Old Blue Brigades were reduced to a small huddle of survivors, many with broken weapons. The Green and Swedish Brigades were also shattered, while Mitzlaff's, Thurn's, and Henderson's units were all depleted. So many officers had been killed that it was impossible to reorganize the infantry that now straggled in a single line of fragmented groups. The units of the original first line of cavalry on both wings were also largely incapable of further action. Bose's and Knyphausen's brigades, together with the single cavalry regiment left in reserve, were the only units still fully operational. The fighting died down sometime shortly before 3 p.m., as both sides disengaged, restricting themselves to desultory artillery fire and long-range musketry. All participants record this lull as lasting a half hour during which the Swedes withdrew the Yellow, Old Blue, and Swedish brigades to the rear, replacing them with Bose's and Kynphausen's. Thurn's Brigade may also have been switched to the extreme right.

News of Gustavus' Death

It is unclear how far news of Gustavus' death contributed to the failure of this second Swedish attack. News travelled slowly and was not immediately believed. Holk's trumpeter presented one of the king's spurs to Wallenstein who doubted Gustavus was dead. Piccolomini brandished Gustavus' gold chain given him by Martinelli, but even this did not convince Wallenstein who only believed it when he received confirmation on 25 November.[75] Reports that the entire imperial army shouted 'Victoria' probably relate to the retreat of the Swedish centre across the highway. Holk certainly believed the battle was won, and imperial morale was high.

Most of the Swedish army remained unaware until Streiff was seen careering riderless out of the smoke and fog. The anxiety was no doubt heightened by the retreat of the Swedish cavalry on the right wing around the same time. A regimental chaplain reported the news, saying the king was merely wounded and using the Latin *Rex vulneratus est* so that the ordinary soldiers would not become alarmed. Dr Fabricius, the royal chaplain, meanwhile went along the ranks asking for news. He later claimed to have rallied the fugitives by singing the psalm 'Sustain us by thy mighty word'.[76] However, various officers were also engaged in steadying the ranks, notably Fleetwood and the Livonian Colonel Tiesenhausen. Meanwhile, Fabricius continued to deny the king was dead, repeating that he was merely wounded. The smoke continued to conceal the extent of the disorganization and demoralization amongst the Swedes.

Gustavus' corpse was found by some of the survivors of his entourage shortly after 3 p.m. around two hours after Streiff had first been spotted.[77] The body was carried to the rear just as the last Swedish units were disengaging from the fighting north of the highway. It was then placed on an artillery pack wagon and brought to Meuchen Church. Alerted that Gustavus was missing, Bernhard left his forces once they had fallen back and rode to consult Knyphausen who was probably still with the centre. Knyphausen was naturally cautious. Now fully certain of the king's death, he urged retreat while it was still possible to save the army. Bernhard, ambitious and reckless, seized his opportunity to save the day. His forceful personality won the argument. He also seems to have been responsible for the decision to release the news of the king's death to the army.[78] Instead of discouraging them, the news filled the soldiers with a desire for revenge, something which Bernhard fanned in order to win the battle or die trying.[79]

The 'Revenge Attack'

The Swedish heavy guns renewed their bombardment of Windmill Hill as the smoke cleared around 3.30 p.m., while those of the captured

Illustration 7: Panoramic engraving of the battle of Lützen by Matthäus Merian, 1637

Illustration 8: Painting of the battle of Lützen by Pieter Snayers

seven-gun battery blasted the imperial left. Both sides' artillery had now been firing at short range for at least three hours. In an age without machinery like cars or jet engines, the loudest man-made sounds most people heard were church bells. A battle would have appeared deafening: 'all one could hear was the thunder and hail from cannon and muskets'.[80] Bernhard returned to his troops on the left, while Knyphausen took charge of directing the centre-right and right wing in a frontal assault. With the way prepared by the artillery, the Green, Mitzlaff, and Knyphausen brigades carried Windmill Hill at their first rush. Their success was supposedly assisted by the explosion of the imperial powder wagons behind the battery.[81] This episode is widely recounted, probably thanks to its depiction in Matthäus Merian's engraving and subsequent inclusion in Friedrich Schiller's history, but is unlikely to have occurred. Though it would have excused their defeat, imperial accounts do not mention it nor is it shown in Pieter Snayers' painting commissioned by Piccolomini, the most accurate visual portrayal of the battle.[82]

While the infantry assaulted the battery, Bernhard's cavalry attacked the gap between Lützen and the hill, soon putting the Trčka cuirassiers under pressure. Wallenstein ordered Hofkirchen to assist with the Sparr Regiment which had remained behind the imperial right since its ignominious retreat earlier in the day. Hofkirchen's officers had been urging him to redeem his and their honour by returning to the battle. Hofkirchen appears to have advanced briefly, before turning his unit around and fleeing, this time for good, shouting to Wallenstein as he went that he should go into the 'Swedish bloodbath' himself. Wallenstein replied that he would soon warm one as hot for Hofkirchen.[83] The renewed departure of the Sparr cuirassiers disordered the other cavalry on the imperial right. Wallenstein's entourage was caught in the confusion as the Swedish cavalry closed in. Count Harrach, his chief chamberlain and a relative of his wife, fell from his horse after being hit in the throat by a musket ball which penetrated to his ear. He survived, despite being trampled by the fugitives. Schweinsberg, the abbot of Fulda, was less fortunate, mistaking the Swedes advancing through the smoke for his own side. Riding towards them, he was recognized as a Catholic cleric and died in a hail of pistol fire.

Holk rallied the imperial right, while Colloredo steadied the centre. All the remaining units were now fully engaged, with the centre now probably forming a single front as the rear battalions moved forward in support of the original first line.[84] The Jung Waldstein and Breuner regiments bore the brunt of the fighting in the centre, supported on the flanks by the Bredow, Holk, Trčka, and Desfours cuirassiers. It was a bitter struggle. 'After the regiments had run out of ammunition, the musketeers upended their muskets and clubbed each other to death.'[85] Officers were no longer taken prisoner, but cut down like ordinary soldiers; something which explains why so few Swedish commanders were captured. Both sides were already exhausted by the time it became too dark to see around 5 p.m. The gun and cannon fire subsided,

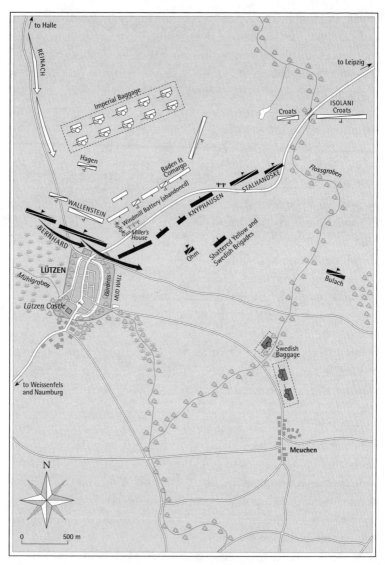

Map 6: Lützen: final positions

though skirmishing continued for another two hours, especially as the Croatians returned to harass the Swedish flanks. The imperialists straightened their line by drawing back their right, abandoning Windmill Hill. Many of them, 'being wonderfull weary man and horse', fell asleep on the cold ground.[86] Most of the Swedes were now well to the south of the highway around 750 m from the imperial line, though it is not clear whether they still held the seven-gun battery.

Wallenstein's Decision to Retreat

Reinach finally arrived with Pappenheim's 2,900 infantry along the Halle road at about 6 p.m. He had already received word of Pappenheim's death and was keen to attack despite the late hour, but was restrained by Holk who rode up to him to summon him to join a council of war convened by Wallenstein.[87] Reinach meanwhile despatched Augustin Fritsch, a captain in his own regiment, to scout ahead. Fritsch recalled going 'with a trusted corporal to reconnoitre and crept on all fours to the Windmill. Because it was fairly quiet, we stood up and looked as far as we could; which wasn't very far in the dark of night. The field was full of lights.' Fritsch at first thought they were the burning matches of enemy musketeers until he realized they were torches carried by soldiers and camp followers plundering the corpses. He promptly returned to Reinach to report that he only needed horses and equipment to recover the imperial battery which stood abandoned on the hill.[88]

Accompanied by Fritsch, Reinach requested to be allowed to occupy Windmill Hill or at least to pull the guns to safety. Wallenstein replied: 'Herr von Reinach, we know more than you. The elector of Saxony and the [duke of] Lüneburg are coming with 16,000 men. We must march immediately.'[89] The elector and Duke Georg only had a quarter of that strength, but the same figure is also reported by Poyntz, suggesting this information was disseminated widely later as the reason for the imperial retreat. Wallenstein may well have believed it, though it is not clear why he now thought the Saxon and Guelph troops at Torgau were a threat, when previously he had been content to remain in the Leipzig area. Already tired and ill, and shaken by the harrowing day, he had clearly already made up his mind to retreat before Reinach arrived. Poyntz recalled 'wee were scarcely laid downe on the ground to rest and in a dead sleep but comes a comment from the Generall [Wallenstein] to all Coronells and Sergeant Majors to give in a note of how strong every Regiment was found to bee'.[90] The roll call had revealed the extent of the appalling losses. Wallenstein believed the army was incapable of further action, writing the next day to Aldringen that 'our people were so desperate that the officers could no longer hold the troopers and privates with their units. Therefore, having consulted the senior officers, I resolved to retire with the army to Leipzig that night.'[91] Holk loyally supported the fateful decision which subsequent official reports further underpinned by reference to officer casualties and lack of supplies.[92]

Wallenstein ordered the army 'to break up without either sound of Trumpet or Drumme' and to abandon the remaining baggage.[93] The earlier flight of the transport personnel and transport animals meant that the Windmill battery had to be left behind as well, though at least three imperial cannon were removed, since the Swedes discovered only eighteen on the battlefield the next day. The retreat began around 6.30 and was well underway within half an hour. The imperialists appear to have been free to take the direct route along the highway over the Flossgraben to Leipzig. Reinach covered the retreat, remaining on the field until 10 p.m. to give time for the main army to clear, as well as his own artillery.

A captured straggler alerted the Swedes that the imperialists were moving, but it was unclear what was happening, especially as the Croatians remained on the battlefield throughout the night. Some sentries were posted on Windmill Hill around 8 p.m. to prevent the imperialists recovering the guns, but otherwise the Swedes kept well out of the way.

5

Military Legacy

Counting the Cost

Dawn on 17 November revealed a grisly sight. The area between
Lützen and the Flossgraben was carpeted with the mangled
bodies of men and horses lying in heaps of twenty or more.[1] The
imperial army left around 3,000 dead on the field, including many who
were simply too badly injured to be brought away and who either died
of their wounds or were finished off by the plunderers. Another 1,160
wounded were abandoned when the army subsequently left Leipzig.
Since these were either murdered or taken prisoner, the army's immediate total loss was about 4,000—a figure which also corresponds to
claims made in contemporary Swedish accounts.[2] At least another
1,000 men would have been wounded, but still able to escape.

Officer casualties were heavy with virtually all regimental commanders being killed or wounded. In addition to Pappenheim, the
senior imperial dead included artillery general Breuner, four colonels,
and ten lieutenant colonels, while Colloredo, Piccolomini, and eight
lieutenant colonels were wounded. Wallenstein and Holk were among
the more lightly injured. The Piccolomini Arquebusiers lost 40 per
cent of their total strength, while the Baden, Breuner, Comargo, and
Alt Sachsen infantry regiments all suffered high losses.[3]

Pappenheim was treated to all the pomp and ritual owing to a
Catholic military hero. His corpse was carried as the army left Leipzig.
Daily masses for his soul were held during the retreat, and his body
was displayed on a wagon in the marketplace, surrounded by burning

candles, during the halt at Chemnitz. Wallenstein held a commemorative service in Prague on 28 February 1633 for both Pappenheim and his own cousin, Berthold von Waldstein. Pappenheim was then finally interred at Strahov Monastery to the pealing of bells from all of Prague's forty-four churches. The costs were borne by Wallenstein who sent his personal condolences together with a gift of 5,000 talers to Pappenheim's widow.[4] This prominence was not sustained, probably because Pappenheim's period of independent command had been too brief and devoid of large battles to attract the attention of later military historians. He was remembered largely through his literary commemoration in Schiller's *Wallenstein* drama trilogy, as well as one of the battle's iconic artefacts: the bloodstained letter retrieved from Pappenheim's corpse which had summoned him from Halle has been displayed at the Viennese army museum since February 1889.

Imperial losses were magnified by additional casualties, prisoners, and stragglers during the retreat to Bohemia, enabling the Swedes to claim Wallenstein lost two-thirds of his army; a figure accepted uncritically by some later accounts as the total incurred in the battle itself.[5] The Swedes found eighteen heavy guns on the battlefield, plus another three which the imperialists had managed to drag away, but subsequently abandoned before reaching Leipzig. Another three cannon were taken later, since twenty-four captured guns are recorded as being moved to Dömitz Fortress in Mecklenburg in April 1633. What was left of the baggage also fell into Swedish hands, along with twenty wagons full of ammunition; the latter giving lie to Wallenstein's claim that shortage of supplies was a factor prompting his retreat.[6]

Imperial officers refuted parts of this trophy list, recording only four to six flags lost, including the colonel's colour of the Hagen regiment abandoned in its rout.[7] Flags and standards had long been considered markers of victory since their capture from men who had sworn to defend them was considered a sign of martial superiority. More directly, they measured how badly an opponent had been defeated, because they were usually only taken from units which had suffered very heavy losses or had fled in battle. The Swedes had collected such trophies since the 1560s, doing so systematically after 1630 when they were housed in the royal armoury. Most Swedish accounts appearing directly after Lützen are surprisingly reticent about the numbers actually captured, though a pamphlet published in 1633 listed twenty-eight standards and fifty flags in addition to thirty cannon. Few imperial units broke in the battle, so the lower figures cited by imperial officers are probably correct for 16 November, with around twenty-five other flags and standards taken from units which surrendered during the subsequent retreat. By contrast, the Swedes lost between thirty and sixty flags and standards, including many that were just bare poles.[8]

The contemporary imperial claim that the Swedes lost 8,000 killed and wounded was an exaggeration, but their casualties still probably totalled around 6,000.[9] At least 1,500 Swedes were killed immediately, while 2,543 infantrymen were badly wounded, of whom a quarter to a half would have died of their injuries. The cavalry had around 1,000 wounded.[10] Losses for individual units ranged from 16 per cent for Thurn and Bose's brigades to around two-thirds of the Yellow and Old Blue brigades. Around 100 senior officers were killed or wounded, including Major General Brahe, three colonels, and two lieutenant colonels dead on the field or shortly after, and another four colonels, two lieutenant colonels, and the Hessian General Uslar who were injured but lived. As with their imperial counterparts, the heavy officer casualties indicate the ferocity of the close-quarter fighting and the degree of degradation of operational capacity during the battle.

Gustavus' death was the one the Swedes felt the most keenly. His corpse had been recovered in the later afternoon and taken by troopers from the Finnish cavalry regiment to Meuchen village where the Swedish baggage had collected. Gustavus was laid on a wooden table in Meuchen's small stone church to be cleaned. The viscera (waste water) was collected in a jar which was placed by the church door and later buried[11]—the first sign of the reverence which henceforth accompanied everything to do with him. After an autopsy, the body was moved that night to Weissenfels where Bernhard disregarded the late king's instructions and had it opened and embalmed in the same room in the inn where Pappenheim had stayed a few days before. Thereafter, the corpse was moved to Wittenberg for public display on 8 December. Gustav Gustavsson, the late king's illegitimate son who was studying at Wittenberg's prestigious Lutheran university, stood watch over his father. The body was then transported to Wolgast in Pomerania where it remained for six months until a sufficiently imposing Swedish fleet had assembled to escort it home.

Arriving in haste from Erfurt, Maria Eleonore collapsed when she met her husband's corpse at Weissenfels. Already regarded as dim, shallow, and silly even by Gustavus, Maria Eleonore's grief has widely been regarded as bordering on madness. Her behaviour included delaying her husband's burial until June 1634 and trying to disinter him later.[12] Her apparent instability has served in later biographies to accentuate Gustavus' masculinity and religiosity, enabling him to appear as a pious warrior single-mindedly pursuing national and spiritual goals without the comforts or distractions of female company. It also served the more immediate political interests of the Swedish councillors led by Chancellor Oxenstierna who swiftly established a regency council to rule in the name of six-year-old Queen Christina, thereby excluding Maria Eleonore and her Brandenburg relations from any influence over Swedish policy.

Around 1,500 Swedish wounded were evacuated with the army to Naumburg, while others capable of being moved were transported to Leipzig. The rest were left in Lützen in the care of the inhabitants who sent them away as soon as possible. Leipzig was still looking after 300 wounded plus abandoned women and camp followers in March 1633. After two months of accommodating the rival armies, the locals were overwhelmed by the task of clearing the battlefield. Lützen officials appealed to Weissenfels to send 200 men to help bury the dead which still covered the area two days after the battle. The bodies were interred in pits along the main road where the bulk of the fighting had taken place. Eléasar Mauvillon, a French Huguenot academic working in Germany, noted in 1738, on his first of many visits to the battlefield, that there were three slight rises which inhabitants told him were burial pits; one where the imperial left had been, one behind their centre, and one where the Swedish centre had stood.[13]

The corpses poisoned the ground water, obliging Lützen also to request beer and food from Weissenfels. Over half the 17 deaths recorded in Meuchen parish for 1632 occurred in November and December. The next six months saw another 64 deaths; an extraordinarily high figure given the small population. Lützen recorded 82 deaths for 1632, compared to 48 the previous year, with 37 inhabitants dying between 17 November and 21 December. Another 21 died during January and February, compared to 17 across the rest of 1633. Malnutrition and hardship were contributory factors, reducing the inhabitants' resistance to illness.[14] Two inhabitants were killed by imperial soldiers prior to the battle. Pastor Stockmann was plundered by the retreating imperialists who stole his books and burnt his larder. Lützen's church organ was smashed and the graves ransacked. Even eighteen years later the town was described as 'burned out'.[15]

The Immediate Aftermath

Wallenstein rode ahead accompanied by eighty cavalrymen, reaching Leipzig around midnight on 16 November. The rest of the army followed, with Reinach and the rear guard arriving at 7 a.m. The retreat was made 'in exemplary order', but demoralization set in as manifest by desertion and marauding.[16] Nonetheless, later claims of a rout are grossly exaggerated. Wallenstein stayed twenty hours in Leipzig, before leaving with his escort for Chemnitz. He was convinced that Arnim was much closer than he really was, and feared the Saxons would either cut him off from Bohemia, or invade that kingdom. He was also conscious that reports of his retreat were encouraging the Saxon population to turn openly hostile, endangering the scattered imperial detachments. Nonetheless, the main factor in his decision was clearly his continuing depression and trauma from the battle.[17]

The imperial infantry followed their commander at 6 p.m. on 17 November, heading south for Bohemia. There was 'no end to the lamentations and cries' from the 1,160 seriously wounded left behind, but they were too badly injured to be moved and the army also lacked sufficient wagons to transport them, though the officers were brought away.[18] The cavalry rested a few more hours in the suburbs before pulling out, followed early the next day by ten companies of Croatians forming the new rear guard. Having reached Chemnitz on 19 November, Wallenstein halted for a few days to concentrate his forces and consult Holk. Orders were despatched to Gallas and other subordinates to secure the Bohemian–Saxon frontier, while Francesco de Grana hurried to Vienna to explain why Wallenstein believed it was now necessary to winter in Habsburg territory. Grana fell ill on route, perhaps reluctant to be the bearer of bad news, so it fell to another Italian in imperial service, Giulio Diodati, to report to Ferdinand II on 29 November. Diodati stressed the significance of Gustavus' death and played up the bravery of imperial officers, especially those who had been injured. His report profoundly shaped the immediate reception of the battle by the Habsburg courts in Vienna and Madrid, which will be discussed later in this chapter. Meanwhile, Wallenstein continued his retreat on 23 November, leaving Colonel Contreras to hold Chemnitz as a base for future operations against Saxony.

The Swedes had remained in a state of alarm, camping in battle order without food or drink throughout the night into 17 November. Bernhard remained undecided whether to renew the fight or withdraw to Weissenfels until dawn revealed that the imperialists had retreated. Swedish morale recovered, but the army was in no position to pursue Wallenstein, especially as the politically sensitive question of command needed to be resolved.[19] The troops formed up at 10 a.m. for an hour to receive the formal news of Gustavus' death, before marching back to Weissenfels with the wounded. Lack of transport and the presence of twenty-five companies of Croatians hovering around the battlefield prevented the Swedes from removing all of the eighteen heavy guns left by Wallenstein. The Croatians remained in the area, ranging as far as Rippach where they intercepted six of the guns, killing the twenty-five Swedish musketeers escorting them and then breaking the wheels of the gun carriages to hinder their further removal. The imperial musketeers in Lützen Castle held out for a further three days, before being violently ejected by Saxon and Guelph troops. Only then could the battlefield be properly cleared. The Swedes took the abandoned artillery, but left the rest of the weapons and equipment for the Saxons who carried off four wagonloads of cannon balls and armour to Leipzig by 25 November.

It was not until 20 November that Bernhard reached Leipzig to join Johann Georg's 3,000 Saxon infantry. A further 1,000 Saxon cavalry and Duke Georg's 3,000 Guelph horsemen arrived the next day. The cavalry belatedly set off after Wallenstein, while advance parties of the infantry broke into the city aided by local militiamen, and murdered 150 imperial wounded and stragglers before taking the others prisoner.[20] Holk had left 700 infantry under Major von Mosen in the Pleissenberg castle to distract and delay the enemy. Mosen's task was assisted by the Saxons' lack of preparation—Johann Georg's troops had to borrow six cannon from the city council to bombard the castle. Having more than discharged his duty by tying down the Saxons for nearly four weeks, Mosen surrendered on 13 December in return for safe passage to the Bohemian frontier.

Meanwhile, Swedish and other Saxon forces mopped up the remaining imperial garrisons. Chemnitz already surrendered on 2 December, much to Wallenstein's annoyance. Freiberg was abandoned without a fight, while Colonel de Suys surrendered Zwickau on 6 January before Holk could relieve him. Like Mosen, each garrison received free passage, though that in Chemnitz was obliged to hand over its flags and artillery. Contrary to their promises, the Swedes forced some of the retreating imperialists to join their own ranks. Mosen deliberately allowed his men to drink before leaving the Pleissenberg, calculating that their temporary good humour would make them less susceptible to Swedish inducements: only twenty of his remaining 669 men defected. Johann Georg had meanwhile mobilized the Saxon militia who, supported by peasants, harried the retreating imperialists. Mosen's party was attacked on 26 December as it crossed the mountains into Bohemia. The official Swedish-Saxon escort stood by as peasants murdered forty-five imperial soldiers along with their families. Others scattered and only 348 men escaped with their commander.[21]

Wallenstein's decision to retreat had exposed his men to the rigours of winter marches. Combined with the loss of cosy Saxon billets, this magnified the sense of defeat. Now that they were no longer wintering in Saxony, the imperialists felt free to vent their frustration on the inhabitants. Forced requisitioning was accompanied by open plunder and deliberate destruction in which the small town of Zschopau and several villages were burned. The bitter small war of skirmishes across the frontier continued over the winter. However, later claims that 'the army entirely disintegrated' are exaggerated.[22] By pulling back, Wallenstein was able to regroup, consolidate, and rehabilitate his forces which still mustered 102,000 overall.[23]

Who Won?

The character of Wallenstein's retreat is a necessary part of any evaluation of Lützen's outcome. The general concept of a 'decisive' victory is that it should have some meaningful impact on the strategic balance, if not actually deciding the outcome of a war. Breitenfeld certainly meets those criteria, and the scale of the imperial and League collapse after that battle contrasts sharply with Lützen where Wallenstein merely evacuated the southwestern third of Saxony his troops had briefly occupied.

Unsurprisingly, Swedish propaganda immediately claimed a great victory. The semi-official account published in Torgau three days later asserted that imperial losses exceeded those suffered by Tilly's army at Breitenfeld and that numerous, mostly unnamed, senior officers had been killed or captured.[24] This verdict was subsequently elaborated in hagiographic accounts of Gustavus and his contribution to the development of warfare which trumpeted Lützen as a 'complete' or at least 'major' triumph.[25] The main qualification such writers were prepared to accept was that Gustavus' death ensured it was a 'mournful victory'.[26] Some felt the king's loss was so significant as to 'negate' the otherwise positive outcome.[27] A more measured version of this view argues that the Swedes won a tactical victory by all contemporary criteria (casualties, trophies, holding the field), but Gustavus' death robbed them of the opportunity to convert it into a strategic one. Exponents of this view generally extend this by excusing Gustavus of any responsibility by treating his actions up until his death as leading towards victory, whilst blaming Bernhard and the other generals for failing to follow up the alleged advantage.[28] The more sober of Gustavus' biographers regard the outcome as undecided, or a draw, only to be converted to a modest Swedish victory through Wallenstein's decision to retreat.[29]

Perhaps equally unsurprisingly, Wallenstein's biographers conclude he won a tactical victory, only to throw it away by retreating. The same criteria cited by Gustavus' partisans for a Swedish victory appear in these accounts of an imperial success: Wallenstein still held the field at the end of the day, and had lost fewer men and flags. Certainly, the feeling among many imperial soldiers present was 'that Wallenston had had the better of the day'.[30] Many feel that Wallenstein's decision to retreat was premature, especially considering the arrival of reinforcements under Reinach.[31] Wallenstein's mental state was clearly a major factor in this fateful decision and he never fully recovered, becoming even more curt and irritable, as well as more battle-averse and inclined towards peace.[32] The sense of disappointment was magnified by the contrast between the battle's outcome and the high hopes accompanying Wallenstein's reappointment as commander at the start of the campaign.[33]

Others interpreted the result as a draw. Again, this was a view held by some participants, like Holk, as well as some later writers.[34] Certainly, Gustavus' death halted Swedish expansion in the Empire, though that was far from clear until the later imperial victory at Nördlingen in 1634.

This has led a few to claim Lützen as a Swedish strategic defeat.[35] Certainly, in a more limited sense, Wallenstein achieved his overall objectives for the 1632 campaign in inflicting serious checks on the Swedes (both Lützen and Alte Veste) and in driving them from Bohemia and Bavaria.[36]

The Follow-Up

The Swedes' inability to capitalize on Wallenstein's decision to retreat further underscored the battle's disappointing outcome. Most immediately, Gustavus' death removed the primary brake on the centrifugal forces within Sweden's alliance system which swiftly emerged in a struggle to determine future operations. Bernhard hastened to Dresden to consult Johann Georg who was already looking for an opportunity to switch sides provided Ferdinand offered sufficient concessions. The Saxons had no interest in an energetic pursuit of Wallenstein into Bohemia which would jeopardize their secret negotiations with the imperialists. Saxon operations accordingly concentrated on improving their bargaining position by ejecting the remaining imperial garrisons from their own territory.[37]

Meanwhile, Bernhard was driven by personal ambition to carve out his own principality from the ecclesiastical land captured during the previous eighteen months and correctly deduced that Gustavus' death would make it harder for the Swedes to resist his demands. In fact, Chancellor Oxenstierna fought hard to retain direct control of the conquered Franconian bishoprics, recognizing their value as bargaining chips in any agreement he might strike with the emperor to extricate Sweden from what now appeared a costly and unwinnable war. At the very least, he was not prepared to cede land until he had achieved Gustavus' goal of corralling Sweden's allies and collaborators within a closer alliance. The disappointing outcome of his negotiations further demonstrates Sweden's weakness after Lützen. Though Oxenstierna persuaded the smaller south and west German partners to form the Heilbronn League in April 1633, the refusal of Brandenburg or

Saxony to commit to this arrangement left the alliance politically impotent and militarily weak. A direct sign of this was the Heilbronn League's failure to prevent Bernhard orchestrating a mutiny of its own army across southern Germany in April–May 1633 which finally forced Oxenstierna to give him Bamberg and Würzburg as a new duchy of Franconia.[38]

News of Gustavus' death was greeted with jubilation by his enemies. Robert Monro, then stationed in Landsberg in Bavaria, noted with puzzlement that the imperial army advanced to the town in battle order and fired three salvoes. It was only once the Swedish garrison received word of their king's death that they understood the reason for this celebration.[39] Having received Diodati's oral report on 29 November, Ferdinand immediately dashed off a personal letter to Wallenstein congratulating him on his victory. Vienna's church bells were rung to announce the good news, while Peter von Strahlendorf, the senior Habsburg official with responsibility for the Empire, wrote soon after to the generalissimo proclaiming Lützen the greatest victory for two centuries.[40] The news reached Madrid at Christmas and was confirmed two days later, triggering twelve days of fireworks, religious services, and theatre performances, including a hastily prepared drama, *Gustavus Adolphus' Death*. Even Pope Urban VIII, who feared the outcome presaged a dangerous growth of Habsburg power, held a celebratory mass in Rome. Wladislaw IV, the new king of Poland, expressed some regret at the death of a fellow Vasa, despite Gustavus being both a political and confessional rival.[41]

The sense of relief at the death of a dangerous foe was palpable in both Habsburg capitals. Ferdinand regarded it as the answer to his prayers, while Count Duke Olivares, in charge of Spanish policy, welcomed it as the first good news to arrive after a difficult year. Both courts also interpreted it as a divine reward for having rejected an earlier offer from a would-be assassin to murder the Swedish king.[42] Yet, unease quickly surfaced. Doubts that the battle had really been a victory were already expressed by the Venetian ambassador in Vienna on 27 November. Elector Maximilian agreed, and refused to congratulate Wallenstein whom he still resented for recalling Aldringen from Bavaria.[43]

Any feel-good factor soon dissipated as Austrian and Spanish planners disagreed over how best to exploit Gustavus' death. Olivares hoped that Lützen had improved Ferdinand's position sufficiently that he could now offer concessions to Sweden's German allies without losing face. Peace in the Empire was a long-running Spanish goal, since it was essential if Austria were to be able to assist in its own war against the Dutch. Olivares accelerated existing plans to despatch a Spanish army from Italy into Germany as part of this strategy. Though the first expedition ended in failure in 1633, a second army arrived in time to join the imperialists in defeating the Swedes at Nördlingen in September 1634. France was already aware of these plans after Lützen and sent an envoy to assist Oxenstierna in rallying the weaker German allies within the Heilbronn League. Once Nördlingen finished the League as a political body, France moved to secure its army under Bernhard in case Sweden made peace with the emperor. This led to France's military involvement in the war in the Empire after 1635, culminating in an active alliance with Sweden across the 1640s.

Meanwhile, Lützen triggered a showdown in Vienna between a narrow zealous faction and a more pragmatic group. The former was represented by Ferdinand's Jesuit confessor, Lamormani, who had been criticized since Breitenfeld for courting disaster by encouraging the emperor's hard line over the Edict of Restitution. Lamormani responded by claiming that Lützen vindicated his faith in Providentialist theology: the victory was a clear sign of divine reward for the emperor's refusal to sacrifice true religion to political necessity after Breitenfeld. Rather than compromising over the Edict to win over Saxony and other Swedish allies, Lamormani urged Ferdinand to make political concessions to France to form a solidly Catholic alliance. The emperor's secular advisors opposed these proposals. Even the overly optimistic Strahlendorf doubted that the imperial army alone had the capacity to evict the Swedes from the Empire, and instead urged capitalizing on the temporary advantage provided by Lützen to open peace talks with the new Swedish regency government under Oxenstierna.

There is a story still repeated today that King Christian IV cried at the news of Gustavus' death, while the Danish chancellor Christen Frijis stayed in his room for two days of mourning. It is far more likely that the king, chancellor, and others were in closed conference debating how Denmark could profit from this opportunity to limit the expansion of their Swedish rival. Certainly, Christian IV wrote directly to Wallenstein on 11 December 1632 offering to mediate.[44] Wallenstein welcomed this, having always regarded military operations as means to pressure opponents into negotiating, rather than as chances to defeat them outright. Ferdinand accepted this course of action by late January 1633, welcoming Danish mediation and opening talks with the Saxons at Leitmeritz in Bohemia two months later.[45] The next two years saw a complex interlocking sequence of negotiations and military operations, both to force Sweden to make peace and to weaken it by persuading Brandenburg and Saxony to change sides. Wallenstein's conduct throughout 1633 was used against him by his personal enemies, since it was far from clear whether he was operating on his own account or on Ferdinand's behalf, culminating in the generalissimo's judicial murder in February 1634. Nonetheless, it was the most sensible course of action, and the absence of quick results was due primarily to Ferdinand's failure to open with a sufficiently good offer to the Swedes who soon felt that continuing the war was the only way to ensure that the blood and treasure they had expended since 1630 were not all in vain.[46]

In retrospect, Lützen emerges as a marginal imperial tactical victory which could have been a significant strategic one had Wallenstein kept his nerve. However, that would have required certain knowledge of Gustavus' death which Wallenstein only received several days later. Wallenstein's decision to retreat opened the possibility for the Swedes to convert it into a strategic victory, but their ability to do so was in turn undermined by Gustavus' death and the underlying weakness of their alliance system and position in the Empire, as well as the continued resilience of the imperial army which recovered still further across the winter. Thus, Lützen scarcely warrants the accolade of a 'decisive victory' accorded it by Gustavus' hagiographers and subsequent military historians.

The Prague Bloody Court

The ambiguity surrounding the outcome of the battle was further encouraged by Wallenstein's subsequent conduct towards his army. Ahead of his arrival in Prague on 2 December 1632, Wallenstein instructed Nicolaus Staffier, the senior military policeman, to institute a court martial, while arrest warrants were soon issued for Bönninghausen, Hofkirchen, Hagen, and other officers accused of cowardice. The officers were incarcerated in the White Tower of Prague Castle and in the prison of the city's Old Town Hall. Meanwhile, the regiments which had fled in the battle were disbanded and the men distributed to other units in a clear indication that a guilty verdict was a foregone conclusion.[47]

Holk opposed this search for scapegoats and assumed oversight of the proceedings only with great reluctance, while Hatzfeldt, Piccolomini, and other officers expressed dissatisfaction.[48] In fact, martial law allowed for immediate punishment without trial for obvious cases of desertion in battle. If Wallenstein had been purely motivated by revenge, as some have claimed, he could have dispensed with a court martial. Instead he hoped that a trial would reveal more about the weaknesses in the imperial army and assist his wider agenda of modest reform in time for the coming campaign, as well as sending a clear signal about the restoration of discipline.

Two tribunals composed of officers and non-commissioned officers convened on 21 January to try the accused from infantry and cavalry units separately. Prague was locked down, with an entire infantry regiment guarding the court house thanks to rumours that the Saxon Colonel Lorenz von Hofkirchen had promised to rescue his brother Albrecht. Albrecht von Hofkirchen's behaviour was criticized later as 'a deliberate sabotage' due to a crisis of conscience.[49] Yet, many Protestant officers served loyally in the imperial army, and Hofkirchen's exact motives are unclear as he allegedly converted to Catholicism whilst in prison.[50] The sentences were read out on 11 February and three days later Hofkirchen, Hagen, nine junior officers, and nine soldiers were executed on the same spot used in 1621 for the condemned Bohemian rebels.

Holk had already interceded for Bönninghausen ahead of the trial, securing his pardon and despatch to Dortmund to raise another cavalry regiment—a unit which promptly fled at the battle of Hessisch Oldendorf on 28 June 1633, demonstrating both Bönninghausen's poor leadership and the fragility of raw troops.[51] Holk was less successful in his intercession for Cavalry Captain Wobersnau whom he described as a 'child', though he was actually 18, who was executed despite last-minute appeals for clemency.

The trial stirred resentment amongst the imperial officer corps, while the ordinary soldiers dubbed Wallenstein the 'hanging duke' and the *Galgensteiner*—a pun on his surname meaning 'Gallowssteiner'. The divisions were short-lived and the establishment swiftly closed ranks. Colonel Hagen's uncle, Elector-archbishop Wamboldt of Mainz, appealed on his behalf, motivated both by familial ties and common membership of the Teutonic Order. However, once it became obvious that the intercession would fail, Wamboldt arranged to have Hagen expelled from the Order so that it would not be tainted by the disgrace of his execution. Meanwhile, the army was mollified by lavish rewards. Piccolomini had already been promoted to major general and given a 10,000 florin cash bonus on 21 December, while Holk was made field marshal ten days later together with the gift of an estate encompassing eighteen villages in Bohemia. His regiment received 2,850 florins, distributed so that wounded officers and men were given two months' pay and the others a single month. Similar bonuses totalling 85,000 florins were given to the other eighteen regular infantry and cavalry regiments which had not fled in the battle, with some individuals being singled out with the reward of promotions, gold chains, or ennoblement.[52]

Change in the Imperial Army

The Prague 'bloody court' martial was part of Wallenstein's wider post-battle analysis which led to a number of modest changes in armament, organization, and tactics. The absence of comprehensive reform was not a reflection of any innate conservatism, but rather the result of a sober assessment of both Swedish and imperial military practice. From this, Wallenstein concluded that Swedish methods were far from universally superior, and overall the changes represented a continuation of the measures he had initiated at the start of his second generalship in December 1631, rather than being solely a response to Lützen as often claimed.[53]

The cavalry was the branch most affected; clearly a consequence of the poor performance of the relatively raw arquebusiers at Lützen. Wallenstein was not simply disappointed at the behaviour of the Hagen and Goschütz regiments, but believed the entire arm was a hindrance, complaining to his senior officers that the German cavalry did not know how to use their carbines properly.[54] His orders to re-equip arquebusiers as cuirassiers were not fully implemented, but the number of regiments was reduced from twenty at the start of 1633 to fifteen by 1634, falling to eight two years later. Meanwhile, the number of cuirassier regiments rose steadily to peak at sixty-one in 1641. The light cavalry were also expanded, perhaps reflecting the success of the Croatians in harassing the Swedish flanks at Lützen, as well as screening the army's movements throughout the campaign. Having already been doubled to six regiments in December 1631, the number of Croatian units rose to nineteen by 1633, while the dragoons were increased from one regiment in 1631 to thirteen by 1634.[55] The uncertainty surrounding Swedish methods was demonstrated by the unevenness of the performance of the imperial heavy cavalry after 1632 as

Wallenstein reduced deployment to five or even four ranks. Thinning the formation adversely affected steadiness and may have been a factor in the precipitous flight of several regiments at the second battle of Breitenfeld in 1642; something which robbed the imperial army of a much needed victory at a crucial stage of the war.[56]

Changes to the other two branches were limited. Infantry officers were ordered to wear more armour to reduce the casualties which were believed to have adversely affected the cohesion of some units at Lützen. Simultaneously, Holk was given 10,000 florins to rebuild the artillery, including ensuring that each regiment had two light cannon.[57]

These changes amounted to tinkering with existing structures, rather than a complete overhaul, yet the cautious approach was vindicated by the battle of Nördlingen fought seven months after Wallenstein's murder, but with the army he had forged. Sweden's south German army was comprehensively defeated, triggering a collapse equivalent to that experienced by the imperialists and Catholic League after Breitenfeld in 1631.[58] Importantly, both sides at Nördlingen were still configured largely as they had been in November 1632, underscoring that the outcome at Lützen (and indeed Breitenfeld) cannot be explained simply in terms of any inherent superiority in Swedish military methods. In fact, it was the Swedes who changed the most, abandoning the checkerboard infantry brigade deployment after Nördlingen in favour of the simpler formation used by the imperialists, albeit in slightly thinner lines. All armies increasingly used broadly similar tactics, with the concept of a distinct 'Swedish system' persisting largely thanks to it being enshrined in printed tactical manuals, such as that produced by William Watts, as well as the numerous British officers who took these ideas back when they returned home around 1638 to fight in the civil wars. The defects of the Swedish brigade swiftly became apparent after its use by the Royalists at Edgehill in October 1642, and both sides converged like their continental counterparts in using the common pattern of pikemen flanked by musketeers, all in five to seven ranks.[59]

News and Images

Full assessment of Lützen's military legacy was hindered by the absence of reliable information about what had actually happened. The reports published in 1632–3 were contradictory and incomplete. The publicly available account of the battle was swiftly reduced to a few essentials which were soon no longer questioned thanks to their constant repetition. Most of these served to underpin the commemoration of Gustavus as a Protestant martyr which will be explored in Chapter 6. Only a minority of publications concerned themselves with the battle in more detail, initially from a professional military interest, but from the mid-eighteenth century onwards also as a subject of academic historical research.

Later perceptions were profoundly shaped by the fact that the bulk of the contemporary published material favoured the Swedes, including printed reports, illustrated broadsheets, and panegyrics on Gustavus. Broadsheets were single, large-format prints combining text with an engraved image which added considerably to their appeal and influence on readers. One prominent example reprinted the pro-Swedish *Erfurt Relation* almost verbatim, but also contributed to much subsequent confusion by recycling an earlier engraving of Breitenfeld which was only superficially altered to correspond with the text about Lützen.[60]

The battle plan produced only slightly later by the famous engraver Matthäus Merian also echoed Breitenfeld by showing a gallows behind the imperial centre, either as an error from copying pictures of the earlier battle or intended as symbolic given the artist's pro-Swedish inclination. This plan was hugely influential thanks to its wide dissemination in the news digest *Theatrum Europaeum*, which became a standard source already while the war was still in progress. Frederick Henry of Orange drew a copy in his notebook around 1640.[61] It formed the basis of battle plans illustrating later Gustavus biographies, such as that by Mauvillon published in 1764. The Swedish deployment appears fairly accurately, reflecting the sources Merian used, and this is

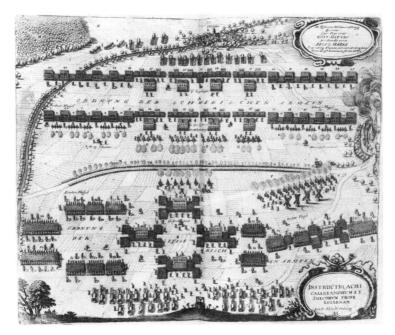

Illustration 9: Engraved plan of the battle by Matthäus Merian (1593–1650)

repeated in other near contemporary material which sometimes omitted the imperial army altogether.[62] However, Merian depicted the imperial infantry in large tercios which bore no relation to the actual formations used and were probably lifted from an old tactical manual in the absence of more accurate information. Wallenstein's actual battle plan was published in 1829, but was long dismissed as depicting camp arrangements rather than fighting formations, not least because the idea of imperial backwardness had become so deeply engrained.[63]

Great Captains

The presence of both Gustavus and Wallenstein was a major factor in sustaining interest in Lützen, not least because the latter's death in 1634 assumed significance as a watershed in later accounts of the Thirty

Years War. None of the generals of the second half of the war achieved comparable prominence in subsequent military history, contributing to the belief that the war descended into 'meaningless violence' after about 1635, devoid of any real interest for future generations of soldiers or historians.[64] The focus on the commanders reflected the general belief that, after God, human events were determined by 'great men'; a view which dominated historical writing prior to the twentieth century and still shapes popular military history today. The moral-theological roots of this conception of history encouraged a preoccupation with the commanders' personal characteristics and motives, since it was believed that it was these attributes that made them 'great'.

The Swedish king was already celebrated in his own lifetime as 'Captaine of Kings and King of Captaines, Gustavus the Invincible'.[65] Later commentators were not always unqualified in their admiration, with Napoleon for example remarking that 'Tilly and Wallenstein were better generals than Gustavus Adolphus'.[66] However, the fact that both he and other renowned commanders like Frederick the Great of Prussia discussed Gustavus alongside Alexander the Great, Turenne, Marlborough, and history's other 'great captains' helped cement the Swedish king's reputation as an outstanding general. Meanwhile, clerical writers continued the line established by Swedish propaganda in 1630–2 that Gustavus' victories were due to his moral and spiritual virtue which imbued him and his army with the courage and skill required to overcome their mighty enemies. Carl Rößler, deacon in Merseburg, called Gustavus the 'greatest general of his age', echoing the secular stadial view of history that each epoch was exemplified by 'world historical' figures.[67] Gustav Rosenthal, another deacon, described Gustavus as 'the bravest of the brave' at the 250th anniversary of the battle.[68]

The Prussian military theoretician, Carl von Clausewitz, also included Gustavus in his pantheon of great generals in his famous book *On War*, but his comments were brief and ambivalent. By likening the Swedish king to a 'new Alexander', Clausewitz drew attention to his conquests rather than celebrated him in the manner of some civilian writers. He noted that, like Charles XII and Frederick the Great, Gustavus depended on his army rather than his own kingdom for his power. Clausewitz's contemporary, Baron Jomini, was even less interested in military history before the mid-eighteenth century and simply mentioned Gustavus' landing in Pomerania in 1630 in his chronological survey of 'maritime expeditions'.[69]

By the time that Clausewitz and Jomini were writing in the 1820s, discussions of Gustavus and Wallenstein were becoming enmeshed in wider controversies over Germany's political future, as we shall see in Chapter 6. Protestant and pro-Prussian writers invariably presented Gustavus as a great general, whereas Catholics, Austrians, and south Germans praised Wallenstein and Tilly. Onno Klopp, a Lutheran convert to Catholicism, denigrated Gustavus in 1861 in order to magnify Tilly's achievements. A statue of Tilly was erected in Munich's Feldherrnhalle ('General's Hall') in 1843 and was part of official efforts to anchor Bavaria's sovereignty in a glorious historical past. Bavaria's royal status dated only from 1806 and had been secured through an alliance with Napoleon against Austria, calling into question the 'German' credentials of the ruling Wittelsbach dynasty. By honouring Tilly, the Bavarian authorities were trying to link their own history to that of the wider German past through a distinctly Catholic interpretation of the Holy Roman Empire.[70]

Wallenstein was the subject of 2,524 publications by 1908, a level of attention only exceeded by that devoted to Gustavus.[71] However, Lützen played a subordinate role in Wallenstein's image, partly because of the widespread later perception of it as a defeat. Additionally, Wallenstein had become remembered primarily as an army organizer and strategist, rather than as a battlefield commander like Gustavus or Tilly. Above all, interpretations were dominated by the circumstances of his death in February 1634 at the hands of a small band of junior imperial officers acting with the prior approval of Ferdinand II. The emperor had sanctioned Wallenstein's judicial murder, because it was believed he was about to defect to the enemy and that it was clear he was now more of a hindrance than a help in securing a deal with

Saxony. The question of whether the generalissimo had betrayed the emperor swiftly dominated assessments of his entire career, including his dispersal of the imperial army into winter quarters prior to Lützen which was presented in pamphlets appearing after his assassination as an act of deliberate sabotage.[72]

As with Gustavus, the basic parameters of these discussions were laid during his lifetime and immediately after his death. Schiller's drama trilogy, written as the French revolutionary wars swept over Germany, then cemented the view of Wallenstein as a victim of his own flaws, notably his personal ambition.[73] Current events clearly influenced Schiller's interpretation and the connections were not lost on his audience either. Clausewitz read various incidents in Napoleon's life through Schiller's portrayal of Wallenstein, and likewise saw both commanders' power as resting on military might rather than political institutions.[74] Underlying such observations were fairly conservative views about the relationship of war to the state. Wallenstein and Napoleon were regarded as illegitimate usurpers who used their military power to overturn social and political conventions. Though Wallenstein was ultimately unsuccessful in his (alleged) political ambitions, his practice of making war pay for itself through the contributions system was interpreted as liberating his soldiers from the conventions of daily life in a manner almost as revolutionary as for the men who served Napoleon. In the final part of Schiller's trilogy, Wallenstein's assassination restores conventional political control over the army through the restoration of the emperor's authority.

Lützen's Place in Military History

The rapid acceleration in changes in military technology around 1870 encouraged a broader view of military history which took more account of the wider context, including the role of the state and of armies as political and social institutions. Nonetheless, the great captains remained as exemplifiers of what were still seen as epochal shifts along a linear path to modernity. This approach is best illustrated by

Hans Delbrück who had fought in the Franco-Prussian War of 1870–1 before becoming a university professor. He wanted to historicize military affairs by rejecting attempts to reduce them to allegedly transcendental precepts. Battles and campaigns should be studied as part of wider human history rather than to provide timeless lessons to educate officers.[75]

Above all, Delbrück popularized the view of early modern European warfare as progressing through a sequence of 'schools', or systems of coherent and self-conscious forms of strategic and tactical practice, each exemplified by particular countries and their great captains. For him, the Spanish were the first to combine pike and shot weaponry effectively in permanent infantry formations which he presented as the large, cumbersome yet resilient tercios. Tilly and Wallenstein were regarded as continuing the 'Spanish School' into the Thirty Years War at a point when it was already being superseded by the 'Dutch School' developed by Maurice of Nassau from the 1580s. This used smaller, thinner units which Delbrück argued were intended to maximize firepower and were capable of more complex tactics thanks to their higher ratio of officers to men. The Swedish system perfected by Gustavus represented a continuation of the Dutch model, combining firepower with a greater emphasis on shock tactics, especially through the introduction of regimental artillery and more aggressive use of cavalry.

Delbrück's idea of a succession of tactical innovations driving warfare fitted conceptions of history as a linear process of modernization which became popular during the later nineteenth century. His thoughts about strategy proved more controversial. By contrasting Gustavus as battle seeker with Wallenstein as battle averse, Delbrück presented them as exemplars of a strategic choice between annihilation and attrition. Lützen might have offered an ideal case to explore this question further had Delbrück not fallen out with the arch-nationalist historian Heinrich von Treitschke, or dissented from official German strategy during the First World War. The General Staff considered the Seven Years War far more relevant than the Thirty

Years War to Germany's current geo-political situation. Frederick the Great's decision to launch a pre-emptive strike against a hostile coalition in 1756 struck a chord with those who believed that Germany was justified in opening a new war in 1914. A first strike policy relied on achieving a swift decisive victory, and its advocates wanted historians to vindicate their recommendations with historical examples. Delbrück was criticized for arguing that Frederick had, in fact, mixed both strategies—indeed, as had Gustavus during 1630–2.[76]

Delbrück's desire to place warfare in its wider context was paralleled by a similar interest among British and American academic and popular historians. Prior to 1914, Anglophone writers generally took a favourable view of Germany and their command of the language gave them access to the voluminous German scholarship on the Thirty Years War. Additionally, they were overwhelmingly Protestant and inclined to accept the positive interpretation of Gustavus which was now firmly fixed by over two centuries of hagiography.

Stephen Crane, author of the *Red Badge of Courage*, devoted one-third of his *Great Battles of the World* to Breitenfeld and Lützen, alongside six other eighteenth- and nineteenth-century engagements. The now routine claim that Gustavus was the most important commander since Alexander the Great was supplemented from the 1890s by the presentation of him as the 'father of modern war'.[77] This assertion was based on the belief that Gustavus had created what later nineteenth- and early twentieth-century Europeans believed armies should be like and how war ought to be conducted. Gustavus' army was considered a permanent force composed of motivated Swedes, controlled by the state and used for the benefit of the nation. Elements of older hagiography were reflected in the view that pious Protestantism contributed to superior discipline and the motivation of fighting for a cause, in contrast to the rootless mercenaries supposedly forming the imperial, League, and Spanish armies. Unlike their opponents, the Swedes supposedly contented themselves with their official rations and did not plunder civilians; something which was also thought to contribute to their greater operational effectiveness. These factors in turn enabled Gustavus to progress to the 'apogee' of pike and shot tactics, especially through allegedly simplified and streamlined training, weapons handling, and the incorporation of technological advances like lighter handguns and regimental artillery.[78] The result was allegedly 'the first disciplined fighting force in Europe since the Roman legions to be able to combine all available combat arms in cohesive action either offensively or defensively'.[79] Many of these admirers accepted that Gustavus' system did not always function perfectly, but blamed any shortcomings on the negative impact of his untimely death and the supposed subsequent dilution of the native Swedish element through the incorporation of 'foreign mercenaries'.

Meanwhile, the Swedish General Staff produced a six-volume history of Gustavus' campaigns using not only their country's own impressive archives of original material, but the latest German scholarship providing new insight into his enemies.[80] Like similar ventures in Germany, Austria, and France, the Swedish officers charged with writing this account were influenced by the ongoing controversy over the respective merits of a strategy of decision versus one of attrition. The former generally found the greatest favour, not least because the 'great captains' approach to military history already presented battle as more honourable than guerrilla warfare, and allegedly more humane in minimizing costs through swift, decisive victory. Such thinking reinforced the verdict that Gustavus was a progressive innovator whose methods looked towards modern war, in contrast to Wallenstein and the imperial army. This conclusion also ensured that Lützen had to be interpreted alongside Breitenfeld as a decisive victory, despite the evidence to the contrary.

The idea of Gustavus as founder of modern warfare was combined with Delbrück's stadial approach in the concept of the Military Revolution coined by the Swedish king's principal English-speaking biographer, Michael Roberts, in 1956.[81] While Roberts did not draw directly on Delbrück, he likewise argued that warfare was transformed through a sequence of innovations passing from one country to another. For Roberts, the key period began in around 1560 and lasted a century during which the transformations were sufficient to consti-tute a 'revolution'. Also like Delbrück, he highlighted the same techno-logical, tactical, and organizational innovations associated with the Dutch army under Maurice of Nassau as initiating this new phase. And again, he likewise argued that these practices reached their culmin-ation under Gustavus. His key contribution was to broaden the dis-cussion even beyond the context envisaged by Delbrück and to articulate a coherent model for how military changes promoted wider historical development.

Roberts argued that new ideas of discipline and tighter command structures developed by Maurice permitted a tactical revolution by making more effective use of the available gunpowder weaponry. Tactical changes in turn promoted a revolution in strategy which culminated in Gustavus' supposed pursuit of decision over Tilly's and Wallenstein's alleged adherence to the older Spanish system of attritional warfare.[82] As armies became more effective, rulers sup-posedly raced to enlarge their own forces to offset their opponents' improved potency. This resulted in an increased scale in warfare which in turn now had a greater social, economic, and above all political impact, ultimately forcing states to adapt or collapse. The ensuing historical debate continues to the present. Initial contribu-tions modified Roberts' time span and shifted emphasis from ideas to technology without fundamentally altering the general thrust of his thesis. Later interventions were more critical, with some arguing that changes were more evolutionary than revolutionary.

This is not the place to follow this debate in detail, but it should be noted that the idea of a military revolution has persisted for so long because it was built on the extensive foundations of nineteenth-century scholarship and the belief that human history can be written as a coherent story of modernization following a single path towards a world fashioned according to European-Western political, social, and economic concepts. This story was also largely secular, reducing religion to part of the ideological 'superstructure' of society. Given that the dominant narrative was written by Protestants, Catholicism

was associated with an earlier 'medieval' phase in human development, whereas Protestantism was regarded as the expression of more
progressive social and economic forces culminating in capitalism and
industrialization. The military reforms of Maurice of Nassau thus
appeared a natural part of the 'early bourgeois revolution' against
Catholic Spain which saw the establishment of the Dutch Republic
as Europe's most dynamic economic and cultural centre around 1600.
The Thirty Years War was also fitted into this story, not least given the
prevailing assumption that the Catholics had lost.[83]

As earlier sections of this book have indicated, the opposing forces
at Lützen cannot be easily aligned into 'progressive' or 'reactionary'
camps. Most of the claims for the Swedes' supposed superiority
have no basis in evidence. For example, the Swedes were not more
technologically advanced than their opponents. While they certainly
deployed more regimental guns than Wallenstein, their infantry had
not adopted lighter calibre muskets which were supposedly easier to
handle. An exhaustive survey of the munitions found on the battlefield
indicates that three-quarters of the Swedish infantry still carried
19.7 mm calibre muskets, significantly heavier than the 17.5 mm calibre
weapons carried by a similar proportion of their imperial opponents.[84] The assertion that Gustavus simplified arms drill because
'reloading required as many as ninety words of command' derives
from a misreading of contemporary printed manuals, such as the
famous *Exercise of Arms* by Jacob de Gheyn which first appeared in
1607.[85] These manuals broke down pike and firearms drill into numerous separate actions, but did so in order to convey movements in
precise detail, rather than as actual sequences of individual commands.
Likewise, the erroneous Merian battle plan is still reproduced to support the stock contrast between the supposedly progressive Swedes
and their opponents.[86] Though now challenged in more specialist
works, this contrast is so deeply entwined with popular assumptions
about the nature of history and modernity that it remains hard to
shift. Whilst acknowledging that Wallenstein may not have actually
deployed his infantry in large blocks, a group of wargamers recreating

the battle in 2011 still chose to deploy their figures representing the imperial army according to the Merian plan.[87]

New Departures

There are signs that such views may shift at last thanks to the archaeological investigation of the Lützen battlefield since autumn 2006, particularly given the current popularity of archaeology and the attraction of the material evidence it unearths. It is indicative of Lützen's wider significance that it is only the second German battlefield to be systematically investigated by archaeologists; the first being the site of the defeat of the Romans in 9AD at Teutoberg Forrest which was examined in 1987. Lützen is also the first location in Germany to be explored using the new techniques of battlefield archaeology. The initial investigations were supported by the Federal Office for the Preservation of Historic Monuments and Archaeology, joined since August 2009 by the Swedish National Heritage Board and part financed by the brown coal-mining firm MIBRAG. Thanks to this support, it has become the largest battlefield archaeology project in Europe.[88]

Battlefield archaeology combines extensive metal detector surveys with localized digging to explore the battlefield and plot finds systematically. Around 1.1 km^2 had been surveyed by 2012, amounting to around a third of the battlefield. Over 13,000 objects were discovered, including 2,500 musket and pistol balls. As the discussion at the start of this chapter indicated, the battlefield was scoured for large objects in the immediate aftermath, meaning that cannon shot, armour, and weapons were already removed in 1632. Small calibre ammunition remained broadly the same from the sixteenth century until the 1840s, making it hard to date the Lützen finds with precision. The Lützen–Leipzig highway saw large troop movements both in 1806 at the time of the battles of Jena and Auerstedt to the southwest, as well as in 1813 during the battle of Großgörschen fought immediately to the south of the 1632 battlefield. One of the items discovered is a button from a

Spanish infantryman in Napoleonic service, strongly suggesting that other finds will date from that era. Moreover, current battlefield archaeology can only plot the fall of shot for the era prior to the use of metal cartridges. This contrasts with the investigation of the Little Big Horn battlefield in the USA where the discovery of cartridges as well as spent ammunition allowed archaeologists to plot both firing positions and targets.

Nonetheless, the finds do assist in locating the areas of fighting more precisely, especially as the relatively flat battlefield means that there has been little soil erosion which might otherwise have shifted objects from their original drop spot. As Chapter 4 indicated, excavation of the drainage ditches alongside the original highway has already challenged the long-standing belief that Wallenstein lined both sides of the road with musketeers. Since 2009 archaeologists have been investigating the mass grave previously known to exist at the east end of the town which had been covered by a car park built in the 1990s. Excavations of a similar grave from the 1636 battle at Wittstock suggest that the Lützen site will add to our understanding of the lives and deaths of ordinary soldiers.[89]

The archaeological investigations are unlikely to resolve all the minor controversies surrounding the actual course of the battle. They have, however, already added a broader human dimension to the story as it is popularly perceived, shifting some of the attention away from the rival commanders and towards the still anonymous ordinary soldiers. This is in line with current trends in military history which seek to reconstruct the experience of battle alongside the traditional interest in what individual engagements can tell us about tactics, strategy, and military institutions. Perhaps most significantly, the recovery of objects from the battlefield allows for new ways to present Lützen to the public, providing opportunities to challenge engrained interpretations of its military significance and moving towards a more nuanced and complex understanding of how it was fought and what it meant.

6

Political and Cultural Legacy

Battlefield Commemoration

The controversy over Lützen's tactical and strategic outcome prevented it from being commemorated as an unqualified victory in the manner of Waterloo. Despite subsequent claims for it being a 'decisive' battle, it clearly did not end the Thirty Years War which lasted another sixteen years. Though it came to be regarded as a Swedish victory, it did not conclude a distinct phase in the conflict, in the manner that White Mountain definitively ended the Bohemian Revolt and restored Habsburg power in their hereditary lands. Instead, its longer-term political and cultural significance derived from how it came to symbolize specific confessional and later nationalist interpretations of the Thirty Years War, especially in Sweden and Germany. Like the military legacy, the basic political and cultural outlines were already formed in the immediate aftermath, but these subsequently underwent a number of subtle, yet significant changes. Initially, the battle symbolized sacrifice for the Protestant cause largely disassociated from its location, but gradually Lützen itself assumed more importance, leading to the physical development of the actual site.

The timing of Lützen also profoundly shaped its subsequent memory, because it was fought when remembrance culture was sharply divided by Christian confession. The papacy claimed a monopoly over official jubilees, while commemoration of secular events remained closely connected to their perceived spiritual significance. Lützen occurred amidst the flowering of Catholic baroque culture which in turn grew from that church's internal renewal and response to the Protestant challenge. The Catholic baroque was a highly visual form of representational culture in which particular messages were manifest in the decorative arts and through imposing religious and secular buildings. White Mountain was commemorated by the construction or rededication of chapels and churches, as well as specially commissioned paintings hung in Rome and Munich.[1] These had considerable meaning for the generation immediately affected by the battle, but rapidly lost that significance after their deaths to become part of the general cityscape. Few of today's visitors to Santa Maria della Vittoria in Rome go beyond Bernini's famous sculpture of the Ecstasy of St Teresa to enter the dimly lit back room decorated with magnificent paintings of White Mountain, the victory that gives the church its name, while the banners from the battle are often erroneously described as Turkish standards taken at the siege of Vienna in 1683.

The general perception of Lützen as an imperial defeat discouraged interest among Catholics beyond the initial outpouring of euphoria at the news of Gustavus' death. This meant that commemoration was profoundly shaped by the Lutheran culture of remembrance which was assuming its definitive form just as the battle took place. Lutherans and Protestants more broadly began celebrating anniversaries, partly in deliberate defiance of the papacy's claim to sanction jubilees, but primarily to build their own identity through history.[2] Lutheran practices were forged by the two centenaries of the Reformation in 1617 and of the presentation of the first definitive statement of their faith, known as the Confession of Augsburg, in 1630. These were officially coordinated by the state churches of the various Lutheran German territories and involved sermons, special religious services, processions, musical performances, and printed broadsheets. The idea of regularly commemorating specific events was thus already deeply ingrained in Lutheran culture and was applied to Gustavus' earlier exploits. For example, a thanksgiving service was held in September 1632 in Swedish-occupied Magdeburg to mark the first anniversary of Breitenfeld.[3]

Remembering Gustavus

Gustavus' death ensured that Lützen could not be commemorated as another Breitenfeld. Instead, it was dominated by the Lutheran concept of sacrifice for a just cause which became established once the king's death was confirmed. Initially, some uncertainty still surrounded Gustavus' fate. Superintendent Möser reported that the news only reached him in Staßfurt on 22 November, Oxenstierna had been informed the day before, but it was only relayed to the Swedish State Council on 18 December. Some pro-Swedish papers were still reporting that the king had merely been wounded, but by late December his death was openly acknowledged and accompanied by a public discussion of its likely negative impact on Protestant unity.[4]

The exiled Bohemian queen and electress Palatine, Elizabeth, immediately realized that Gustavus' death was a chance for her husband Frederick V to step out from under the Swede's shadow and assume his former role as personification of the Protestant cause. More immediately, she hoped that her brother, England's King Charles I, would switch the aid he had promised Sweden and instead fund the Palatine exile government directly.[5] Elizabeth's plans were wrecked by Frederick V's death from plague on 29 November. The elector's passing was at least noted, but not widely mourned, and he remained eclipsed in death as in life by Gustavus.[6] Georg Leopold, the Lutheran mayor of Marktredwitz in the Upper Palatinate, blamed Frederick V as the 'cause of this bloody war' and recorded the deaths of Gustavus and Pappenheim equally as 'the two splendid heroes the like of which have never lived under the sun'.[7]

Some contemporaries failed to mention Gustavus' death at all in their diaries or memoirs, such as the Lutheran pastors in Erlangen who noted Breitenfeld and Alte Veste in their church books, but omitted Lützen.[8] However, for many of those who had fought at Lützen, their presence at the site of their beloved king's death was the defining moment of their lives. Lützen forms the centrepiece of Jöns Månsson Teitt's otherwise sparse account of his career as a

Swedish soldier.[9] His claim that the sun stopped shining for a month afterwards was also voiced widely by others in Sweden.[10] Most pious Protestant observers consoled themselves that at least Gustavus had fought 'chivalrously and firmly against the enemy of the Evangelicals', and although he had been killed, he had nonetheless served as God's instrument and 'had achieved much and given the cause a good start'.[11] Some pastors claimed that their parishioners mourned the Swedish king's death more than if it had been that of their own prince.[12]

Others found the thought of Gustavus' death so hard to bear that they clung to hopes that he was still alive. Rumours circulated in the Lutheran city of Augsburg during January 1633 that the king was on his way to finish off Maximilian of Bavaria.[13] A succession of prints appeared throughout that year explaining his continued absence by reporting he had returned to Sweden. Rather less piously, it was wagered at the Stuart court in December 1632 that Gustavus was still alive and would soon reappear.[14]

The Lion of Midnight

These sentiments and anxieties were responses to the high expectations stoked by two years of pro-Swedish propaganda. A key element in this was the identification of Gustavus as saviour of the Protestants of the Empire, thus unwittingly setting up the martyrology that would follow his death at Lützen. Frederick V and Christian IV had already successively been identified in pamphlets and broadsheets as stepping forward to deliver the Empire's Protestants from the dangers posed by the alleged conspiracy of the Habsburgs, Jesuits, and papacy to extirpate their religion.[15] The defeat of these two would-be saviours was followed by Ferdinand's imposition of the Edict of Restitution in March 1629, further giving weight to claims that Protestantism was in mortal danger. From spring 1629 broadsheets appeared reporting the alleged prophecy of an eleven-year-old girl from Cottbus that a new prince would appear as God's instrument to save German

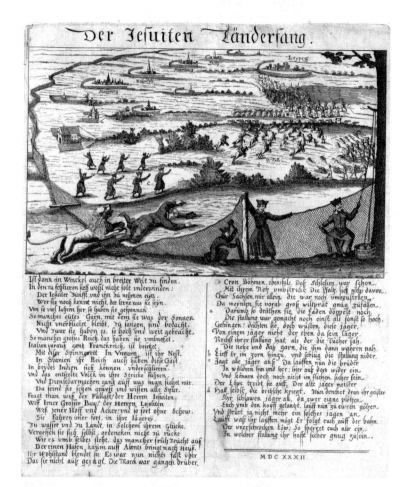

Illustration 10: Gustavus Adolphus as 'Lion of the North' chasing the Jesuits out of Germany

evangelicals. Thus, the ground was well prepared by the time Gustavus actually landed in June 1630. His appearance from the north also conveniently fitted the trope of the Lion of Midnight, the metaphor for the apocalyptic King of the North in the Book of Revelations who had appeared in a succession of prophesies since the late fifteenth century as the defender of the true faith. The prominence of lions as a Swedish heraldic device further reinforced the analogy.

The Swedes were initially hostile to these pamphlets which were not part of their official effort to justify their invasion of the Empire. Like its counterparts in Germany, the Swedish Lutheran church establishment regarded prophesies as theologically unsound and the country's government had censored, banished, and even executed a number of native wandering prophets during the 1610s and 1620s.[16] Gustavus and his closest advisors refused publicly to endorse the concept of holy war, which they rightly regarded as open-ended, ill defined, and politically disadvantageous at a time when France was their main ally and Spain a key trading partner. Yet, they did appreciate the value of accepting and even encouraging Germans to think that Gustavus was coming to their aid.

Around 200 pro-Swedish broadsheets appeared in 1630–2, far more than were produced by Habsburg or Catholic partisans.[17] Many of these presented Gustavus as being on a divine mission to rescue the Empire's Protestants. One prominent example showed him on his landing in Pomerania, receiving the holy sword direct from God to smite a papal-Habsburg monster depicted as a seven-headed dragon threatening the true church. This and other prints hailed Gustavus variously as a new Judas Maccabeus, Joshua, Samson, David, or Josiah. The first of these figures was especially important, because it was Maccabeus who had restored Jewish worship in ancient Jerusalem, suggesting that Gustavus would reverse the Edict and liberate German Protestants from a new Roman imperial oppression, represented by the Habsburgs as Holy Roman emperors. Johannes Botvides, one of Gustavus' military chaplains, issued a print combining the texts of the Swedish army's prayers with the apocryphal book of Judas Maccabeus. Verses from that book were used in the commemorative religious service held in Bernau on 17 December after Gustavus' death, while Oxenstierna also referred to Maccabeus in his fruitless efforts to console Maria Eleonora. These comparisons with Old Testament heroes were also intended to convince Germans that Gustavus had the necessary qualities and divine backing to become the new Protestant champion. Given the absence of allies and his still unproven military reputation in 1630, such ideological support was particularly necessary.[18]

Perhaps unsurprisingly, Protestant clergy were the most enthusiastic audience for this message. Martin Feilinger, pastor near Schlüchtern in Franconia, wrote that Gustavus was 'the Roman Empire's general against the tyranny of the tyrannical emperor Ferdinand from the house of Austria'. He later thanked God for sending 'this brave hero and warlike Gideon'.[19] Pamphlet production spiked after Breitenfeld, reaching a crescendo with the Swedish capture (presented as 'liberation') of Augsburg on 24 April 1632, which was also a key centre for printing in southern Germany.

The pamphlet campaign stoked expectations way beyond what could reasonably be met. Well before Lützen, many Protestants were disillusioned by their actual encounters with the Swedish army which was far from the godly force they had been led to believe. Transgressions were often initially excused by blaming Gustavus' subordinates rather than the king himself. The Saxon church establishment questioned whether Gustavus was the 'right Gideon', reflecting their elector's extreme reluctance to ally with the Swedish invaders.[20] Theological reservations continued to encourage scepticism, despite the enthusiasm of individual pastors. In particular, the church leadership feared some of Gustavus' supporters risked confusing his role as divine instrument with his actually being semi-divine. One image played on the Latin *Gustav Sued* (Gustavus of Sweden) as the reverse of *Deus* (god).[21]

This sense of unease permeated into Gustavus' inner circle, as exemplified by stories circulating soon after the king's death which appear to have originated with his chaplain, Johann Fabricius. Reportedly, Gustavus told Fabricius a few days before Lützen that 'I fear that God will punish me, since the people exalt me so high, and would make a god of me'. Most accounts date this incident to 10 November when Naumburg's inhabitants knelt before him as he rode into their town.[22] Many of the posthumous broadsheets disseminated this story which conveniently exonerated Gustavus from the theologically problematic aspect of the earlier hagiography. It also helped distinguish between Gustavus as mortal, a human sinner who would certainly die at some point, and as God's instrument which could not fail. This was exemplified in another widely disseminated print entitled *Der Schwede lebet noch* (The Swede Still Lives) which distinguished between the king's mortal remains, whilst arguing his spirit lived on in the cause his armies still fought for and eternally in heaven as reward for his efforts. Such prints also presented Gustavus as an example to emulate so that, in the words of one Westphalian pastor, God would 'bring Joshua and Maccabeus again to smite proud Babylon to the ground'.[23]

Nonetheless, the king's death without full victory raised the possibility that he might be considered a failure. Lutheran clergy sought to counter such suggestions by shifting any blame for Lützen's outcome onto the Swedish army which had allegedly become distracted by plunder, or alternatively criticizing German Lutherans for failing to support Gustavus adequately. Some soldiers even expressed this view, with one Scottish officer remarking that the king had died 'becaus [*sic*] we was not worthie of him'.[24] Robert Monro quoted Proverbs 28:21 that Gustavus had died 'for our sinnes and the sinnes of the land' to refute charges that he carelessly lost his life through his own recklessness, as well as rebut Catholic claims that his death proved that he had lacked divine favour.[25]

The public discussion and commemoration of Gustavus in print subsided after 1633, not least because the second anniversary of his death coincided with the crushing imperial victory at Nördlingen, precipitating a collapse of Swedish positions across southern Germany. It became much harder to believe in the imminent arrival of a new saviour. Hope gave way to despair as the war dragged on without any prospect of a Protestant victory. There was a growing sense among moderates of all confessions that foreign interference was only prolonging the war at the Empire's expense. Ferdinand II finally made substantial concessions in the Peace of Prague in May 1635, including effectively suspending the Edict of Restitution. Saxony,

Brandenburg, and most of Sweden's other German allies now joined the emperor in what was explicitly presented as a patriotic war to drive out the Swedes as foreign invaders.[26]

Gustavus the Martyr

The Swedish government's development of Gustavus' image as Protestant martyr was the ideological accompaniment to military and diplomatic moves to shore up their crumbling position in the Empire. The official position was that Lützen had been nothing short of a complete victory, since anything less would have implied the king had died in vain. The tone was set already in the *Declaration* published in 1633 which depicted Gustavus as receiving both the victor's laurels and the martyr's palm branch. Another semi-official publication presented Gustavus' death as a heroic sacrifice 'to Lord Jesus and to save the religion and to recover the lost liberty of the Evangelical German electors and Estates'.[27]

This had always been part of the rhetoric surrounding the Swedish invasion, but the language of sacrifice now assumed new significance with Oxenstierna's demands for 'compensation' for his country's efforts on behalf of the Empire's Protestants. Sweden clearly expected to be rewarded with German territory, above all the Lutheran duchy of Pomerania which it had occupied since 1630 and the possession of which was now considered essential to safeguarding the security of its wider Baltic empire. Compensation was joined by 'satisfaction' after Sweden's numerous German officers held Oxenstierna hostage in August 1635 until he agreed that their pay arrears be included in any peace settlement.[28] Further Swedish successes in 1643–5 encouraged the Swedish government to widen its demands to include the secularized ecclesiastical territories of Bremen and Verden, acquisition of which would not only extend their presence in Germany, but outflank their Danish rival to the south. Three more years of fighting eventually secured these demands in the Peace of Westphalia, including the massive sum of over 5 million talers paid by the Protestant imperial

Estates to enable Sweden to meet the pay arrears and discharge its army.

The strong religious character of the language of sacrifice ensured that the image of Gustavus the martyr outlived the achievement of Sweden's political objectives at the end of the war. This also ensured that Gustavus' death was remembered more as that of a martyr than as a secular hero. The biblical references were already prominent in the images and texts appearing shortly after his death. Several of these compared the king to a pelican, since it was believed these birds fed their blood to their young. Pelicans were thus used to symbolize Jesus' gift of his life and blood for humanity, and a golden pelican adorned Gustavus' tomb in Stockholm.

Martyrdom swiftly extended to saint-like veneration for Gustavus' body and personal effects. A person's physical attributes were believed to indicate their virtues. The autopsy recorded that the king had 'a heart as large as those of two people'.[29] Jöns Teitt recorded that it weighed 40 Lott, or about 2 kg, while Monro said it was 'the heart of a lion' in an even clearer reference to the contemporary association of a large heart with courage and magnanimity.[30] Captain Philippi, who worked in Lützen as a district official in the early nineteenth century, recalled that his great grandfather had been the village carpenter in Meuchen and had made the coffin to transport Gustavus' corpse. Drawing on family stories and local lore in January 1832, he discovered a decomposed oak urn under the floor of the west nave of the church beneath a mural of the Swedish coat of arms. He concluded the urn had contained the viscera washed off Gustavus' body during the autopsy.[31] The urn was rediscovered in 1855, and then sealed in a lead cylinder and reinterred in its original spot when the church was renovated in 1912. The table on which the corpse had lain was still in use in a nearby house throughout the nineteenth century, before being moved into the church for permanent display in 1902 with the encouragement of Pastor Sielaff who was keen to promote Meuchen as the location which 'gave King Gustavus Adolphus his first resting place and established his first memorial'.[32] As a good Lutheran, Sielaff wanted to avoid comparisons with the Catholic cult of saints, writing that the viscera was 'not martyr's blood', but rather evidence of Gustavus' sacrifice 'pro Christo'. More prosaically, he wanted to ensure that his parish was not overshadowed by the new Swedish chapel being constructed on the battlefield to the north and in 1913 he secured an imperial decree from Wilhelm II renaming Meuchen church as the King Gustavus Adolphus Memorial Church.

Meanwhile, the king's personal effects had been preserved like holy relics. Ironically, this practice was initiated by Gustavus himself after he had been wounded in the campaign in Prussia against the Poles. The first injury occurred as he was hit by a musket ball in the right shoulder whilst crossing the Vistula near Gdansk in May 1626. Initially he was convinced he was dying, but soon realized the wound was relatively superficial. He sustained his second wound in August 1627 when he was recognized by the Poles and deliberately targeted as he led a charge. He was shot in the neck and the bullet lodged in his right shoulder blade, forcing him to abandon his attack. After this injury he stopped wearing body armour, leaving him unprotected at Lützen. He already decided in autumn 1627 to preserve his blood-stained clothing, and in March 1628 sent it back to Stockholm to be placed in the royal armoury.

He clearly wanted to monumentalize himself and demonstrate his self-sacrifice on behalf of good causes. He was very proud of the musket ball still lodged in his shoulder and allegedly allowed Christian IV to feel it when they met subsequently.[33] The clothing and wounds were also interpreted as signs of divine favour which had spared him otherwise certain death, and the two incidents were soon woven with others, such as a story of a cannon ball entering his tent, but swerving to miss him. Preservation of the clothing thus represented a votive offering of thanks for his life being spared, very similar to Catholic practice during the Thirty Years War. It also fitted the general late-Renaissance passion amongst European monarchs for collecting weapons, armour, and other items associated with prominent family members or famous people. The Swedish armoury was decorated with paintings seized by Gustavus from art collections in Würzburg and Munich, as well as flags and other trophies which could not be recycled like cannon.

The imperialists had already removed the elk leather coat from Gustavus' corpse on the battlefield. Keen to ingratiate himself with the Habsburgs, Piccolomini sent this trophy to Vienna where it remained until 1920 when it was returned to Stockholm by the new Austrian government in thanks for aid from the Swedish Red Cross during the First World War. Gustavus' gorget, or metal neck protector, was also plundered by imperial soldiers and eventually ended up in the armoury of the small principality of Schwarzburg.[34] The other items still with the corpse were taken with it back to Sweden. The Regency Council eventually allowed the distraught Maria Eleonora to keep the

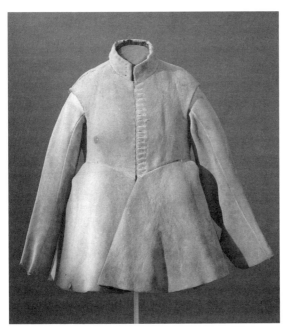

Illustration 11: Elk leather coat worn by Gustavus at Lützen, now in the Royal Armoury, Stockholm

cloth which had been wrapped around her husband's heart after it had been removed in Weissenfels, as well as the heart itself which she preserved in a silver casket. The remaining clothes, including a blood-stained shirt, were placed in the armoury where they were later shown on public display. Gustavus' sword had been missed by the plunderers, because it was only that of an ordinary officer and he had dropped it when first wounded, rather than where he finally fell.[35]

His horse Streiff died of its wounds shortly after the battle. It was skinned and sent to Stockholm where it joined the display in the armoury. Streiff was a bay, but the display failed to prevent the misconception that Gustavus had ridden a white horse at Lützen 'like an angel of God', as claimed by John Durie, a Scottish cleric attached to the ex-patriot merchant community in the Prussian port of Elbing.[36] This was how the king was depicted by the history painter Wilhelm Carl Räuber in 1886 on a large canvas acquired by Lützen museum. Though the Swedish military artist Carl Wahlbom showed a bay in his 1855 painting of Gustavus' death, his other work depicting the battle of Stuhm presents the king on a white horse. The imagery linked directly back to the presentation of Gustavus as saviour in 1630–2 through 19:11 of Revelation which recounts how the victorious Christ will appear on a white horse on Judgement Day.

Images also offered a substitute for those who could not possess or see items directly relating to the king. Some images were produced from life, such as the portrait commissioned from a local artist by the council of the imperial city of Dinkelsbühl during his stay there in October 1632. The rapid and extensive dissemination of his portrait through the broadsheets produced in 1630–2 provided readily available templates for artists to copy after his death. The Swedish general Carl Gustav Wrangel had a portrait painted based on a copperplate engraving, while Wittenberg town council commissioned a similar portrait in February 1633. Johann Cleffmann, an official in the Swedish army, painted miniatures of both Gustavus and his wife around the same time which he bound into his own family chronicle. Likewise, various commemorative medals were struck after Gustavus' death.[37]

Illustration 12: Gustavus' stuffed horse, Streiff, in the Royal Armoury, Stockholm

Illustration 13: Death of Gustavus Adolphus, by Wilhelm Karl Räuber, 1886

A Warrior-King

Lützen as the physical battle site remained secondary to the image of Gustavus' martyrdom for several centuries. It was enough to know that he had died there. The actual location was in any case problematic, since the town was in Saxony which switched sides in the Peace of Prague in 1635 in return for territorial concessions and the suspension of the Edict of Restitution. After a further decade of fighting, the Swedes forced Saxony to declare neutrality, while their troops treated it as an occupied hostile land for another seven years before finally withdrawing after the conclusion of peace.

With the image of Gustavus largely detached from the place of his death, Lützen the battle was largely forgotten within a much broader, more generalized commemoration of the Thirty Years War promoted by the governments and church establishments of the imperial Estates, especially in Protestant areas after the early 1650s. Annual ceremonies were held on 24 October, linking commemoration directly to the anniversary of the signing of the Peace of Westphalia. Peace was celebrated as the deliverance from the horrors of war. Regardless of confession, all churches had already preached that the war was divine punishment for the sins of the population. This message continued after 1648, and was combined with other secular measures intended to restore authority. The population were admonished to be pious, thrifty, and obedient in accordance with the will of God to ensure such devastation did not return.[38]

The Peace of Westphalia was interpreted positively as stabilizing the Empire, in sharp contrast to how it was viewed in Germany after the early nineteenth century. Far from fragmenting into a loose federation of independent states, the Empire remained effective in defending itself against renewed aggression after the 1660s, and in resolving internal conflict prior to 1740. Even thereafter, the bulk of its inhabitants continued to identify with it as their natural home, because the overarching imperial structure helped anchor and protect local identities and liberties.[39] Protestants were explicit in their celebration of the imperial constitution which guaranteed their religious as well as political rights. The centenary of the Peace of Westphalia and the bicentenary of the Peace of Augsburg were marked by large-scale official events in 1748 and 1755, respectively.

By contrast, in Sweden the image of Gustavus as Protestant hero-king persisted more clearly than that of the Thirty Years War, because it became integral to a wider sense of national identity. This was not unique, as late seventeenth-century Europe saw other overtly confessional hero-kings, notably William III in Britain and the Dutch Republic, and the Catholic Jan Sobieski of Poland-Lithuania. However, Gustavus' image burned particularly brightly because his successors Charles XI and Charles XII self-consciously projected similar personas as warrior monarchs serving a Protestant nation.[40] Both claimed to be building on Gustavus' achievements and were influenced in their statements and actions by their own understanding of his campaigns and his death at Lützen.

This was illustrated most clearly by Charles XII whose accession in 1697 aged just 14 was followed shortly by the existential challenge of the Great Northern War (1700–21). Augustus the Strong, elector of Saxony, had converted to Catholicism in order to secure election as king of Poland in 1697 after Sobieski's death the previous year. Augustus wanted to strengthen his rule by recovering lands lost by Poland to Sweden in the 1620s. Sweden appeared weak after setbacks under Charles XI, while Augustus enlisted Danish and Russian support in a seemingly overwhelming coalition. Charles XII confounded expectations by winning a series of spectacular victories, enabling him to topple Augustus with the aid of discontented Polish aristocrats and to install one of these, Stanislaus I Leszczynski, as pro-Swedish king of Poland in 1704. Having consolidated his position, Charles turned west, advancing through Habsburg Silesia to invade Saxony on 27 August 1706, intending to force Augustus to renounce the Polish throne.

The Swedish advance into the heart of the Empire precipitated a major crisis, because it threatened to merge the Great Northern War with the parallel War of the Spanish Succession, which began in 1701 when Austria challenged the French-backed candidate to succeed the defunct Habsburg line in Spain. Britain and the Dutch Republic were allies of Austria, but objected to Emperor Joseph I's treatment of his largely Protestant Hungarian subjects who had rebelled in 1703. The British and Dutch urged concessions, both from a sense of religious solidarity and because they rightly believed that the revolt was diverting Austrian military efforts away from the primary struggle against France. Additionally, both powers declared their support for the Lutheran minority in Lower Silesia whose limited rights of toleration granted by the Peace of Westphalia were being ignored by the Habsburgs. Added to this complex mix was the fact that Habsburg Austria regarded Augustus as a key ally in the Empire who was currently providing auxiliaries for the allied armies fighting France. Augustus' conversion to Catholicism in 1697 had alarmed German Protestants, some of whom claimed it undermined the religious balance in the Empire secured by the Peace of Westphalia. The electors of Hanover and Brandenburg used the conversion of their Saxon rival and his subsequent embroilment in Poland as an opportunity to expand their influence at his expense across northern Germany.

As this brief outline suggests, the situation was complex and differed substantially from that in 1630 when Gustavus had invaded the Empire. Yet, some of the anxieties surrounding religious and political rights were similar. Moreover, all the actors were conscious of the earlier example, notably Charles XII who pursued Augustus' army from east to west across Saxony. Having overrun the electorate, Charles turned back to lodge in Altranstädt Castle just outside Leipzig on 11 September 1706. His visit to Lützen the next day provided an opportunity for the young king to impress his staff with his knowledge of the battle, including naming the Swedish units which had been present. He also took the opportunity to interview two elderly burghers to whom accounts of the battle had been passed down the generations. Concluding his visit, Charles remarked 'I have always endeavoured to live as he [Gustavus] did; may God give me grace to die as he did'.[41]

The visit was far more than purely personal. The Swedish transit of Silesia and occupation of Saxony breached the peace of the Empire, entitling Augustus to call on the other imperial Estates for military assistance, just as the Brandenburg elector had done when the Swedes invaded his territory in 1674. To pre-empt such a move, Charles employed arguments similar to those voiced by Gustavus in his official manifesto justifying his invasion of the Empire in 1630: threats to the rights of the Protestant imperial Estates had allegedly necessitated Swedish intervention. This time, Charles additionally cited rights deriving from Sweden's role alongside France as guarantor of the Peace of Westphalia, even though the actual clause scarcely legitimated an invasion. The real power came from Charles' battle-hardened army whose presence in Saxony obliged both Augustus and Joseph to despatch envoys to Altranstädt. A series of agreements were concluded over the following eleven months in which Augustus renounced Poland and agreed additional safeguards for his Lutheran Saxon subjects, while Joseph promised to allow the Lower Silesians to use the churches guaranteed them in the Peace of Westphalia.[42]

The treaties of Altranstädt inserted Charles into the pantheon of Protestant Germanic heroes, and his image now appeared alongside that of Gustavus as 'rocks of the church'. However, in contrast to his predecessor, Charles' image as a warrior-king always overshadowed his Protestant credentials as he appeared more Spartan than Lutheran. In many ways, he embodied Gustavus' personal contradictions in even more extreme form, especially through his relentless wars against his many foes which were already interpreted by many contemporaries as unnecessarily aggressive. He outdid Gustavus as a risk taker, invading Russia with wholly inadequate forces in 1708 and suffering a crushing defeat the following year at Poltava. Ultimately, his risk taking fulfilled his wish expressed at Lützen, as he was shot dead inspecting siege trenches outside Frederiksten in Norway in 1718. This avoidable death did not conform to conventional ideals of heroism and, like that of Gustavus, raised suspicions that he had been murdered by one of his own soldiers.

Illustration 14: Gustavus Adolphus and Charles XII as 'Rocks of the Church', depicted in a copperplate *c*.1706

Charles' flaws and his country's eventual defeat in the Great Northern War ensured that Gustavus re-emerged during the later eighteenth century as the preferred symbol of the Swedish monarchy. Gustavus was the first Swede to be monumentalized through an equestrian statue, though this was only completed in 1796, forty-one years after it was initiated, and it was not until 1854 that a statue was also erected in Göteborg, the city he had founded. Gustavus III, who ruled in 1771–92, and the contemporary Swedish historian Sven Lagerbrink, saw Gustavus as a useful symbol in their desire to overcome the aristocratic factionalism which was undermining Sweden's political stability. The bicentenary of Gustavus' birth in 1794 provided additional stimulus, but attention remained focused on Swedish history with little reference to Lützen beyond being the site of the king's death.

German Politics

Prussia's new king, Frederick II, not yet dubbed 'the Great', used the opportunity of a succession crisis in the Habsburg lands and the Empire to conquer Silesia in 1740, thereby opening rivalry with Austria. The subsequent War of Austrian Succession (1740–8) was followed by the Seven Years War (1756–63), again begun by Prussia, but as a pre-emptive strike against a hostile coalition assembled by Austria hoping to recover Silesia. These events provided the immediate context for renewed discussions of both Gustavus and Lützen that would run well into the nineteenth century and involved the use of the German past to legitimate rival visions for the country's future.

Catholic and Habsburg views remained largely unchanged from those already expressed during the Thirty Years War that Gustavus had been a foreign invader who met a well-deserved end at Lützen. Protestant interpretations were more complex, largely given the ambiguous role of Prussia's ruling Hohenzollern family and their chequered past. As a new warrior-king who defied the Habsburgs, Frederick immediately invited comparisons with Gustavus, but he was personally conscious of how the Swede had bullied his ancestors and cheated them of their inheritance in Pomerania. In his history of the Hohenzollerns, Frederick argued that Gustavus was a secular opportunist who used religion to cloak his ambitions in the Empire.[43] Yet, the Prussian king behaved precisely this way when he attempted to claim Gustavus' mantle of protecting German religious and constitutional liberties against the Habsburgs during the Seven Years War.

Frederick's self-fashioning as champion of 'German liberty' did not go unchallenged among the lesser princes of the Empire who saw their autonomy endangered as much by the rise of Prussia as Austria's more established power. After the 1740s there was a succession of attempts to forge an alliance among the middling and smaller principalities as a 'third Germany' to counterbalance Austria and Prussia. These efforts grew after 1772 when Prussia, Austria, and Russia combined to deprive Poland of around a third of its territory. Fearing they faced a 'Polish future', several minor princes began corresponding on ways in which the imperial constitution might be strengthened to check Austria and Prussia. Leopold III of Anhalt-Dessau was one of the leaders of this group and the most imaginative in trying to project its political programme through architecture and landscape gardens. His 'Gothic House', built in the 1780s near his extensive Wörlitz Gardens, contained a collection of Gustavus' memorabilia and a massive sandstone relief of the king whom he singled out as a hero of German freedoms. Ultimately, the princes were outmanoeuvred by Frederick who assumed leadership of their league in 1785 and proceeded to use it to disrupt Habsburg management of the Empire.[44] Even in its original conception, the league bore no relation to the actual alliances forged by Gustavus, but Leopold's fascination with the Swedish king is indicative of how the Thirty Years War was becoming instrumentalized in contemporary politics.

The Swedish Stone

The mid-eighteenth-century wars in the Empire also stimulated a new historical interest in Lützen as more than merely the site of Gustavus' death. Several biographies appeared during or shortly after the Seven Years War, including that by Walter Harte, canon of Windsor, whose work was swiftly translated into German, as well as works by two Frenchmen working in Germany: Eléazar Mauvillon, who had visited the battlefield twenty times between 1738 and 1757, and André Dufresne de Francheville, who published a French translation of an account of Gustavus' German campaigns by Galeazzo Gualdo Priorato, Wallenstein's earliest biographer.[45] Mauvillon tried to present the battle in more detail, while Francheville's book included a plan of Lützen drawn by a Prussian officer. Nonetheless, Gustavus remained the dominant figure and all these works were hagiographic, especially that by Harte who, as a clergyman, continued the earlier tradition of ascribing the king's bravery and successes to his morality and piety. Lützen remained primarily Gustavus' death site, but the writers were now less concerned by the story of sacrifice and martyrdom than with how he had died and who fired the fatal shot; a topic on which Francheville wrote another book.[46]

Interest in the course of the battle and the precise circumstances of Gustavus' death encouraged greater attention to the actual battlefield. Local legend recounted how Nils (or Jacob) Eriksson, the cavalryman accompanying the royal entourage, had been helped by thirteen peasants from Meuchen after the battle to roll an irregular block of 'Scandinavian granite' approximately 120 cm tall to mark the spot where the king had died. The rock had become known as the Swedish Stone (*Schwedenstein*) by the time Mauvillon visited the battlefield, but the story was already disputed during the late eighteenth century. Francheville rejected both Mauvillon's claim that Gustavus had been murdered and his acceptance of the Swedish Stone as the death site, arguing instead that the king had fallen 700 paces away on the other side of the road where the imperial centre had stood. Another author soon rejected both, saying the Swedish Stone was really an old milestone, and that Gustavus had died 83 paces away in a different direction.[47]

By that point, the stone had become popularly accepted as the death site, despite continued rumours that the real location was further west.

Gustav Adolph der IV.te besucht die Stelle wo Gustav Adolph der I.te seine rühmliche Laufbahn endigte

Illustration 15: Gustavus Adolphus IV visiting the Lützen memorial, 1803

The general consensus was the essential prerequisite to developing the Swedish Stone as a memorial, and it now became the focal point of all public commemoration of the battle. There were already calls for a more fitting monument prior to the visit of the new Swedish king, Gustavus IV, in 1803. The stone was now inscribed with 'GA 1632' and eight poplar trees were planted. Six of these were subsequently cut down during the Napoleonic Wars, but another four smaller trees were put in their place. The Swedish general Karl Gottfried von Hellwig arranged for four benches to be placed in a semi-circle around the stone after he visited in 1813. Hellwig had a relatively unusual background for a senior officer at the time, being the son of a Saxon master carpenter and the husband of the poet Amalia von Imhoff. The arrangement of the trees and benches fitted the

139

prevailing Romantic sensibilities with their emphasis on nature and quiet contemplation.

The Romantic View of the Thirty Years War

The Holy Roman Empire crumbled under the combined impact of the French invasion after 1792 and continued political rivalry between Austria and Prussia. The latter's retreat into neutrality in 1795 effectively partitioned the Empire, leaving a southern rump to fight on alongside Austria against France. Having been defeated at Austerlitz, Emperor Francis II abdicated and dissolved the Empire in August 1806 to prevent its legacy being usurped by Napoleon. Isolated, Prussia was then crushed by Napoleon at the battles of Jena and Auerstädt that October, freeing the French emperor to complete his reorganization of the 'third Germany' as the Confederation of the Rhine. Napoleon's defeat in Russia in 1812 opened the way for Austria and Prussia to rejoin the anti-French coalition and defeat France in what became known in Germany as the Wars of Liberation 1813–15.

These events shaped how Lützen was remembered in two important ways. First, the profound and rapid political changes affecting central Europe more firmly confined the Thirty Years War to history whilst stimulating interest in it as a parallel tale of suffering. This trend was closely connected to the intellectual and literary currents known as Romanticism which peaked roughly in 1770–1830 and which saw historical writing as a way to forge emotional connections between past and present. The memory of the Thirty Years War as an unmitigated disaster and unparalleled horror now became definitively fixed in the popular consciousness. A key element in this was the renewed interest in, and wider dissemination of, Grimmelshausen's *Simplicissimus*, a semi-autobiographical account of the war first published in 1667 which now became celebrated as the first German novel.[48] Grimmelshausen was read through the experience of the renewed trauma of invasion, war, and occupation since 1793, as well as Romanticism's fascination with horror.

Some of these themes fed into Friedrich Schiller's history of the Thirty Years War which first appeared in serial form in 1791–5, and was followed by his Wallenstein drama trilogy in 1799.[49] Gustavus Adolphus is the central figure in Schiller's discussion of the period 1629–32, reducing all others to supporting roles, and already conveying a sense of the Swedish king as a 'world historical man' before this term was applied by Ranke, Droysen, and other nineteenth-century historians to mean individuals who changed or personified the course of history through exemplary lives or taking appropriate decisions.[50] Schiller reiterated seventeenth-century pro-Swedish propaganda to argue that Gustavus had intervened in the Empire to save German Protestantism. However, he departed from the established tropes of sacrifice and martyrdom to recount the king's death in gruesome detail without any heroic last words. His verdict was far more ambivalent than the earlier hagiography, arguing that Gustavus had died at the right time, having recovered Protestant political and religious rights, but before he could establish Swedish hegemony in Germany. If he had lived, Gustavus would have become a tyrant like his opponent, Ferdinand II.[51]

Schiller's view of Gustavus as flawed yet still dying for a noble cause proved hugely influential and continues today as the mainstream historical verdict on the king's intervention in the Thirty Years War. It also cemented the idea of Lützen as a 'turning point' in the war, providing new arguments for it to be interpreted as 'decisive' without it necessarily being a clear victory for either side. The battle now became a watershed between the first half of the war which supposedly had been a struggle over religious and constitutional principles between clearly defined parties led by 'world historical figures', and the second half when it allegedly spiralled out of control into meaningless violence. Like Schiller's verdict on Gustavus, the sense of Lützen as a turning point has also persisted, not least because it chimes with other, later grand narratives. The most important of these is that of the conflict starting as the last and greatest of an age of 'religious wars', but burning itself out after 1635 to pave the way for an allegedly purely secular settlement in the Peace of Westphalia.[52]

Lützen in Swedish and German Nationalism

Alongside this sense of the Thirty Years War and Lützen in particular as a cathartic turning point, a more obviously nationalist interpretation was the second consequence of the period 1792–1815. The view of the nation remained highly confessionalized in the early nineteenth century, with identity and national mission tied closely to faith and morality. Nationalism was regarded as a positive force in a world which was increasingly conceived as a 'family of nations' living in harmony, not rivalry. Such sentiment had yet to penetrate official policy making which remained wedded to more conservative concepts of legitimate rights associated with monarchy, not popular sovereignty. The Congress of Vienna 1814–15 sought to stabilize Europe by relatively modest territorial adjustments intended to prevent France from threatening the continent's peace again. The Confederation of the Rhine was replaced by a German Confederation combining thirty-five medium states with Austria and an enlarged Prussia, all under the nominal presidency of the Austrian emperor.

These changes compelled Sweden to relinquish Stralsund to Prussia in 1815, whilst allowing it to retain Norway which it had gained from Denmark by siding with the anti-French coalition the year before. The loss of Sweden's last German outpost suggested that the country was now merely a Scandinavian rather than a major European power, and prompted a discussion of what its identity and future role should be. It took some time for this to be worked out, but the generally pacific orientation was already signalled in 1833 by Anders Fryxell's comparison between Charles XII and Gustavus. Whereas the former was condemned as a militarist who had endangered Sweden, the latter was praised for allegedly serving the broader European good by selflessly intervening in the Thirty Years War to stem the threat posed by the Habsburgs.[53]

Fryxell's positive interpretation was popularized by the playwright and novelist August Strindberg so effectively that few questioned its validity. The power of this consensus was demonstrated in 1882 by the outrage directed at Julius Mankell, an ancestor of the Swedish crime writer Henning Mankell and an army captain, liberal politician, and amateur historian. Mankell was a national hero after his bravery as a volunteer in the abortive Polish rising against Russia in 1863. After leaving the army, he turned his attention to history, arguing that Sweden's intervention in the Thirty Years War was driven by Gustavus' personal ambition. Mankell was roundly condemned in Sweden for voicing such a 'Catholic' opinion, and King Oscar II wrote that he was not worthy to wear a Swedish uniform.

Opinion in Germany was more polarized and complex due to the reluctance to confront the realities of the recent French Revolutionary and Napoleonic Wars. These were commemorated as national 'Wars of Liberation', but in fact had elements of a civil war, just like the Thirty Years War.[54] Most of the surviving medium states still forming the 'third Germany' after 1815 had benefited from backing Napoleon with some, like Saxony, sticking with him well into 1813. Prussia's failure to support Austria after 1795 directly contributed to the collapse of the Empire, while Austria arguably had demonstrated better 'German' credentials by briefly renewing the war against France in 1809. The war after 1813 had entailed the mobilization of thousands of reservists and volunteers across all German states, stoking hopes that their service would be rewarded by political reforms once peace was achieved. These aspirations were not met at the Congress of Vienna which established the German Confederation, incorporating much of the old corporate social order, including the feudal powers of princes and aristocrats. The inclusion of both Austria's multi-ethnic empire to the east and south, as well as Prussia's millions of Polish and Lithuanian subjects, all clashed with the integral ideals of nationalism articulated by Romantic intellectuals with their emphasis on language and culture as primary determinants of identity.

The authorities' reluctance to allow public discussion of these issues forced Germans to debate them obliquely, with many choosing the more distant past as a way to articulate hopes and fears for the future. Interpretations of the Thirty Years War divided broadly into two camps, each associated with a vision of how best to organize a German state. The so-called 'Greater German' school was represented primarily by Catholics such as Johannes Janssen and converts from Protestantism like Onno Klopp who broadly regarded Germans as one of several peoples inhabiting central Europe. They saw the German Confederation as an acceptable continuation of the old Holy Roman Empire which combined Austria, Prussia, and the third Germany without requiring either of the two German great powers to sever ties with their non-German subjects. The Thirty Years War was interpreted as the last opportunity to unite the Empire under Habsburg leadership which had been frustrated by the selfishness of the princes, especially the Protestants who were blamed for inviting foreign powers to invade. The Peace of Westphalia was regarded as condemning Germany to weakness and disunity from which the country was only just emerging.

The alternative 'Lesser German' view was held by Protestant authors who saw the nation in more exclusive cultural and linguistic terms, and who regarded Catholics with suspicion because of their ultramontane loyalties to the pope. From this perspective, the Reformation was the last opportunity to unite the Empire which had been squandered by the Habsburgs' refusal to embrace Protestantism as the true 'German' faith. The Thirty Years War thus became part of the 'Counter-Reformation' driven by the Habsburgs as Europe's leading Catholic power with the alleged intention of destroying Protestantism in the Empire. The most politicized form of this approach was the Borussian School exemplified by Droysen and Treitschke who identified Prussia as the power best suited to forge national unity.[55] Swedish intervention in the Thirty Years War was interpreted through the lens of the more recent Wars of Liberation as a parable of liberation and an attempt to unify Germany through Gustavus' network of alliances with Protestant princes. A typical example of this was the work of Friedrich Ludwig von Rango, who had won the Iron Cross whilst serving as a junior officer in the Prussian army in 1813 and subsequently wrote poetry and a hagiographic biography of Gustavus, presenting him as the direct spiritual link between Arminius' defeat of the Roman legionaries at Teutoberg Forrest and the Wars of Liberation against Napoleon.[56]

Lützen and the Myth of Religious Freedom

Rango's book was an early example of generally short biographies appearing across the next 150 years aimed at a broad readership and largely eschewing the academic standards simultaneously being set by contemporary professional historians like Ranke. The authors' purpose was often explicitly didactic and their works bore a strong resemblance to the long tradition of exemplary Christian lives, including their recycling of existing stories and anecdotes in place of original research. Quotations from contemporary material were inserted without acknowledgement or context, and sometimes entirely fabricated dialogue was used to personalize events and catch readers' attention.[57] These books were usually titled *Gustavus Adolphus the Great*, signalling their positive assessment of the king as a world historical figure who shaped human development. Gustavus was uniformly praised as a Protestant hero who intervened in the Thirty Years War supposedly because his heart was moved by the plight of German Protestants.[58] Swedish wartime propaganda was accepted uncritically, notably its presentation of Protestant liberties as universal religious freedoms. Already sometime shortly after 1813 a wooden sign was placed near the Swedish Stone at Lützen with the explanation 'Here fell G.A. [*sic*] in battle for religious freedom'. The stone monument erected at Breitenfeld in the bicentenary year 1831 was inscribed:

> On 7 September 1631/1831,
> saved at Breitenfeld,
> religious freedom for the world,
> Gustavus Adolphus Christian and hero.

This equation of Protestant rights with universal ones was further underpinned by recycling stories already current during Gustavus' lifetime which purported to demonstrate his religious tolerance, such as his willingness to engage in theological debate with Jesuits and his alleged patience in dealing with conquered Catholics.[59] In part, this represented an attempt to modernize Gustavus following the Enlightenment which had rationalized religious identity as part of a proper social order rather than its defining characteristic. For many in nineteenth-century Germany, religion should provide the moral foundation of the new German nation which they hoped would be forged through political unification.[60] Anglophone writers often accepted this image of a tolerant Gustavus uncritically, presenting it as further evidence for his progressive thinking and as a factor in his military success.[61] The arguments were advanced in revised form by Günther Barudio, a former factory worker turned freelance historian who published commercially successful books on Gustavus and the Thirty Years War.[62] In these, Swedish intervention is presented as the equivalent of the Allied invasion of Germany in 1944–5, while Gustavus dies as a martyr for German liberty. The reality of Swedish religious policies during the Thirty Years War was rather different in occupied Catholic areas, and until 1866 any Swedes who converted from Lutheranism lost their inheritance and were obliged to emigrate.

Far more than academic scholarship, these popular works entrenched the belief that the origins of the Thirty Years War lay in Catholic opposition to the Lutheran Reformation and subsequent Jesuit and Habsburg machinations to reverse the Peace of Augsburg of 1555. Like the seventeenth-century pamphlets, their account of Lützen is brief and largely reduced to the pre-battle prayers and Gustavus' death. Works published in the 1820s and 1830s often repeated folkloric elements, such as Gustavus' oversized heart, his 'magic' sword, and the alleged involvement of Franz Albrecht von Sachsen-Lauenburg in his 'murder'. Such elements were dropped from later books, no doubt because they detracted from the otherwise pristine image of Gustavus as pious Protestant hero. The latter was further sustained by the continued reprinting into the 1880s of seventeenth-century broadsheets showing the Swedish king as 'rock of the church'.[63]

The political dimension also drew uncritically from Swedish propaganda and the immediate reactions to Gustavus' death. The king's demise was blamed on the 'sins' of his followers and their alleged failure to back him adequately. The Saxon elector and other princes were criticized for being too weak and divided to defend Protestantism, thus necessitating Swedish intervention.[64] The parallels with nineteenth-century politics were clear: as the successors of these lesser principalities, the minor states of the 'third Germany' were seen by many as obstacles to national unity that should be swept away.

The Growing Importance of Place

The new ways of thinking about the nation emerging around 1800 encouraged a greater interest in Lützen as the physical location of the battle and Gustavus' death. The town was close to another eleven battle sites in the wider Leipzig area, including the two Swedish victories at Breitenfeld (1631, 1642). This proximity already drew comment in the immediate aftermath of 16 November 1632 when pro-Swedish accounts mentioned King Henry I's victory over the Magyars at Riade near Merseburg in 933. There were traces of what was thought to have been the Magyar camp near the Schkölzig wood on the edge of the Lützen battlefield.[65] Though not made explicit, it is possible that the authors wanted to associate Gustavus' alleged defence of 'German liberty' with Henry's defeat of the Magyar raiders. Henry also came to be regarded as the first king of what eighteenth-century writers began presenting as a German national monarchy, rather than simply one of several post-Frankish kingdoms.

Only 19 km west of Lützen lies Rossbach, the site of Frederick the Great's spectacular victory over a combined Franco-imperial army during the Seven Years War in 1757. This assumed a significant place in the nineteenth-century 'Lesser German' historiography trumpeting Prussia's alleged mission to unite Germany. Closer still was Großgörschen, a village just 4 km further up the Flossgraben southeast of Lützen where Napoleon had scored a minor victory on 2 May 1813 over a combined Russo-Prussian army at the start of the Wars of Liberation. Unlike Riade or especially Rossbach, Großgörschen did not fit the wider nationalist narrative and was only commemorated locally. Significantly, German-language accounts almost invariably name this battle after Großgörschen which indeed had been at the centre of the action, whereas English and French accounts call it 'Lützen' and generally note the proximity of the Napoleonic battle to the site of Gustavus' death.[66]

The most recent and greatest of the nearby battles was that fought at Leipzig in October 1813 which broke Napoleon's power in Germany. For that reason and thanks to the presence of Prussian, Russian, Austrian, Swedish, and even British troops in the Allied army, it came to be known as the Battle of the Nations. Rather than overshadowing Lützen, it contributed to the growing interest in that battle, because the theme of Gustavus' sacrifice for German liberty could be woven into a longer narrative linking the Reformation through to the Wars of Liberation. The fact that Wittenberg, birthplace of the Lutheran Reformation, was only 60 km away reinforced these connections in the minds of many nineteenth- and twentieth-century observers.

The boundary changes enacted at the Congress of Vienna in 1815 were also significant. Saxony had delayed too long in 1813 in abandoning its alliance with Napoleon and was punished by the transfer of the northern half of its territory to Prussia. Lützen now became Prussian as the frontier moved almost to the gates of Leipzig. Detaching Lützen from Saxony distanced commemoration of the battle from discussion of Saxony's controversial role in the Thirty Years War. However, Borussian historians also had no immediate use for Lützen, since Brandenburg-Prussia's role in the Thirty Years War was also difficult to fit easily into the narrow Lesser German nationalist interpretation.

Indeed, most of the German past remained controversial in the immediate aftermath of the Wars of Liberation, as demonstrated by the anxieties stirred by a few hundred students commemorating the tercentenary of the Reformation in 1817 at the Wartburg, the castle in Wittenberg where Luther first published his attack on the papacy. Virtually all the states of the German Confederation were governed by conservatives who, rightly, feared that any moves towards the liberal-nationalist vision of a unified Germany would remove them from the map. The Austrian chancellor, Metternich, coordinated a crack-down on public demonstrations in 1819 and imposed tighter censorship laws. In fact, the liberal nationalists were repeatedly frustrated by the lack of popular support, with their gatherings attracting only hundreds compared to the tens of thousands participating in Catholic pilgrimages. Nonetheless, the authorities remained nervous thanks to continued popular unrest caused by a variety of social, economic, and political grievances.

The bicentenary of Swedish intervention in the Thirty Years War occurred at the start of a succession of often violent protests across much of Germany in 1830–3. For example, the palace of Brunswick's unpopular duke was burned down, while an assembly in Hambach in May 1832 attracted a crowd of 30,000, often identified as Germany's first mass political demonstration. Though localized and ill coordinated, these events accelerated the pace of modest reforms in some medium and smaller states. Rioting in Dresden forced the Saxon king to change his government and issue a new constitution on 4 September 1831 which added an elected lower house to the kingdom's parliament.

The Bicentenary in 1832

The battle's centenary in 1732 had been marked only by local clergy with religious services, and by 1832 it had been forgotten whether it had been commemorated at all.[67] Such apparent neglect was not acceptable in the current atmosphere. Whereas visitors had previously been content with the Swedish Stone as a site for quiet contemplation, local activists now felt a more imposing monument was required. Their ideas reflect a transition from the ideals of the later eighteenth century and of Romanticism with their focus on the natural environment, to those of the more strident nationalism later in the nineteenth century which would demand massive statues striking heroic poses.

The prime mover was Captain Eduard Philippi who lived in Leipzig, but was driven by his personal interest in Gustavus to secure a transfer to Lützen as an official in the Prussian revenue service. By March 1830 he had collected 101 supporters for his proposal for a larger monument which was endorsed by the town council. Recognizing the cost implications and keen to attract external interest, the council wrote to the Swedish government requesting support.[68] However, Philippi's project only gathered momentum with the erection of monuments at Breitenfeld in 1831 and Alte Veste the following year.[69] Local opinion was galvanized by a desire not to be outdone by their neighbours to the north at Breitenfeld, as well as the rapid approach of Lützen's own bicentenary. Philippi and his supporters favoured placing an imposing yet unadorned granite block behind the Swedish Stone, considering this as in keeping with Gustavus' character and that of his Lutheran faith. Philippi donated the proceeds of his new book on the battle, while further money was gathered through subscription and donations from units of the Second and Fifth Federal Army Corps which were stationed nearby.[70] However, these efforts raised only 450 of the 3,000 talers estimated costs by late summer 1832.

Undaunted, the activists decided to go ahead with a commemorative ceremony even without a monument to unveil and placed articles in local papers to attract participants. The event established a format, the essentials of which are still observed annually in Lützen today. The proceedings began on 5 November with memorial services at Meuchen Church and other sites where, according to local lore, Gustavus had stopped on his way to Lützen.[71] By staging their event according to the Old Style Julian calendar dating of the battle, the organizers subtly excluded Catholics and signalled the self-consciously Protestant character of their commemoration. The main event opened at a leisurely 10 a.m. the next day; subsequent ceremonies would begin earlier at 7 a.m. with hymn singing on Lützen marketplace. Participants were summoned by the tolling of Lützen's church bells.

Around 12,000 assembled, including the French ambassador to Saxony, local clergy, and 800 students from the Weissenfels seminary and local schools who were dressed in the Swedish colours of yellow and blue. Gustav von Rochow, the regional administrator, was there on behalf of the Prussian government, while the Lutheran church establishment of both Prussia and Saxony were represented by Heinrich von Holleufer, provost of Merseburg, and Dr Goldhorn, archdeacon of the Thomaskirche in Leipzig.

The crowd processed along the highway accompanied by Prussian and Saxon gendarmes and the Lützen civic militia, with the town's poorer inhabitants bringing up the rear. This formalized order was reminiscent of seventeenth-century civic ceremonies and reflected the persistence of the early modern corporate social structure into the nineteenth century. The absence of regular troops followed a warning from the Prussian culture minister not to make it an overtly nationalist event.

Swedish participation was indirect at this stage, but would become a major presence later. The earlier request for assistance had led to the donation of a silk flag which was displayed in Meuchen Church during the 1832 ceremony. The origins of this were soon forgotten and by the later nineteenth century it was mistakenly believed to have been an imperial banner captured by the Swedes. The Swedish royal arms were freshly repainted on the wall above the urn containing Gustavus' viscera which Philippi had recently rediscovered.[72] Parallel celebrations were also held in Sweden, inaugurating 6 November as an unofficial national day. Circumstances there were very different than in Germany, as there were no political constraints on celebrating Gustavus as a heroic king who personified what was then believed to be the country's golden age. A crowd of 7,000 gathered in Uppsala, a town with only 4,500 inhabitants, in the presence of Crown Prince Oscar and his sons Karl and Gustav. School children led a torchlight procession to the church for a commemorative service and patriotic speeches.[73]

Having reached the Swedish Stone at Lützen, the Weissenfels seminarians performed Handel's *Messiah*. The crowd then prayed, before young women laid wreaths and placed a blue silk cushion decorated with the three Swedish royal crowns at the Stone. These elements directly referenced the Swedish connection and the official character as a primarily religious ceremony. The following speeches were more openly nationalist. Johann Haasenritter, a prominent member of the Merseburg Consistory, urged those assembled to remember Gustavus' sacrifice to re-establish the German constitution and to deliver the land from slavery. Dr Grossmann, the Thomaskirche's superintendent who had presided at the Breitenfeld commemoration the previous year, was a surprise guest. Allegedly, the local schoolmaster was so overcome with emotion that he was unable to deliver his planned speech, allowing Grossmann to step forward and deliver a stirring address in which he expressed the hope that the event would help raise German national consciousness.[74]

While the nationalist element would grow more pronounced across the nineteenth century, the first ceremony also displayed another feature that many contemporary observers preferred to ignore. Having stood patiently throughout the music, prayers, and speeches, the crowd happily returned to enjoy the more prosaic delights of Lützen's taverns which welcomed the event as a significant boost to their trade. Meanwhile, the local and visiting dignitaries were entertained at a banquet which mirrored those at modern charity events designed to solicit funds. Carried by the heady atmosphere of the day, those present agreed to constitute Philippi's band of enthusiasts as a formal organizing Comité to promote the planned monument.

The Gustavus Monument

The subsequent discussions revealed tensions between the secular and religious aspects of commemoration which would persist to the present day. Though he had publicly called for national unity, Grossmann was actually more concerned with religious consciousness and favoured a 'living monument' over a physical one. He saw the bicentenary of 1630–2 as an opportunity to associate Lutherans more closely with Germany as the birthplace of the Reformation by attracting them as pilgrims to the sacred soil of the Lützen-Wittenberg area. For him, the image of Gustavus' sacrifice was a means to solicit donations which could be used to promote the spiritual and material welfare of Protestants living elsewhere in Europe under what he regarded as oppressive Catholic rule; notably in Habsburg Bohemia and in Prussia's newly acquired province of Westphalia. The result was the Gustav-Adolf-Verein (GAV: Gustavus Adolphus Foundation) incorporated on 4 October 1834, but with a formal foundation date of 6 November 1832. The name not only associated the organization with Lützen, but attracted strong Swedish support; Swedish donations accounted for 78 per cent of the funds raised by 1841 and by 1882 the organization was providing aid to over 1,500 Protestant communities across central Europe.[75]

Catholics swiftly condemned the GAV as an attempt to present Gustavus as a benevolent humanitarian in order to hide the horrors inflicted on Germany by the Swedish invasion. The organization was initially banned in Bavaria, while Prussian Catholics were so incensed when their king Frederick William IV assumed patronage of the GAV in February 1844 that they proposed establishing a rival 'Tilly Foundation' to support poor Catholic parishes. Even some Lutherans were uneasy. The Prussian conservative Leopold von Gerlach complained in June 1866 that it was as if the Catholics had established an 'Alba Association'—the Duke of Alba being the Spanish general who, at the start of the Dutch Revolt in 1567, had instigated the infamous 'Council of Troubles' which had led to the judicial murder of thousands of Protestants.[76] The GAV continually struggled with its name, but the organization continued to distribute hagiographic material on the Swedish king into the twentieth century, and retained reference to him when it was reorganized after the Second World War as the Gustav-Adolf-Werk (Gustavus Adolphus Work) in 1946.[77]

More secular currents were represented by Christian Schild, a Leipzig merchant who spotted a business opportunity and spearheaded the drive for a physical monument. Copying the mass fundraising techniques pioneered in late Georgian Britain, Schild placed an advert in the Leipzig paper on 7 November 1832 for a 'penny subscription' which would be entirely separate from Grossmann's efforts.[78] This was worded deliberately to appeal to broad nationalist sentiment across Germany by arguing that a 'more fitting monument' would provide a focus for unity. Subscribers' names were published in subsequent editions of the regional papers. The Duke of Weimar sent a mere 9 talers, probably from jealousy that Gustavus was distracting attention from his own ancestor, Duke Bernhard. However, the large turnout at the November ceremony, together with the avowedly Lutheran character of the project, made Schild's appeal safe for Protestant German states to endorse. The Saxon government pledged 1,000 talers, and though Prussia's King Frederick William III sent only 100, he nonetheless directed his court architect, the renowned Karl Friedrich Schinkel, to design the new monument.[79]

Schinkel's original design was for a neo-classical open stone and masonry temple to be erected over the Swedish Stone. This was abandoned as too expensive in favour of a 10 metre high cast iron 'baldachin' (canopy) inspired by the design of the new spire of the Riddarholm church in Stockholm, built in 1835–40 to replace the original which had been destroyed by fire. The cheaper monument ensured that sufficient funds remained from the subscription to purchase the Swedish Stone site and the immediate surrounding land, as well as to erect a small caretaker's hut.[80]

The unveiling ceremony on 6 November 1837 demonstrated just how far official attitudes had shifted in the past five years. The event now had the official backing of the Prussian government which despatched the Thuringian Hussar Regiment, a local unit, while Saxony sent its Second Rifle Battalion and Sweden provided an eight-man squad from its army. The martial element was reinforced by Lützen's civic militia and uniformed university students from Leipzig, Halle, and Jena. Four guns of the Saxon 4th Artillery Brigade fired a salute during the unveiling itself. Prussia and Sweden were directly represented by their king and crown prince, respectively. The

Illustration 16: The Swedish Stone and Chapel

church was also now more prominently represented in the person of Johann Dräseke who, as the general superintendent of the Prussian province of Saxony, was the head of the regional Lutheran church. Up to 6,000 people marched out of Leipzig to attend, while separate columns of school children and parishioners converged from Meuchen and Lützen. Contemporaries reported up to 25,000 people present, and it is likely that overall numbers exceeded those present in 1832.[81]

The crowd gathered around a pulpit erected at the monument site for the occasion and sang the Lutheran chorale *Nun danket alle Gott*. Unlike 1832, there was little restraint on explicitly nationalist rhetoric. Dräseke called Gustavus' campaigns of 1631–2 Germany's 'first war of liberation' delivering Protestants from the Catholic-Ultramontane tyranny personified by Wallenstein, and proceeded to link this to 1813 when Germans had risen again to defeat another 'foreign oppressor'.

Illustration 17: Inauguration of the Gustavus Adolphus Memorial, 1837

This contrast of Wallenstein with Gustavus as the incorruptible hero was now firmly part of the Protestant church's promotion of bourgeois morality. Dräseke concluded by calling on the audience to finish what Gustavus had begun.[82] Given the presence in the audience of the veteran nationalist, the famed gymnast Friedrich Jahn, some might have expected Dräseke to envisage political union. In fact, like the political establishment backing the event, his national vision was still profoundly conservative and was limited to a broadly Protestant-influenced development of government, education, and society. At the banquet that evening, Dräseke pronounced Gustavus and Frederick William III as so united 'by piety, love and chivalrous spirit' that they could be honoured by a single toast. While this presented the Prussian king as continuing the work of his Swedish forebear, it was also probably an attempt to stop proceedings becoming too alcoholic.

The Monument as Destination

The link to 1813 was further personified through the employment of David Blume, who had lost a leg at the Battle of the Nations, as caretaker for the monument and unofficial guide. His successor, Friedrich Altenkirch, had lost an eye in the same battle.[83] The new monument gave people a reason to visit Lützen at any time and not just on 6 November. Over 1,000 visitors signed the guest book during 1838, while those arriving across the following decade included Sweden's Prince Karl, the governor of the Danish West Indies, a Russian vice admiral, and numerous Scandinavian, German, and Russian officers. Christian Günther, who had become a local celebrity after emigrating to the USA in 1814 and making a fortune, made two visits in 1839 and 1850, before eventually leaving 30,000 marks to the Lützen poor in his will.[84] The activity offered new opportunities for locals, and not just the innkeepers. The town's militia petitioned the council to provide them with a flag in 1839 on the grounds of their participation in the unveiling ceremony two years earlier.[85]

In retrospect, however, 1837 emerges as the peak of the Romantic nationalist association with Lützen, as public attention focused increasingly on more practical ways to forge unity. The bicentenary of the Peace of Westphalia coincided with the Revolutions of 1848–9 which revealed the depth of divisions over Germany's future. As the precursor of the German Confederation, the Holy Roman Empire was increasingly blamed for contemporary problems. The Peace of Westphalia was now regarded as a source of national shame, in place of the earlier praise of it as stabilizing the Empire and securing Protestant rights. The critical interpretation threatened Gustavus' positive image, since Sweden had benefited materially from the Peace at Germans' expense. Matters were settled in the three conflicts of 1864, 1866, and 1870–1, collectively known as the 'Wars of German Unification', which saw Prussia forge the German Empire on the basis of the Lesser German solution by excluding Austria and its numerous non-German speaking subjects. There was now a new crop of battles to celebrate, notably the victory over France at Sedan on 2 September 1870 which became the new German Empire's national holiday.[86]

These developments threatened to leave Lützen's new Gustavus memorial without a clear purpose at a time when practical problems of organization and maintenance became more obvious. Philippi's original Comité dissolved itself as its elderly members died and its funds were spent. The elected members of Lützen's town council initially blocked a proposal that they assume responsibility. However, the Prussian provincial government based in Merseburg refused to help, forcing the town reluctantly to take the place of the defunct Comité.[87] Funds were invested to generate interest in the monument's maintenance, but the council was repeatedly called on to meet additional specific costs, for example providing two flags for the annual November ceremony in 1865. The GAV continued to provide occasional donations, such as 500 talers in 1858, while the Berlin military pensions office paid the caretaker.[88] By 1874, the GAV was no longer prepared to assist, preferring instead to devote all its efforts towards its 'living monument' of supporting Lutheran church activities in Catholic areas. Having prepared a cost estimate, the Merseburg authorities formally approved the council as successor of the defunct Comité, which at least resolved some of the legal ambiguity surrounding questions of responsibility for the monument and ownership of the land.[89] However, all Merseburg would contribute was the 2 marks 40 pfennigs for the fire insurance premium on the caretaker's house.

1882–1914

The revival of Lützen as a commemorative site demonstrates how anniversaries can be a powerful stimulus to historical imagination. The 250th anniversary of the battle in 1882 was of course also the 50th anniversary of the GAV which held its annual general meeting in Leipzig to coincide with the annual ceremony at Lützen to which it also sent a delegation.[90] The event revealed just how far the conflicts of 1848–71 had failed to resolve the controversies of German national identity. The organizing committee had wanted to invite the Prussian and Swedish monarchs, but were blocked by Chancellor Bismarck who feared that the overtly Protestant character of the ceremony would endanger his rapprochement with German Catholics to whom he was now turning as potential allies against the rising socialist movement. Nonetheless, the Merseburg government paid for the monument's renovation and erected a 1,000-seat grandstand for the more distinguished guests. The latter included Sweden's ambassador and a Finnish delegation which arrived with its own ceremonial banner. Their participation was also not without controversy, since Finland had been conquered from Sweden by Russia in 1808. The Russian authorities regarded any expression of a separate Finnish identity with suspicion.[91] However, the 250th anniversary of Gustavus' death was marked by meetings in Turku (Abo) and Porvoo (Borga), though neither attracted anything like the 20,000 people who assembled in Lützen.

The success of the 1882 event was also due to an economic upturn and a surge of local pride and interest. As in 1832, individual enthusiasts played a disproportionate part in promoting commemoration and in developing the battlefield as a visitor destination. Oscar Planer, a local wood trader, was inspired to become an avid collector of Gustavus memorabilia and would be one of the key figures in Lützen into the twentieth century.[92] A neo-Renaissance town hall was built in 1884–5 to replace an actual sixteenth-century building now deemed impossible to repair. Not only was this style currently fashionable, but it reinforced the town's association with the seventeenth century, and it was also used for the Protestant orphanage, called the Gustav-Adolf-Haus, built in 1903. A 2.5 metre tall statue of Gustavus inaccurately dressed in full armour was placed high on a prominent corner of the new town hall.

The new building was a sign of wealth and confidence. Initially, the council had planned to convert Lützen Castle which it bought in 1884 from a publican who had acquired it when the town passed to Prussia

Illustration 18: Gustavus Adolphus statue on the corner of Lützen Town Hall

in 1815. The interim owner had demolished the upper storey, sold off the copper roof, and filled in the moat, but sufficient remained of the original building to act as a further reminder of the events of 1632, as well as providing another visitor attraction. The monument had already been enhanced by using the former exercise ground of the local reservists to expand the surrounding park in the 1860s.[93] A major boost came in 1897 when the town was connected to the national rail network, greatly increasing accessibility. Extra services were laid on for each November ceremony, and numbers were especially large when the date fell on a Sunday, as in 1910.[94]

These developments exacerbated tensions already present since the 1830s between competing secular and spiritual forms of commemoration. First, the town's success directly threatened the battlefield itself. Three of the windmills were removed in April 1903 to make way for the

Illustration 19: Historic postcard from Lützen

new Hahn Brothers' factory.[95] Second, increased visitor numbers inevitably encouraged commercialization which was meanwhile fed by new manufacturing techniques capable of supplying highly decorative yet affordable goods. The expanding middle classes were keen to demonstrate learning and morality within the setting of the bourgeois home, and Gustavus' life appeared a suitably edifying story in tune with their national and religious concerns. Manufacturers were happy to provide popular prints, tablecloths, and cups emblazoned with the king's image or that of the new monument, while a Göteborg confectioner began producing Gustavus marzipan for the Swedish market in the 1890s.

The 1882 event already had elements of a Volksfest. Alongside the singing of traditional Lutheran hymns, the crowd were entertained by the band of the 96th Prussian Infantry Regiment playing a specially composed *Gustavus Adolphus March*, as well as a recently composed overture to Schiller's *Wallenstein's Camp*, plus hits of the day like Strauss waltzes, Liszt's *Second Hungarian Rhapsody*, Brahms' fifth and sixth *Hungarian Dances* and Wagner's *Tannhäuser* overture.[96] The band's presence also exemplified the martial character which the event had acquired since 1837, but which now grew with the militarization of German society after the accession of Wilhelm II in 1888. This also meant attention was paid to the battle as more than just the occasion of Gustavus' death. The local paper published an account of the action, including orders of battle, in time for the 1905 ceremony.[97] By then, it had become clear that the ceremonies were a pleasant country excursion for the inhabitants of the nearby metropolis, Leipzig, and newspapers praised it as an opportunity to enjoy 'the quiet of autumnal nature far from the bustle of daily life'.[98]

The tensions soon became obvious between what the authorities considered proper and the economic opportunities and pressures of those actually running the monument and associated events. One caretaker was already dismissed in 1877 for 'gross dereliction of duty'.[99] The Merseburg government then complained that his replacement had 'over the course of the years surreptitiously expanded his permission to dispense harmless refreshments into a formal publican's trade' which 'had caused offence amongst certain sections of the public'.[100] The business had the backing of Otto Lenze, the town's long-serving mayor. When the Merseburg government forced it to close, Lenze's friend, the landowner Karl Louis Martzsch, provided funds to demolish the caretaker's house and replace it with a purpose-built restaurant opposite the monument in 1896. The pair secured official approval for their venture by opening a small, free museum. Additionally, Martzsch donated 13.5 hectares to expand the park supported by a foundation established by his will in 1893.

Late Nineteenth-Century Controversies

The Lutheran Church remained determined to preserve the religious character of the Lützen ceremonies and the wider commemoration of Gustavus.[101] Despite abandoning its openly anti-Catholic measures of the early 1870s, the Prussian government remained partisan in its religious sympathies and the tercentenary of Gustavus' birth in 1894 received official backing, with Wilhelm II summoning all Protestant schools to mark the event on 9 December. Lützen's population was 98 per cent Protestant and the town now assumed the name Gustav-Adolf-Stadt (Gustavus Adolphus Town), echoing the title of Luther-Stadt given to Wittenberg.

The Centre Party, the main political organization of German Catholics, denounced the 1894 celebrations. Their publisher, Germania, issued a pamphlet drawing on Droysen and other recent historical scholarship to argue that Gustavus had misused religion to hide his selfish political ambitions in Germany. Bavarian Catholics meanwhile responded in their customary fashion by staging rival ceremonies to honour Tilly and Maximilian I, as well as celebrating a mass to commemorate the Wittelsbach dynasty as defenders of Catholicism. Protestants reacted angrily, with the Leipzig daily paper dismissing any criticism of Gustavus as 'Jesuit lies'.[102]

The emergence of socialism added to these debates a third voice which had been absent earlier in the century. Franz Mehring worked as a journalist in Leipzig and was familiar with the Lützen ceremonies and Gustavus cult. The initial print run of 30,000 copies of his pamphlet sold out quickly in 1894 and its arguments circulated more widely still through precis disseminated in socialist papers. Ironically, Mehring echoed many of the criticisms levelled by Catholics, arguing that Gustavus was a militaristic imperialist monarch who plundered Germany to sustain his own unstable Swedish empire. His treatment of Wallenstein was also favourable, presenting him as seeking peace through compromise. However, his central argument was aligned with that of Karl Marx and Friedrich Engels: since religion was the opium of the masses, it was irrelevant which religious group had behaved better than another in the Thirty Years War, and the real issues were to do with class.[103]

The controversy revealed the deeper divisions over what it meant to be German in the later nineteenth century. The lack of consensus was a major source of political anxiety, because it suggested that the new German Empire forged in 1871 had not resolved the problems of unity and identity.[104] This issue was already present during the 1882 ceremony when the question of Gustavus' nationality was addressed more explicitly. The committee organizing parallel celebrations in Helsingfors (Helsinki) wrote that the battle's memory was 'dear to all those who value the high ideal of religious freedom, but above all among those peoples whose ancestors fought under the banners of Gustavus Adolphus'.[105] This appeal to a common brotherhood in arms became central to the articulation of Lützen as representing a common Nordic-Germanic identity uniting Germans and Scandinavians. The playwright Otto Devrient presented Gustavus in his five-act drama from 1891 as teaching Germans how to behave by uniting rather than dividing their lands. Others argued that 'Gustavus Adolphus thought and felt more German than the Habsburg Ferdinand ... [and] was a better German and would have been a better ruler than Charles V'.[106]

Pan-Nordic-Germanic identity was fostered by continued Scandinavian-German connections after 1882. Swedish and Finnish delegations attended the annual November ceremonies, while King Oscar II presented a large painting for the mayoral office in Lützen's new town hall in 1887. Later, in 1903–4, he arranged for trees to be sent from Sweden to be planted on the land donated by Martzsch to extend the memorial park. The 130-strong Hanover male voice choir cooperated with Lützen's council during the 1894 tercentenary of Gustavus' birth to ensure they would perform at the king's tomb in Stockholm on the right day.[107] A German naval squadron commanded by Prince Heinrich, the Kaiser's brother, visited Stockholm that year. Meanwhile, Lützen's mayor, clergy, and leading citizens like Oskar Planer learned Swedish, and the speeches at the November ceremonies were now given in that language as well as in German.[108]

Swedes were broadly pro-German after 1871. German became the main foreign language taught in schools, while the country's army and sciences looked to Germany for models. The prominent Swedish historian, Martin Weibull, used the 1882 celebrations in Lund to argue that the true German culture was that of a common Nordic-German Protestantism. Though Ferdinand II and Maximilian of Bavaria had been born German, their Catholic upbringing led them to act against the country's interests, whereas Wallenstein was even less representative because he was a 'Slav'.[109] Weibull's interpretation was part of a wider later nineteenth-century trend to read the past through a national identity defined narrowly by language and culture. The leading Swedish papers commented during the anniversary year of 1894 that Gustavus had forged a German-Swedish-Protestant union. Unity extended even to geology. The GAV's central committee chair celebrated the Swedish Stone in 1907, exclaiming 'How holy this stone is! Transported in ancient times from Swedish icebergs to German fields.'[110]

Lützen and Swedishness

However, as with all late nineteenth-century articulations of national unity, there were severe cracks underneath the surface. The continued focus on Protestantism excluded German Catholics from any positive association with Lützen's commemoration, while associating Swedishness with pan-Germanism threatened to submerge it within what many Swedes still saw as a distinct culture. Swedish identity became directly political with the dissolution of the political union with Norway on 7 June 1905. Sweden had always ruled at least one other Scandinavian country since 1319, with control over Norway dating from 1814. Regional hegemony was integral to Swedes' belief in themselves as the leading Nordic power and many initially clamoured for war to prevent Norwegian independence. Though partition eventually proceeded peacefully, Swedes were forced to rethink a narrower, more explicitly Swedish identity.

The political split affected the new Victoria Congregation (*Viktoriagemeinde*), established in 1903 to serve Swedes and Norwegians living in Berlin and named after the Swedish crown princess who came from Baden. As the two new nationalities moved to organize their religious life separately, the Congregation's Swedish pastor saw the by now traditional Swedish presence at the Lützen ceremonies as a way to promote Swedish language and culture in Germany. He invited Per Pehrsson, pastor of Göteborg's largest parish who was currently visiting Hanover, to address the eighty-strong Swedish group attending the November ceremonies in 1905. The recent division was symbolized by the Swedes holding their new national flag, now only blue and yellow because the Norwegian colours had been removed from the top quadrant. Pehrsson was enthused by the experience and became the key figure in the use of Lützen to promote the new Swedishness, especially after his election to the Swedish parliament in 1906. The well-established Lutheran component of Lützen's commemoration lent itself to his project. Pehrsson found an ally in Nathan Söderblom who became archbishop of Uppsala in 1914 and proclaimed Swedes to be God's chosen people. The pair believed that the new Swedishness would in turn assist a religious awakening. To symbolize this, they persuaded Oskar Ekman, a wealthy industrialist, to fund the construction of a Swedish chapel next to the Gustavus monument at Lützen.[111]

Lützen's council initially opposed the plan which involved the demolition of the newly built restaurant, but were persuaded when the Swedes offered to pay to rebuild the restaurant a few hundred metres away where its presence would not detract from the solemnity of the site. In return, the council allowed the Swedes and local pastors to establish an independent administrative board to oversee the construction and management of the chapel. The mayor would simply be a member; an arrangement the council would come to regret. The chapel's design by Lars Israel Wahlman stressed Swedish motifs and used some imported materials. It was completed in time to be consecrated at the November ceremony in 1907 attended by 20,000 people, including Sweden's crown prince, the Kaiser's son Eitel Friedrich, and Paul von Hindenburg, the future field marshal and German president.[112]

Pehrsson used the momentum generated by the chapel project to establish the National Association for the Preservation of Swedishness Abroad (*Riksförcningen för svenskhetens bevarende I utlandet*) in December 1908 with the backing of government ministers. Pehrsson's co-founder, the linguistic nationalist Vilhelm Lundström, believed that Swedes were the purest among a common family of Nordic-Germanic races. Pehrsson's involvement in the National Association projected commemoration of Lützen to the wider Swedish diaspora, especially in the United States where the Chicago chapter of the Augustana Synod, the organization established in 1860 to oversee the Swedish Lutheran church in North America, now introduced an annual commemoration of Gustavus each November.[113]

A Finnish delegation also attended the consecration of the Swedish Chapel and from 1908 onwards 6 November was celebrated by Finland's Swedish minority as 'Sweden Day'. Commemoration of Gustavus found little resonance with the wider population once Finland secured independence from Russia in 1917, and instead memories of the Thirty Years War focused on the Hakkepeliten, or Finnish horsemen known by their war cry 'hack 'em down'. Meanwhile, Perssohn's other collaborator, Archbishop Söderblom, tried to steer the commemoration of Lützen in a less sectarian direction after 1912, establishing an international ecumenical movement in 1925 for which he later won the Nobel Peace Prize. He was opposed by the GAV which defended the narrowly Lutheran character of the event and ultimately foundered on his own inability to reach beyond Protestants to engage Catholics and other Christians.[114]

From 1914 to the 1932 Tercentenary

The strongly Germanic character of Lützen's commemoration by the early 1900s ensured it became an expression of patriotism after the outbreak of the First World War. The 1914 November ceremonies were attended by war wounded on leave. Pastor Gustav Jödicke attempted to present the current war as a continuation of the fight for the 'freedom which was once saved by Gustavus Adolphus', and suggested that the Swedish king was 'a faithful model for our glorious Kaiser'.[115]

The Chapel Board placed advertisements in newspapers throughout Germany to ensure a good attendance despite the war. The ten Swedes from Berlin's Victoria Congregation at the November 1918 ceremonies just made it home before the revolutionaries paralysed the rail network in what was part of a general overthrow of the old order that led to the establishment of the democratic Weimar Republic in 1919. Post-war poverty and depression proved more disruptive than the war. Only seventeen people visited the battlefield monument during 1919. Lützen's new left-wing mayor removed the Swedish flags and bust of Gustavus from his office. The hyperinflation of 1921–4 eroded the value of the Ekman endowment supporting the chapel and the monument, and the caretaker's post was left vacant.[116]

Four factors converged in 1928–32 to ensure a dramatic revival of Lützen's commemoration. As in 1832, local enthusiasts played a significant role. Initially, this was not obvious. A local history magazine, the Lützener Heimatblätter, was begun in 1924 and eventually produced forty-three issues by the time it folded three years later. These scarcely mentioned the battle, indicating that the population's sense of the past was both broader and more parochial with stories on numerous other, yet always local topics. However, Oskar Planer and other citizens saw the battle as the defining moment in their community's history and made it the centrepiece of their local and regional museum (*Heimatmuseum Lützen und Umgebung*) which they established in July 1928. This enterprise represented a continuation of the secular currents already present during the nineteenth century which regarded the battle as central to the area's past and a means to connect this with wider events. The approach of the tercentenary prompted Max Brauer, a teacher in Weissenfels, to devote over two years to making a huge diorama of the battle using tin soldiers. His model proved too big to fit into the museum, so Lützen enthusiasts hastily made their own with 3,000 figures showing the battle at the moment of Gustavus' death to be ready for 1932.

Religion formed a second, parallel factor promoting the revival, as the local pastors and their Swedish contacts in the National Association were concerned that the November ceremonies were becoming an excuse for music, drinking, and dancing. A parish newsletter *Around the Swedish Stone* (*Rings um Schwedenstein*) was launched in February 1929 as an attempt to reconnect the ceremonies with local religious life.[117]

Faced with local indifference after 1918, the Chapel Board increasingly expected Swedes to pay for the maintenance of the Swedish Chapel and Gustavus monument. Pehrsson eventually organized the Lützen Foundation (*Stifelsen Lützenfonden*) in 1931 to coordinate fundraising in Sweden. His initiative coincided with the easing of the Depression and a new donation from the Ekman family, enabling plans already prepared in 1908 to be realized. A new caretaker's hut was pre-fabricated in Sweden and shipped to Lützen where it was erected in time for the 1932 November ceremonies. Hans Svensson, a Swede, became the new caretaker. Initially he was supposed to be paid from fees and postcard sales, but from 1938 the Foundation assumed responsibility for his salary. Having surveyed the battlefield in 1929 as part of their six-volume history of Gustavus' wars, the Swedish

General Staff supplied a copy of their map to be reproduced as a colour handout for visitors to the memorial.[118]

The tercentenary in 1932 had a catalytic effect similar to the 1832 anniversary. The Swedish media gave the 1932 events more attention than the German or American elections that year, while parallel ceremonies were held by the Swedish diaspora in Finland, Latvia, Estonia, and the USA. Matters were more complex in Germany where the tercentenary coincided with the Weimar Republic's death-throes. The July 1932 elections saw the Nazis increase their representation in the Reichstag from 12 to 230 seats. Amidst escalating political violence, it proved impossible to form a stable government and new elections were called for 6 November. Though the Nazis polled 2 million fewer votes and lost thirty-four seats, the results polarized German politics further as other right-wing parties and the Communists made further gains.

The Prussian regional government feared that the sectarian character of the November ceremonies might contribute to public disorder and agreed only to fund the restoration of Meuchen's church in April 1932. Any hopes that the tercentenary would pass quietly proved illusory. A succession of religious, sporting, and youth groups held meetings in Lützen throughout the summer of 1932, culminating in a mass rally of 100,000 people at the Battle of the Nations monument outside Leipzig in October. Attended by Nazi stormtroopers and members of the veterans' organization Stahlhelm, this was a darkly nationalist event with speeches openly denouncing France and Western democratic values. Lützen's mayor hoped to get the annual November ceremonies moved to avoid their coinciding with the Reichstag elections, but they went ahead as planned amid a large military presence. The crowd of up to 15,000 included many sporting Nazi insignia. German and Swedish socialists revived Mehring's earlier critique of Gustavus as a 'foreign' imperialist, but their objections were lost in the generally nationalistic mood encapsulated by a local newspaper headline as 'Germans, Protestants, Fellow-believers!'[119]

Illustration 20: 11th Saxon Infantry Regiment lining the route during the tercentenary celebrations, 6 November 1932

Commemoration under Nazism

Further national elections on 3 March 1933 saw the Nazis achieve a majority in coalition with another right-wing party. Twenty days later they seized power through the Enabling Act which allowed Hitler to rule by decree. Events in Lützen mirrored national trends. The Communists and Social Democrats split the opposition vote allowing the Nazis to secure a majority of the council's fifteen seats and to depose the incumbent mayor. The *Lützener Heimatblätter*, revived following the tercentenary, responded indirectly in its first new issue in November 1933 by asking rhetorically whether, after three centuries, it was time to stop commemorating the battle. 'The answer to this question is eased by the fact that the Swedes themselves will not stop doing so.' However, the local history society was dissolved in 1939 as part of the wider 'consolidation' of all civic life within Nazi party organizations.

The GAV and the Lützen Foundation were allowed to continue because the Nazis were not threatened by their by now monotonous refrain of Lützen as the 'consecrated place of pilgrimage for all evangelical believers from the whole world'.[120] Pehrsson was an ardent anti-communist, while Karl Mannborg, the Lützen Foundation's representative in Germany, had served in the right-wing Freikorps against the German Revolution of 1918 and openly compared Gustavus to Hitler. Mannborg was succeeded by another conservative, Otto Link, who was prepared to cooperate with the Nazis to ensure the November ceremonies continued during the Second World War. Pehrsson did fear the Nazis' antipathy towards religion and strove to preserve the strictly Lutheran character of Lützen's commemoration. Backed by the Ekman family, the Foundation managed to remove the town's Nazi mayor from the Chapel Board in 1935, but the significance of this was greatly lessened by the political sympathies of Pastor Hagemeyer, the new Board chair, who invited Goering's sister-in-law to speak at one of its events. Erling Eidem, Soderblöm's successor as archbishop of Uppsala, knew of the death camps, but despite his hostility to Nazism, refrained from using his presence at the 1942 ceremonies to criticize the regime.

The conservative historian Johannes Paul had already presented Gustavus as a military strongman who prefigured the Nazi ideal of a leader. This line was developed further by Wilhelm Koppe, who argued that Gustavus had pursued the kind of 'German freedom' supposedly represented by the Nazi policy of subsuming individuals within a single national will.[121] The Nazi interior minister Wilhelm Frick took the opportunity of visiting Sweden in December 1937 to describe Gustavus as 'the pure-German hero-king who had influenced Germany like no other'.[122] Attempts to co-opt Gustavus as an Aryan role model culminated in plans to replace the nineteenth-century monument with a grandiose equestrian statue. Though some Swedish fascists laid wreaths on the king's coffin during the 1932 tercentenary, their country's government preferred to use each 6 November as an opportunity to cement national solidarity against all external threats, including those posed by Germany.

Nazi interest in promoting the Gustavus cult quickly faded when it became obvious that Sweden would not join Germany in the Second World War. Gustavus was just too Christian to be fully Nazified, and the planned new monument was abandoned after 1939 in favour of renovating the monuments commemorating victories at Tannenberg and Lodz in 1914. Official assistance was provided to ensure the November ceremonies continued after 1939, and Swedish and Finnish troops paraded with Wehrmacht soldiers during those held in 1941. However, by 1943 only 150 people attended, compared to crowds of 6,000 to 12,000 during the 1930s. Numbers dropped to fifty in 1944, and just five the following year.[123]

Commemoration under Communism

Lützen's main employer, the chemical plant at Leuma, was bombed on 4 April 1945. Ten days later, US troops took the town after brief fighting during which the Swedish Chapel was damaged. The area was soon transferred to Russian control. Soviet troops pulled down the Kaiser's statue in the main square, but spared that of Gustavus on the corner of the town hall after locals interjected 'that was no German imperialist! It is a neutral Swedish king'.[124] Meanwhile, the caretaker Hans Svensson kept both US and Russian troops out of the monument park by flying the Swedish flag and displaying a notice that it was 'Swedish property'. This unofficial extension of Sweden's actual neutrality to the monument would become a major factor preserving Lützen's commemoration across the next forty-five years.

Some attempts to benefit from connections to Sweden failed. A local book dealer was unable to import Swedish books about the battle, while Otto Link's application for Swedish nationality was rejected on the grounds he had never lived there.[125] The new German Democratic Republic (GDR), established in Soviet-occupied Germany

Illustration 21: Hans Svensson's notice of the memorial as 'Swedish property',
1945

in 1949, blocked the Chapel Board's attempts to transfer exclusive
control of the monument site to the Lützen Foundation on the
grounds that all land belonged to the people. Nonetheless, over a
century of growing Swedish involvement had fostered the local belief
that the land was somehow Swedish territory. Crop-spraying aircraft
avoided the site because their owners thought it would be too much
bother to apply for overflight permits from the Swedish embassy.[126]
The local Lutheran pastors recognized that their connections to
Sweden offered some protection from the new government's interference in church affairs. Locals also had more prosaic reasons to

continue the November ceremonies, since the regular arrival of Swedish guests provided clandestine access to food, cash, and otherwise hard-to-obtain goods like a sewing machine.

After a decade of some plurality, official GDR interpretations of the Thirty Years War solidified along orthodox Marxist-Leninist lines. Structural forces like socio-economic change were believed to determine history, marginalizing the role previously ascribed to individuals like Gustavus. Within another decade, the Thirty Years War was held to have been a disaster, not for the traditional nationalist reason for having frustrated German unity, but for allegedly delaying the economic progress believed necessary to move history forward. The direction of Weissenfels Museum informed the town's mayor that 'the bourgeoisie were completely ruined as the "rising class", thereby removing them as carriers of future capitalist development'.[127]

Nonetheless, the GDR still needed to claim the German past as part of its wider strategy to legitimate itself as a sovereign state alongside the rival Federal Republic established in the west on the other side of the Cold War divide. Promoting Lützen's commemoration appeared a good way to assist efforts to secure Swedish recognition of the GDR as a state. The communist authorities cooperated with the National Association to finance another renovation of the Gustavus monument in 1957–61. The construction of the Berlin Wall in 1961 actually encouraged the authorities to take a more relaxed attitude to the November ceremonies, since tighter control of their frontiers made it easier to police foreign visitors. The coincidence of the ceremonies with the annual Leipzig trade fairs provided another incentive, since attracting further visitors allowed the regime to showcase its form of socialism.

The appointment of Erich Honecker as general secretary of the ruling Socialist Unity Party in 1971 entailed a tacit recognition of the post-1945 division of Germany and led to efforts to foster a distinct East German 'national' identity. This allowed greater scope for local and regional history. Lützen's museum reopened in 1973 and within a decade a new diorama with 3,600 tin figures was built by local enthusiasts to replace the one damaged in the war. The local history magazine resumed publication and short brochures were produced to give visitors a brief history of the castle and battlefield monument.[128]

As previously, personal initiatives and connections remained significant at the local level. Per Pehrsson continued to organize the annual convoy of Swedish visitors until his death in 1953. Otto Link knew Dr Rudolf Stöwesand, a former pastor, playwright, and Gustavus enthusiast who became the regional administrator with responsibility for building materials and was able to help repair the wartime damage to the Chapel. However, Link soon feared arrest and fled with his family to the West in 1950, while the caretaker Svensson refused to return from his holiday in Sweden after the Berlin Wall was erected in 1961. His German replacement was swiftly removed after refusing to cooperate with the Stasi in monitoring visitors to the battlefield. Though the Lützen Foundation eventually found another caretaker, neither it nor the National Association was now directly represented in Germany and the Chapel Board devolved entirely to locals.

Management of Lützen's commemoration now became a microcosm of the general struggle to maintain autonomous spheres in the GDR. The Chapel Board used its 1907 charter to deny the Communist mayor his seat on the grounds that all members had to be Lutherans. However, the dispute revealed divisions between the competing secular and spiritual visions of commemoration which extended back into the nineteenth century. Disagreements between Lützen's pastors and their Swedish counterparts in the Victoria Congregation added another layer of complexity. Meanwhile, many in the town's now large non-church-going population resented their religious neighbours' access to coffee, chocolate, and other foreign goods smuggled along with bibles by the Swedes attending the annual November ceremonies.[129]

Wider post-war attitudes also changed how people regarded the battle. The kind of overt militarism characterizing commemoration between 1871 and 1945 was clearly out of fashion. Several of the local pastors were genuine pacifists who used the November ceremonies to warn against the horrors of war. This created space for them to retain the religious character of the event without challenging the GDR regime which, by the early 1980s, was presenting itself as a bastion of world peace.[130] The tensions inherent in this approach emerged with preparations after 1977 for the 350th anniversary of the battle in 1982. The Lützen Foundation opposed the local pastors' didactic pacifism, favouring instead a traditional historical exhibition without any direct reference to contemporary events. The GDR authorities had more directly material goals, seeing the event as an opportunity to present a positive image to Western visitors. Whereas annual visitor numbers averaged only a few hundred in the two decades immediately after the war, they soared to 50,000 in 1969 which was the town's own 700th anniversary. This was not matched again, but many of the 35,000 or so visiting each year during the 1970s and 1980s were currency-rich foreigners whom the regime was keen to attract.[131] Though official efforts concentrated on the much bigger international draw of the 500th anniversary of Luther's birth in 1983, the government nonetheless renovated the chapel, monument, castle park, and the 3 km road to Meuchen used in the ceremonial procession each November.

Changes in Sweden also favoured renewed engagement. The National Association had already renamed itself the National Association for Sweden Contact (*Riksföreningen Sverigekontakt*) in an effort to distance itself from its nationalist origins. The pacifist spin on the battle suited the Swedish government's own desire to promote the country as a neutral friendly to all. It joined the Lützen Foundation and several businesses in raising 350,000 kroner to build a new Swedish-style wooden visitor centre next to the 1932 caretaker's hut. Swedish royalty boycotted the event in protest at the GDR's persecution of Ernst Sommerlath, a theologian related to Sweden's queen, but over 15,000 people attended the 1982 November ceremonies, including twenty Swedish clergy, while an accompanying historical conference organized by Greifswald University allowed space for Protestant, Catholic, and Marxist interpretations.

Commemoration in Reunified Germany

The subsequent management of the commemorations reflected the growing dysfunctionality of the GDR regime and society that culminated in the mass protests of autumn 1989. The council, clergy, and Lützen Foundation proved incapable of cooperating, while the town's Lutheran congregation continued to dwindle. The end of the GDR in 1990 posed an existential crisis. The inhabitants rejected incorporation in Leipzig and instead voted to become the administrative centre for a rural district immediately west of that metropolis. Some infrastructural improvements followed, such as road resurfacing, but the town otherwise suffered like many other rural areas from the collapse of the socialist command economy. The agricultural collective was privatized, local factories closed, followed by the high school in 1999. Meanwhile, the population contracted by over a third to just 3,700 by 2007.[132]

Now that East Germans were free to travel abroad, Lützen's attraction as a visitor destination drastically declined. Whereas 40,000 people arrived each year during the 1980s, numbers fell to 25,000 the following decade. The real cost of the caretaker's salary tripled after 1990, because the Swedish kroner was not as strong relative to the deutschmark as it had been to the former GDR currency. With neither the Lützen Foundation nor the National Association able to cover the increased costs, the local pastors were finally forced to allow the town council a greater role in organizing the commemorations. The election of Maik Reichel, an art historian, as mayor in 1999 confirmed the official efforts to redress Lützen's economic decline by promoting the battlefield as a heritage site and tourist destination.

Though the Swedish ambassador no longer attended the November ceremonies, members of the royal family were present in 1991, 1993, and especially at the 400th anniversary of Gustavus' birth in 1994. Access was improved with a car park at the monument, while a new historical exhibition opened in the 1982 building. The castle and town museum were comprehensively renovated in 1991–5 and since 1996 have been supported by a new local history society. The first serious attempts to discuss the battle's interpretation and meaning were informally initiated in 1998 and broadened into a series of historical conferences after 2007. That year was the battle's 375th anniversary, which was sufficiently prominent to attract sponsorship from the new regional government, state lottery, and local banks. A three-month-long exhibition in the castle museum drew 11,000 visitors, and led to another major display, organized in collaboration with Czech museums in 2012, which at last paid attention to Wallenstein as the opposing commander in the battle. A preliminary event was organized two years earlier in conjunction with Greifswald University, thus connecting Lützen indirectly to the faint public memory of Wallenstein as Duke of Mecklenburg.

The religious element has persisted alongside these economic and academic aspects. The November ceremonies remain in the form established in 1832, though since 1990 they have been renamed the Day of Encounter (*Tag der Begegnung*) in place of the more overtly sectarian Gustavus Adolphus Day. It is clear that neither this ecumenical approach nor the academic reinterpretation of the battle has penetrated the wider popular consciousness. Many visitors to the 2007 exhibition expressed sectarian opinions on the Thirty Years War, the battle, and its commanders that would not have been out of place in the nineteenth century. Others echoed Mehring's critique of Gustavus as using religion as a cloak for secular ambition; perhaps a legacy of this interpretation being reiterated during the GDR.[133] It is hoped that the present book will go some way towards a more reflective and nuanced interpretation of the battle and its significance.

7

Conclusion

Lützen was not the most important battle of the Thirty Years War in terms of its military and political impact. That dubious honour probably goes to White Mountain (1620) which changed the political balance across much of Central Europe, stabilizing the Austrian Habsburg monarchy and creating a set of property arrangements lasting into the 1940s. Breitenfeld (1631) and Nördlingen (1634) both made a profound immediate impact, even if their results were eroded in the medium term. The second battle of Breitenfeld (1642) and Jankau (1645) also probably outweigh Lützen in political significance, since they successively forced the Habsburgs to open serious talks at the Westphalian congress which ultimately settled the war. Lützen, thus, cannot be considered 'decisive' in the way that term is customarily applied.[1]

Nor did Lützen mark a shift to a more modern form of warfare as claimed by proponents of the Military Revolution thesis. Most of the tactical innovations employed by Gustavus were abandoned soon after his death, such as the Swedish brigade in checker-board deployment, or the practice of interlarding musketeer detachments between cavalry squadrons. Where the battle perhaps did mark a change was as one of several engagements producing a gradual convergence among all belligerents during the Thirty Years War towards a composite 'German' method of deploying and using tactical formations.

Lützen was certainly not a Swedish victory. Wallenstein scored a tactical success, inflicting serious losses on Sweden's main field army, virtually destroying some of its best units. The imperialists held the field at the end of the day and, with Reinach's arrival, had sufficient fresh infantry to have recovered their artillery. Gustavus' death temporarily imperilled Sweden's fragile network of allies and collaborators which would almost have certainly unravelled without the belief that the day had been won. Wallenstein handed this to his opponents through his decision to withdraw, based partly on exaggerated fears of approaching Saxon and Guelph troops, but mainly due to his own mental state and loss of nerve. His subsequent retreat into Bohemia damaged his army which abandoned its artillery and wounded, and suffered further losses through desertion and the capitulation of small garrisons in Saxon towns. All this added credence to Swedish claims of a significant victory. In reality, the wider strategic situation remained stalemated until the imperial triumph at Nördlingen, but by then the myth of the Swedes' success had been entrenched through their effective propaganda.

The belief in a great victory was the essential pendant to Gustavus' heroic martyr's death, since it made his sacrifice appear worthwhile. Initially, this was used to legitimate Sweden's claims for 'compensation' for the cost of its intervention in the Thirty Years War, but later the idea of sacrifice was woven into a dynastic, and then broader national Swedish identity. Protestantism was a significant component from the start, not least because it was already part of Gustavus' image before his death. The martyrology forged bonds between Swedish and German Lutherans, as well as ensuring a sympathetic reception across the rest of Protestant Europe. Much of the later image in the Anglophone world of Gustavus as a 'Great Captain' is largely a secularized version of the seventeenth-century hagiography of him as a Christian warrior.

Lützen differs from the way many other battles are commemorated and especially from the general assumption that war commemoration involves a fading memory once the initial century or so has passed and after those who were either there, or knew someone who was, are dead. 'After that, it's quarter centuries, then halves, then—perhaps after 200 years—only centenaries remain'.[2] By contrast, the memory of Lützen faded well before its first centenary which was scarcely marked at all, but then it experienced a dramatic revival with the bicentenary and has been commemorated with varying intensity annually ever since.

Some other battles have also experienced a similar resurgence of interest long after they were fought. Naseby, fought on 14 June 1645, was a genuinely decisive battle, because the rout of the main Royalist field army made it clear that the king's cause was hopeless and that Parliament would win Britain's civil wars. Despite the clearer outcome than at Lützen, Naseby's remembrance was interrupted by the Restoration in 1660, since the monarchy had no wish to remember a defeat. Interest revived during the 1820s for reasons quite similar to those at Lützen. The desire of local enthusiasts to link their locality to a wider national story coincided with larger political and religious trends; in this case, connections between British liberalism and a resurgence of Non-Conformism, especially between the 1860s and 1910s.[3] Despite this, Naseby never achieved the same level of interest or support and, unlike Lützen, still lacks a visitor centre and other facilities normally associated with a heritage site of national importance.[4]

Despite its distinctive features, Lützen's commemoration illustrates important general issues in European remembrance culture. The first concerns the plasticity of history; how far a story can be made to serve different agendas over time. Behind this lurks a more fundamental question about the nature of history itself and how far distinctions can be made between an 'objective' past and the subjective world of fiction. Here, Lützen illustrates the limits to the postmodernist critique that historians merely tell stories and that there is little or nothing to choose between their competing interpretations. Among other things, Gustavus was just too Christian and too foreign for the Nazis and East German Socialist Unity Party to co-opt commemoration for their own purposes.

Nonetheless, the comparison with fiction is useful in highlighting the elements which ensure that some historical events are better remembered than others. As Chapter 4 indicated, it is impossible to reconstruct the actual course of the battle with complete accuracy, and uncertainty still surrounds even the sequence and timing of the main events. However, details matter far less in remembrance culture than drama. Indeed, historical scholarship on the battle lagged considerably behind propaganda and hagiography in terms of both volume of output and the reach and significance of its impact. The course of events was almost immediately reduced to a few essentials: Wallenstein on the defensive attacked by Gustavus, the pre-battle prayers, Gustavus' charge, his death and that of Pappenheim, the 'revenge attack' and capture of the Windmill battery, Wallenstein's retreat.

These core elements were all personified by figures whose broader historical role reinforced Lützen's place in wider events. While Gustavus was always the most prominent, Wallenstein and Pappenheim remained important 'supporting characters' throughout, if only as foils to help magnify the Swedish king's virtues. All three remained significant as carriers of the core narrative and none could be removed without undermining the rest of the story. Confusion over the details of the battle allowed Gustavus' death to emerge as the defining moment and ensure that this has dominated how Lützen has been remembered. Until only recently, Gustavus' martyrdom for the Protestant cause eclipsed the other 6,000 or so other deaths in the battle which was commemorated largely as the story of one man's sacrifice. This contrasts with other famous engagements like Waterloo or Gallipoli where the general death toll has always been a prominent feature in their legacy. The other deaths are only now penetrating public consciousness, thanks to the recent discovery of the mass grave at Lützen, as well as the widely publicized excavation and preservation of bodies found on the Wittstock battlefield which is now the site of a national Thirty Years War museum.[5]

Though the main characters and core features have remained fixed, the fact that all are open to different interpretations has helped keep Lützen's story alive across the centuries. A major element of this is the simple fact that it is a battle, rather than some other kind of historical event, that is being remembered. Battles are inherently uncertain human activities involving multiple decisions taken under extreme conditions with potentially fatal consequences for those involved. It is this which accounts for the perennial popular interest in military history—and battle history in particular—over that of collective human endeavours of lasting significance, such as accounts of bridge construction or other major engineering projects. The inherent uncertainty captures the imagination, drawing in those who were not present and who, thankfully, have largely not known war themselves. There are always the personal questions: how would I have reacted under those circumstances? What would I have done when faced with that decision? And like most battles, Lützen, even when reduced to its core essentials, is sufficiently complex to prompt many questions in the minds of subsequent observers. Broader, long-standing controversies have surrounded the circumstances and location of Gustavus' death, Wallenstein's decision to retreat, and the exact nature of the battle's outcome and strategic significance.

Thus, it seems that to be remembered, a battle does not need to be decisive in the conventional sense, but does require the presence of a few prominent participants whose moral characters and personalities are at least as important as their military skills. The sequence of events does not have to be fully established, but should be sufficiently clear to permit a fairly stable narrative to emerge. However, this story should not be fixed too tightly or otherwise it might grow stale in the retelling. Some aspects need to remain controversial to allow subsequent generations to reinterpret events and to attach new meanings more in tune with their immediate concerns.

In Lützen's case it is clear that the symbolism surrounding Gustavus' death allowed generations of Germans and Swedes to internalize commemoration as part of their own identity expressed through Protestantism and various forms of nationalism. This in turn helped simplify the story of the battle as it was popularly remembered, reducing it to a basic outline which could be related to idealized visions of morality and national identity. Commemoration thus became 'owned' by people espousing certain kinds of confessional and national identity, even if they in fact often disagreed on defining that identity. The sense of ownership reinforced the belief that this was a Protestant victory, since to do otherwise entailed implicit criticism of the validity of the identities associated with the dominant narrative of the battle. As the descendants of the 'losing' side, Catholics were excluded from official commemoration, but that did not stop them, or later also socialists, from joining debates about the battle.

The proliferation of particular images assisted in perpetuating remembrance of Lützen. It was important that the battle occurred during the 'media revolution' associated with modern print culture, since the dissemination of contemporary pictures helped imprint the key personalities and events on the popular consciousness. Merian's battle map and panoramic engraving were particularly important in fixing general perceptions of how the battle had been fought, especially once these became woven with teleological linear narratives of military developments in which the Swedes were allegedly at the forefront. Likewise, the numerous engravings of Gustavus provided later generations with a readily identifiable figure associated with the battle. It also proved significant that Schiller, Germany's equivalent of Shakespeare, wrote prolifically about the battle's rival commanders and the war in general. The widespread reproduction of these images and texts mirrored the repetition of the commemorative rituals developed in 1832 as annual events. Often, these elements were combined further, as in the recycling of texts about the 1832 ceremony or the 1837 monument unveiling in pamphlets issued during subsequent important anniversaries, like 1882, 1894, or 1932.

The production of images and pamphlets reveals the significance of economic motives in sustaining Lützen's commemoration. This was a big battle for a very small town. Like Waterloo, the battle put Lützen on the map—literally, as it is the only reason why it appears in historical atlases. Gustavus' death gave it even greater reach and resonance. The development of large-scale public ceremonies after 1832 enabled Lützen to step out of Leipzig's shadow as a destination in its own right. The significance of the 1632 battle is underscored by the lack of any comparable attention paid to Großgörschen, fought in May 1813 and involving five times as many combatants with seven times the number of casualties.

Finally, Lützen demonstrates the significance of local people to commemoration. The regional authorities based in Merseburg, the evangelical church, and the GAV were indeed important as intermediaries between the town and the wider world, particularly in attracting wider interest and material support. Here, again, Gustavus proved significant, because, as a foreign monarch, his death connected the battle directly to Swedish history. The practice of commemorating Gustavus primarily on the day of his death, rather than his birth or accession, helped link Swedish identity to the battle and ensure continued interest in Lützen across Sweden and to a lesser extent Finland. This proved especially significant between 1945 and 1990 when the traditionally religious character of commemoration was threatened by the secularizing aspects of Communist rule.

However, important though these intermediaries and wider interest groups were, local activists and enthusiasts exercised a disproportionate influence on developing and sustaining commemoration. For the most part, they were people outside the higher power structures of church and government. While senior clergy were prominent during the 1830s, the initial impetus was provided by Eduard Philippi. Moreover, it was Philippi's tangible monument that focused commemoration on the actual battle site, whereas Grossmann's vision of a 'living memorial' produced the GAV, an organization associated with Gustavus but not primarily Lützen. Similarly, Oskar Planer and those involved in establishing the Lützen museum were clearly people who caught the 'history bug' and wanted to know more about the battle and its associated personalities. Their involvement was sustained by their own passion. Planer, having been forced by straitened financial circumstances to sell his original collection of Gustavus memorabilia at the end of the First World War, then proceeded to sink a second fortune in rebuilding it during the 1920s.

Pastors like Paul Sielaff were another important local element alongside officials like Philippi and businessmen like Planer, and they likewise shared broadly common middle-class backgrounds and enjoyed sufficient social standing and cultural capital to take the lead in organizing and sustaining commemoration. Like the coincidence of the battle with the print revolution, the broader timing of the commemorative activities was important, because these emerged around 1830 alongside a surge of local middle-class activism directed at political reform, economic development, social welfare, and educational improvement. All these groups shared similar forms of activism: organizing committees, penny subscriptions, fundraising banquets, public events, and forays into journalism and popular publications.

The higher authorities were suspicious of such activities, since these were used by those seeking radical political and social change. However, in Lützen's case, these fears were allayed by the activists' broadly middle-class character and the conventionality of their methods. The strong religious element was also significant, as the initial character of the November ceremonies as a Lutheran commemorative event ensured they received official permission at a time when other grassroots activities were proscribed. Involvement in the commemoration allowed activists to acquire additional status and prestige. The town also benefitted economically from the influx of visitors; something which has resumed importance across the last two decades. How far this will continue remains to be seen, but it is likely that recent efforts at a more inclusive remembrance culture and attention paid to casualties other than Gustavus will compensate for the declining interest in the battle among Lutherans and Swedes. Nonetheless, there are limits to how far Lützen or any other engagement can be universalized as examples of human experience of warfare since, as this book has shown, remembrance of individual battles rests on their distinctive stories and the meanings subsequent generations attach to them.

NOTES

Chapter 1

1. For example, F. L. Petre, *Napoleon's Last Campaign in Germany 1813* (London, 1912), p.70.
2. Swedish General Staff, *Sveriges Krig 1611–1632* (8 vols, Stockholm, 1936–9), VI 18–29; W. Watts, *The Swedish Intelligencer* (3 parts, London, 1633–4), II 89b–91b; R. Monro, *Monro, His Expedition with the Worthy Scots Regiment called Mac-Keys* (Westport, CT, 1999), pp.250–1.

Chapter 2

1. Further discussion of these debates in P. H. Wilson, 'The Causes of the Thirty Years War 1618–48', *English Historical Review*, 123 (2008), 554–86, and 'Meaningless Conflict? The Character of the Thirty Years War', in F. C. Schneid (ed.), *The Projection and Limitation of Imperial Powers 1618–1850* (Leiden, 2012), pp.12–33. For a succinct account of the conflict, see R. G. Asch, *The Thirty Years War. The Holy Roman Empire and Europe, 1618–48* (Basingstoke, 1997).
2. Further discussion in P. H. Wilson, *The Holy Roman Empire. A Thousand Years of Europe's History* (London, 2016).
3. P. H. Wilson, 'Atrocities in the Thirty Years War', in M. O'Siochrú and J. Ohlmeyer (eds), *Ireland 1641. Context and Reactions* (Manchester, 2013), pp.153–75.
4. A. Ernst and A. Schindling (eds), *Union und Liga 1608/09* (Stuttgart, 2010).
5. J. Polišenský, *Tragic Triangle. The Netherlands, Spain and Bohemia, 1617–1621* (Prague, 1991).
6. P. H. Wilson, *Europe's Tragedy. The Thirty Years War* (London, 2009), pp.269–313.
7. G. Mortimer, *The Origins of the Thirty Years War and the Revolt in Bohemia, 1618* (Basingstoke, 2015), pp.165–75.
8. O. Chaline, *La bataille de la Montagne Blanche* (Paris, 1999).
9. P. D. Lockhart, *Denmark in the Thirty Years War, 1618–1648* (Selinsgrove, 1996); P. H. Wilson, 'The Stuarts, the Palatinate, and the Thirty Years War', in S. Wolfson and V. Caldari (eds), *Marriage Diplomacy. Early Stuart Dynastic Politics in Their European Context, c.1604–1630* (Woodbridge, 2017).

10. T. Brockmann, *Dynastie, Kaiseramt und Konfession. Politik und Ordnungsvorstellungen Ferdinands II. im Dreißigjährigen Krieg* (Paderborn, 2011).

11. G. Mortimer, *Wallenstein. The Enigma of the Thirty Years War* (Basingstoke, 2010); R. Rebitsch, *Wallenstein* (Cologne, 2010); J. Polisensky and J. Kollmann, *Wallenstein* (Cologne, 1997).

12. M. Kaiser, *Politik und Kriegführung. Maximilian von Bayern, Tilly und die Katholische Liga im Dreißigjährigen Krieg* (Münster, 1999).

13. J. H. Elliott and L. W. B. Brockliss (eds), *The World of the Favourite* (New Haven, CT, 1999).

14. I. Schurbeth, 'Zwei ehrgeizige Fürsten. Wallenstein und Gustav Adolf', in I. Schurbeth and M. Reichel (eds), *Wallenstein. Die blut'ge Affair' bei Lützen* (Dößel, 2012), pp.157–70 at 165–8.

Chapter 3

1. E. Ringmar, *Identity, Interest and Action. A Cultural Explanation of Sweden's Intervention in the Thirty Years War* (Cambridge, 1996); J. P. Findeisen, *Axel Oxenstierna* (Gernsbach, 2007), pp.128–41; S. Goetze, *Die Politik des schwedischen Reichskanzlers Axel Oxenstierna gegenüber Kaiser und Reich* (Kiel, 1971).

2. D. Böttcher, 'Propaganda und öffentliche Meinung im protestantischen Deutschland, 1628–36', in H. U. Rudolf (ed.), *Der Dreißigjährigen Krieg* (Darmstadt, 1977), pp.325–67. Sweden's official justification is printed in P. H. Wilson, *The Thirty Years War. A Sourcebook* (Basingstoke, 2010), pp.122–30.

3. H. Langer, *Stralsund 1600–1630* (Weimar, 1970), pp.242–62.

4. T. Brockmann, *Dynastie, Kaiseramt und Konfession* (Paderborn, 2011), p.436; L. Höbelt, *Ferdinand III (1608–1657)* (Graz, 2008), p.56.

5. J. Glete, *Swedish Naval Administration 1521–1721* (Leiden, 2010), pp.96–102, 405.

6. M. Kaiser, *Politik und Kriegführung. Maximilian von Bayern, Tilly und die Katholische Liga im Dreißigjährigen Krieg* (Münster, 1999), pp.303–445.

7. M. Puhle (ed.), '...*gantz verheeret!' Magdeburg und der Dreißigjährige Krieg* (Magdeburg, 1998); *Konfession, Krieg und Katastrophe. Madgeburgs Geschick im Dreißigjährigen Krieg* (issued by the Verein für der Kirchenprovinz Sachsen, Magdeburg, 2006).

8. D. Albrecht, *Maximilian I. von Bayern 1573–1651* (Munich, 1998), pp.777–8.

9. W. P. Guthrie, *Battles of the Thirty Years War from White Mountain to Nordlingen, 1618–1635* (Westport, CT, 2002), pp.19–43; F. Pira, 'Slaget vid Breitenfeld', *Ny militär Tidskrift*, 16 (1931), 236–42.

10. P. H. Wilson, *Europe's Tragedy. The Thirty Years War* (London, 2009), pp.461–4, 476–87.

11. Findeisen, *Oxenstierna*, pp.186–92.

12. Swedish General Staff, *Sveriges Krig 1611–1632* (8 vols, Stockholm, 1936–9), VI 82.

13. The most likely version of this agreement is printed in P. H. Wilson, *The Thirty Years War. A Sourcebook* (Basingstoke, 2010), pp.183–4.

14. Strength in September 1632: General Staff, *Sveriges Krig*, VI 240. For Pappenheim's campaign, see G. Droysen, 'Das Auftreten Pappenheims in Norddeutschland nach der Schlacht bei Breitenfeld', *Zeitschrift für preussische Geschichte und Landeskunde*, 8 (1871), 410–28, 601–22.

15. Examples in G. Droysen, 'Der Krieg in Norddeutschland von 1632', *Zeitschrift für preussische Geschichte und Landeskunde*, 9 (1872), 245–55 at 252.

16. W. Watts, *The Swedish Intelligencer* (3 parts, London, 1633–4), II 73a–74b.

17. Ibid. II 113a.

18. Findeisen, *Oxenstierna*, pp.226–9; P. Suvanto, *Die deutsche Politik Oxenstiernas und Wallenstein* (Helsinki, 1979), pp.58–9.

19. H. Weigel, 'Franken im Dreißigjährigen Krieg', *Zeitschrift für bayerische Landesgeschichte*, 5 (1932), 1–50 at 39.

20. Albrecht, *Maximilian*, pp.834–5.

21. H. Mahr, 'Strategie und Logistik bei Wallensteins Blockade der Reichsstadt Nürnberg im Sommer 1632', *Fürther Heimatblätter*, new series, 50 (2000), 29–53; General Staff, *Svriges Krig*, VI 155–69.

22. Goetze, *Die Politik des schwedischen Reichskanzlers*, pp.82–3.

23. F. Taeglichsbeck, *Das Treffen bei Steinau an der Oder am 11 Oktober 1633* (Berlin, 1889), pp.2–30; General Staff, *Sveriges Krig*, VI 268–81.

24. H. J. Arendt, *Wallensteins Faktotum. Der kaiserliche Feldmarschall Heinrich Holk 1599–1633* (Ludwigsfelde, 2006), pp.118–44.

25. Guthrie, *Battles*, pp.187–93, 220–1; General Staff, *Sveriges Krig*, VI 202–17.

26. M. Roberts, *Gustavus Adolphus. A History of Sweden 1611–1632* (2 vols, London, 1953–8), II 748–63; J. Pekar, *Wallenstein 1630–1634* (Berlin, 1937), pp.227–31; Suvanto, *Die deutsche Politik*, pp.64–9.

27. See for example, Ferdinand to Wallenstein 31 October 1632, H. Hallwich (ed.), *Brief und Akten zur Geschichte Wallensteins 1630–1634* (4 vols, Vienna, 1912), III 386–93 (hereafter BA).

28. R. Rebitsch, *Matthias Gallas (1588–1647)* (Münster, 2006), pp.62–3.

29. R. Sennewald, *Das Kursächsische Heer im Dreissigjährigen Krieg* (Berlin, 2013), p.149.

30. There were another 5,400 men defending Bavaria where they faced 9,500 Swedes and allies: General Staff, *Sveriges Krig*, VI 326–8.

31. J. Krebs, 'Zur Beurteilung Holks und Aldringen', *Historische Vierteljahrschrift*, 3 (1900), 321–78 at 347–52; Albrecht, *Maximilian*, pp.838–40.

32. Sennewald, *Das Kursächsische Heer*, pp.148–9; BA III 187–8, Wallenstein to Gallas 30 September 1632.

33. Arendt, *Wallensteins Faktotum*, pp.151–2.

34. O. Rudert, 'Der Verrat von Leipzig', *Neues Archiv für Sächsische Geschichte und Altertumskunde*, 35 (1914), 68–87; J. Krebs, *Aus dem Leben des kaiserlichen Feldmarschalls Grafen Melchior von Hatzfeldt 1632–1636* (Breslau, 1926), pp.17–19; Arendt, *Wallensteins Faktotum*, pp.156–9.

35. Holk to Wallenstein, 1 November 1632, BA III 397.
36. It is clear that this is the reason for Holk's recall, and not the news of Gustavus' advance northwards towards Saxony as widely stated in the secondary literature. See B. Holl, 'Wallensteins angebliche Skizze für die Schlacht bei Lützen', in *Der Dreissigjährige Krieg* (issued by the Heeresgeschichtliches Museum, Vienna, 1976), pp.59–78 at 64.
37. G. Fleetwood, 'Letter from George Fleetwood to his Father Giving an Account of the Battle of Lützen and the Death of Gustavus Adolphus', *The Camden Miscellany*, vol. I (London, 1847), pp.5–6.
38. Quotation from Colonel Dalbier's report, National Archive, SP81/39 part 2, fol. 250–3. Gustavus' camp is described in the 1633 *Relation* printed in G. Droysen (ed.), *Gedruckte Relationen über die Schlacht bei Lützen 1632* (Halle, 1885), p.26.
39. Wallenstein to Gallas 10 November 1632, BA III 457–8. Wallenstein had also sent repeated requests to Maximilian to return Aldringen's imperial corps on the grounds that Gustavus' return north meant Bavaria was safe, but the elector refused.
40. Sennewald, *Das Kursächsische Heer*, p.150.
41. 1638 *Declaration*, printed in Droysen, *Lützen*, pp.35–6.
42. Reproduced, for example, in Sennewald, *Das Kursächsische Heer*, p.156.
43. Diodati's report, printed in J. Heilmann, *Das Kriegswesen der Kaiserlichen und Schweden zur Zeit des Dreißigjährigen Krieges* (Leipzig, 1850), pp.379–89 at 381. There are good discussions of the reasons behind Wallenstein's decision in G. Mann, *Wallenstein* (Frankfurt, 1983), pp.730–2; G. Mortimer, *Wallenstein* (Basingstoke, 2010), pp.165–70.
44. Arendt, *Wallensteins Faktotum*, p.163.
45. Time from Superintendent Möser's diary, F. Winter (ed.), 'Mösers Aufzeichnungen über den Dreißigjährigen Krieg', *Geschichtsblätter für Stadt und Land Magdeburg*, 9 (1874), 11–69, 165–220 at 44.
46. Most accounts claim it was delivered by a Saxon shepherd called Assmus, or Assmussen. Others have this individual later guiding the Swedes across the Rippach stream. It is extremely unlikely that it was a deliberate leak to goad Gustavus into battle, as suggested by Sennewald, *Das Kursächsische Heer*, p.158.
47. Dalbier's report.
48. Quotation from General Staff, *Sveriges Krig*, VI 400. About 1,250 infantry and all but 100 of the army's wagons were left in Naumburg.
49. Strength from Sennewald, *Das Kursächsische Heer*, p.158. Other sources give 500 light cavalry and 100 musketeers. Contemporary Swedish accounts give the impression of facing a much larger force.
50. According to the official Swedish campaign diary: E. Zeeh/N. Belfrage (eds), *Dagbok ford I det svenska fältkansliet, 26 maj–6 november 1632* (Stockholm, 1940), p.62.

51. For example, R. Monro, *Monro, His Expedition with the Worthy Scots Regiment Called Mac-Keys* (Westport, CT, 1999. First published 1637), p.294; Dalbier's report; 1632 *Relation* in Droysen, *Lützen*, p.17. Examples of such cavalry standards in A. and J. Lucht, *Fahnen und Standarten aus der Zeit des Dreißigjährigen Krieges*, vol. II (2nd ed., Freiberg, 2015), pp.131–3, 155, 167.

52. This is claimed by Arendt, *Wallensteins Faktotum*, p.165, but these units were definitely in Altenberg and Zwickau after the battle, to where they had gone to secure the roads to Bohemia.

53. A. Geiger, *Wallensteins Astrologie* (Graz, 1983), esp. p.42.

54. Holk's report in G. Lorenz (ed.), *Quellen zur Geschichte Wallensteins* (Darmstadt, 1987), p.252. for Wallenstein's illness, see Mann, *Wallenstein*, pp.753–4.

Chapter 4

1. Meuchen is called Chursitz in some accounts, a name possibly deriving from the fact that it was on the old boundary of *Kursächs* (i.e. electoral Saxony): J. Heilmann, *Das Kriegswesen der Kaiserlichen und Schweden zur Zeit des Dreißigjährigen Krieges* (Leipzig, 1850), p.354.

2. S. Poyntz, *The Relation of Sydnam Poyntz 1624–1636* (ed. A. T. S. Goodrick, London, 1908), p.72 records only three, but all other accounts give four. Two originals were still there by the mid-nineteenth century, along with two replacements: Heilmann, *Kriegswesen*, p.353.

3. Windmill Hill is about 123 m above sea level. The ground slopes slightly along the highway to about 119 m at the extreme left of the imperial position, falling a further 4 m by the point where the highway crosses the Flossgraben. It rises southwards to 130 m at Meuchen.

4. G. Droysen (ed.), *Gedruckte Relationen über die Schlacht bei Lützen 1632* (Halle, 1885), pp.28, 37; J. M. Teitt, *Meine I[onas] M[ånsson] T[eitt] Kriegszüge, so ich mit Ihr Kön. Maijth, Gustavo Adolpho ...*: http://www.amg-fnz.de/quellen/teitt/T-edit. htm. Examples of those accepting such inflated figures include T. N. Dupuy, *The Military Life of Gustavus Adolphus, Father of Modern War* (New York, 1969), p.139; J. F. C. Fuller, *The Decisive Battles of the Western World* (2 vols, St Albans, 1970), I 494; M. Clodfelter, *Warfare and Armed Conflicts. A Statistical Reference to Casualty and Other Figures 1500–2000* (Jefferson, NC, 2001), pp.35–7, 39. The imperial army is detailed in the Orders of Battle.

5. For example, the map used by the West Point cadets: http://www.westpoint. edu/history/SiteAssets/SitePages/.

6. Examples in G. B. Malleson, *The Battlefields of Germany* (London, 1884), pp.89–90; G. Barudio, *Der Teutsche Krieg 1618–1648* (Frankfurt, 1998), p.343; Fuller, *Decisive Battles*, I 491.

7. The thinner formation is suggested by T. M. Barker, *The Military Intellectual and Battle. Raimondo Montecuccoli and the Thirty Years War* (Albany, NY, 1975), pp.90–1, 190.

8. F. Chauviré, 'Le problème de l'allure dans les charges de cavalerie du xvie au xviiie siècle', *Revue historiques des armées*, 249 (2007): http://rha.revues.org/index553.html; P. Englund, *The Battle of Poltava* (London, 1992), pp.101–2, 164.

9. B. Holl, 'Wallensteins angebliche Skizze für die Schlacht bei Lützen', in *Der Dreissigjährige Krieg* (issued by the Heeresgeschichtliches Museum, Vienna, 1976), pp.59–78 at 63–4, 71–2; R. Sennewald, *Das Kursächsische Heer im Dreissigjährigen Krieg* (Berlin, 2013), pp.153–6, though his plan shows some units which were unlikely to have been present.

10. As suggested by W. P. Guthrie, *Battles of the Thirty Years War from White Mountain to Nordlingen, 1618–1635* (Westport, CT, 2002), pp.202–3.

11. A. Schürger, 'The Archaeology of the Battle of Lützen' (University of Glasgow PhD, 2015), pp.208–24, and his 'Die Schlacht von Lützen 1632: Archäologische Untersuchungen auf dem linken kaiserlichen Flügel', in H. Mellor (ed.), *Schlachtfeldarchäologie* (Halle, 2009), pp.135–49 at 138–41.

12. S. Bull, *The Furie of the Ordnance. Artillery in the English Civil Wars* (Woodbridge, 2008), p.25. See generally P. Engerisser, *Von Kronach nach Nördlingen. Der Dreißigjährige Krieg in Franken, Schwaben und der Oberpfalz 1631–1635* (Weißenstadt, 2004), pp.570–91.

13. Swedish General Staff, *Sveriges Krig 1611–1632* (8 vols, Stockholm, 1936–9), VI 419; R. Sennewald, *Das Kursächsische Heer*, p.169.

14. Engerisser, *Von Kronach*, pp.588–91. For Sweden artillery production, see J. *Swedish Naval Administration 1521–1721* (Leiden, 2010), pp.505–73. For cartridges, see Bull, *Furie*, pp.18–23.

15. Droysen, *Lützen*, p.7.

16. F. Winter (ed.), 'Mösers Aufzeichnungen über den Dreißigjährigen Krieg', *Geschichtsblätter für Stadt und Land Magdeburg*, 9 (1874), 11–69, 165–220 at 45.

17. This claim was made in an imperial account published nine years after the battle, and seven years after Wallenstein's assassination: J. Seidler, *Untersuchungen über die Schlacht bei Lützen 1632* (Memmingen, 1954), p.47. Some secondary accounts doubt the presence of the false troops, but they are recorded by Poyntz, *Relation*, p.126, and are shown clearly on the Snayer's painting commissioned by Piccolomini who was at the battle.

18. J. Le Roger sieur de Prade, *The History of Gustavus Adolphus Surnamed the Great* (London, 1689), pp.213–14, 221; H. J. Arendt, *Wallensteins Faktotum* (Ludwigsfelde, 2006), p.169; F. Watson, *Wallenstein. Soldier under Saturn* (London, 1938), pp.365–6.

19. Droysen, *Lützen*, p.29.

20. Most sources record 12,800 infantry and 6,200 cavalry, but the musters from 14 November list the so-called *prima plana* of officers, non-commissioned officers, etc. at full strength whereas they were certainly under strength. Included in the total are 600 dragoons who were probably deployed covering the route to Naumburg.

21. L. E. Wolke, 'die Schlacht bei Lützen', in M. Reichel and I. Schuberth (eds), *Gustav Adolf* (Dößel, 2007), pp.61–70 at 64.
22. His infantry brigade still formally bore his name, but was also identified by its actual commander, Colonel Bose.
23. W. Watts, *The Swedish Intelligencer* (3 parts, London, 1633–4), III 125; Droysen, *Lützen*, p.17. This would suggest around 5 a.m.
24. Droysen, *Lützen*, p.17.
25. G. Fleetwood, 'Letter from George Fleetwood to His Father Giving an Account of the Battle of Lützen and the Death of Gustavus Adolphus', *The Camden Miscellany*, vol. I (London, 1847), p.7; Droysen, *Lützen*, p.12. Superintendent Möser at Staßfurt to the west recorded a fine, still day: Winter, 'Mösers Aufzeichnungen', p.44. See also Schürger, 'Archaeology', pp.249–52.
26. The horse was named after Colonel Streiff von Lauenstein who had bought it for a colossal 1,000 Swedish talers in November 1631 before presenting it to the king.
27. Examples of contemporary reporting include B. P. von Chemnitz, *Königlichen Schwedischen in Teutschland geführten Kriegs* (2 vols, Stettin, 1648–53), I 462–3; Droysen, *Lützen*, pp.17–18.
28. N. Ahnlund, *Gustavus Adolphus the Great* (New York, 1999), pp.144–5; H. Berg, *Military Occupation under the Eyes of the Lord. Studies in Erfurt during the Thirty Years War* (Göttingen, 2010), p.239.
29. K. Deuticke, *Die Schlacht bei Lützen* (Gießen, 1917), p.68.
30. C. L. Scott, A. Turton, and E. Gruber von Arni, *Edgehill. The Battle Reinterpreted* (Barnsley, 2005), p.114. For Swedish organization, tactics, and equipment see R. Brzezinski and R. Hook, *The Army of Gustavus Adolphus* (2 vols, London, 1991–3). Further discussion in K. Roberts, *Pike and Shot Tactics 1590–1660* (Oxford, 2010).
31. The ten detachments were formed from the Löwenstein and part of the Brandenstein regiments and were probably each only fifty to seventy men, rather than 200 each as widely reported in secondary accounts.
32. General Staff, *Sveriges Krig*, VI 505. Using the known effective strengths, and allowing for tactical deployment and standard frontages per man, with gaps between the units, the first line was probably 867 m for the cavalry right, 1050 m for the infantry, and 767 m for the cavalry left. Based on information in R. Ward, *Animadversions of Warre* (London, 1639), pp.212, 295; A. Schürger, 'Die ersten Minuten der Schlacht von Lützen', in M. Reichel and I. Schurberth (eds), *Leben und Sterben auf dem Schlachtfeld von Lützen* (Lützen, 2011), pp.103–20 at 107; Barker, *The Military Intellectual*, pp.87, 230, 295; Scott et al., *Edgehill*, pp.193–9.
33. It is more likely that their posting here was due to insufficient space than a deliberate decision as claimed by the General Staff, *Sveriges Krig*, VI 430. Schürger, 'Archaeology', pp.287–8, 308–11 argues that they managed to fit north of the canal and only moved east of it to confront the Croats in the

early afternoon, but this is highly unlikely as there is no obvious place they could have crossed in the face of a rapidly approaching enemy.

34. This space was about 2,150 m, compared to the 2,700 m-long Swedish line.

35. Droysen, *Lützen*, p.9. See also General Staff, *Sveriges Krig*, VI 430. C. V. Wedgwood, *The Thirty Years War* (London, 1957), p.289 has the cannonade starting at 8 a.m., but that is very unlikely.

36. E. Zeeh and N. Belfrage (eds), *Dagbok förd I det svenska fältkansliet, 26 maj–6 november 1632* (Stockholm, 1940), p.63. Seidler, *Untersuchungen*, pp.44–5 estimates the imperial artillery fired eighty shots.

37. Schürger, 'Die ersten Minuten', pp.110–16.

38. Zeeh and Belfrage, *Dagbok*, p.63.

39. Seidler, *Untersuchungen*, pp.59, 98–9; Guthrie, *Battles*, p.213; Arendt, *Wallensteins Faktotum*, p.171; Schürger, 'Archaeology', pp.276–7, 325, 329.

40. Sennewald, *Das Kursächsische Heer*, pp.162, 170. One near contemporary account says the imperial cavalry were seconded by commanded musketeers: Droysen, *Lützen*, pp.38–9. If so, these were probably those which had been posted to protect the battery.

41. Droysen, *Lützen*, p.10.

42. Seidler, *Untersuchungen*, pp.47–9, 65–70. For Priorato, see A. Strohmeyer, 'Zwischen Kaiserhoff und französischen Hof. Wallensteinbilder in den Biographien des Conte Galeazzo Gualdo Priorato', in J. Bahlcke and C. Kampmann (eds), *Wallensteinbilder im Widerstreit* (Cologne, 2011), pp.51–74.

43. Droysen, *Lützen*, pp.38–9.

44. The smoke appears to have returned around the time Gustavus rode into the imperialists: ibid, p.32.

45. General Staff, *Sveriges Krig*, VI 440–1. This fact further supports the hypothesis that Gustavus simply blundered into the enemy, rather than leading a rescue mission, because his infantry were not endangered at that point.

46. Leslie to the Marquis of Hamilton, in C. S. Stanford, *The Life and Campaigns of Alexander Leslie, First Earl of Leven* (London, 1899), p.30. The various contemporary accounts of Gustavus' death are discussed in G. Barudio, *Gustav Adolf der Grosse* (Frankfurt, 1982), pp.610–15; B. Eriksson, *Lützen 1632. Ett ödesdigert beslut* (Stockholm, 2006), pp.285–6; H. Ritter von Srbik, 'Zur Schlacht von Lützen und zu Gustav Adolfs Tod', *Mitteilungen des Instituts für österreichische Geschichtsforschung*, 41 (1926), 231–56; Seidler, *Untersuchungen*, pp.63–77. Leublings's account is printed in B. Kitzig, *Rätsel um Gustav Adolfs Tod* (Stockholm, 1954).

47. *Johann Georg Mauls Diarium aus dem Dreißigjährigen Krieg* (Naumburg, 1928), p.6. More on the duke's extortion in L. Radler, *Das Schweidnitzer Land im Dreißigjährigen Krieg* (Lübeck, 1986), pp.31–42.

48. Four were definitely there at some point: Nils (or Jacob) Eriksson, a cavalry trooper; Wolf Siegmund von Lüchau, the duke's stable master; Franz von Henning, a Lorrainer also on the duke's personal staff; and a chamberlain

called Truchsess who may also have been a French spy. Karl Gustav Wrangel, the future Swedish field marshall, had originally been present, but was sent off at some point with a message. Leubelfing supposedly wrote an account before he died of wounds, but it is also possible that this was a later forgery: G. Droysen, 'Die Schlacht bei Lützen 1632', *Forschungen zur deutsche Geschichte*, 5 (1865), 69−264 at 193−8.

49. G. Irmer (ed.), *Die Verhandlungen Schwedens und seiner Verbündeten mit Wallenstein und dem Kaiser von 1631 bis 1634* (3 vols, Stuttgart, 1888−91), III 391.

50. The term used by the 1633 *Declaration* printed in Droysen, *Lützen*, p.39.

51. Some accounts combine this sequence with the earlier encounter with the Götz cuirassiers. In this version, it is that regiment's adjutant, Johann Schneeberg, who either shot or stabbed Gustavus and then took the king's gold chain. On his subsequent return home to Bökendorf near Paderborn, he bought a house which was still known by his name in the twentieth century: T. Hamacher, 'Der Tod Gustav Adolfs', *Westfälische* Zeitschrift, 109 (1959), 273−81; Lützener *Heimatblätter*, 1 (November 1933).

52. T. M. Barker, 'Generalleutenant Ottavio Fürst Piccolomini', *Österreichische Osthefte*, 22 (1980), 322−69.

53. Quoted in Sennewald, *Das Kursächsische Heer*, p.174.

54. Arendt, *Wallensteins Faktotum*, p.174.

55. General Staff, *Sveriges Krig*, VI 441.

56. Möser in nearby Staßfurt reports a trumpet signal being given at 11 p.m. to summon the regiments to assemble: Winter, 'Mösers Aufzeichnungen', p.44.

57. Chemnitz, *Königlichen Schwedischen*, I 467. Möser clearly favoured Sweden and noted the bad behaviour of imperial troops throughout his account, yet makes no mention of plundering delaying the infantry. Other near contemporary accounts place the cavalry's departure at 2 a.m., and imply the infantry left at the same time, but were unable to keep pace with their mounted comrades: Droysen, *Lützen*, pp.9, 37.

58. There is no evidence to support the claim that Pappenheim went via Leipzig which would have added 23 km to his journey and placed his point of arrival to the east of the battlefield, rather than at Lützen: M. Roberts, *Gustavus Adolphus. A History of Sweden 1611−1632* (2 vols, London, 1953−8), II 768. Accounts placing his arrival later between 2 and 3 p.m. appear to have confused it with the later imperial counterattack.

59. Guthrie, *Battles*, p.219 believes 12.45, while Sennewald, *Das Kursächsische Heer*, pp.171, 174 thinks 1.15.

60. J. Krebs, 'Zur Beurteilung Holks und Aldringen', *Historische Vierteljahresschrift*, 3 (1900), 321−78 at 331 puts Pappenheim's strength as high as 7,000. Given that the heavy cavalry units of the original imperial left wing were engaged in counterattacking the Swedish infantry, Pappenheim had around 1,100 of his own cuirassiers and arquebusiers, plus 1,800 light cavalry including the

Croatians who had rallied. The Swedes had about 2,400 battle cavalry, of whom 390 were still on the east side of the Flossgraben, plus at least 450 commanded musketeers and possibly five regimental guns.

61. H. Jessen (ed.), *Der Dreißigjährige Krieg in Augenzeugenberichten* (Düsseldorf, 1963), p.319; M. Merian, *Topographia superioris Saxoniae*... (Frankfurt, 1650), p.131; Droysen, *Lützen*, p.31. Other reports record the projectile as a falconet ball, i.e. roundshot from a small calibre field piece.

62. As suggested by R. Brzezinski, *Lützen 1632* (Oxford, 2001), p.80 n4.

63. Ehinger's report in BA IV 133–4.

64. Poyntz, *Relation*, pp.72–3. See also J. P. Findeisen, *Gustav II. Adolf von Schweden* (Gernsbach, 2005), pp.288–9.

65. Arendt, *Wallensteins Faktotum*, p.175.

66. Droysen, *Lützen*, p.10.

67. Seidler, *Untersuchungen*, pp.56–9 is among many arguing the infantry were saved by the mist.

68. R. Monro, *Monro, His Expedition with the Worthy Scots Regiment Called Mac-Keys* (Westport, CT, 1999), p.296. One Swedish account records that the light cavalry 'attacked from behind in two places', leading Seidler, *Untersuchungen*, pp.55–6, 90 and others to claim that Wallenstein simultaneously launched the Croatians from his command in a separate attack against the Swedish left. It is highly improbable that such an attack could have been pre-arranged and coordinated with Pappenheim's over 2 km away. Moreover, the Croatians would have had to ride through Bernhard's troops, since there was no gap between these and the Mühlgraben, unlike the situation at the canal. Finally, all other Swedish accounts only refer to regiments which were stationed on their right wing being affected by the attack. The reference to 'two places' must thus refer to Pappenheim's light cavalry moving along both sides of the canal.

69. Roberts, *Gustavus*, II 768.

70. As admitted by the semi-official Erfurt Relation of 1632: Droysen, *Lützen*, p.19.

71. As suggested by Brzezinski, *Lützen*, p.65, rather than General Staff, *Sveriges Krig*, IV 442–3 which puts this move three hours later at 4 p.m. With the rest of the army now fully committed, it would have made more sense to have these two brigades in close support rather than about 1 km to the rear. The first line's reserve of Henderson's musketeers was now also merged with the reorganized front.

72. Droysen, *Lützen*, pp.10–11.

73. Diodati's report in Heilmann, *Kriegswesen*, pp.385–7.

74. Colonel Dalbier's report, National Archive, SP81/39 part 2, fol. 2503.

75. J. Pekar, *Wallenstein 1630–1634* (Berlin, 1937), p.236.

76. Roberts, *Gustavus*, II 769–70.

77. Dalbier's account and Teitt, *Kriegszüge*.

78. One eyewitness claims it was still concealed: Kitzig, *Rätsel*, pp.5, 33.
79. Contemporary Swedish accounts emphasize the desire for revenge as motivating the final attack, not as an attempt to recover the royal corpse, as claimed by Seidler, *Untersuchungen*, pp.79ff. See Droysen, *Lützen*, p.32; Chemnitz, *Königlichen Schwedischen*, I 466.
80. Erfurt Relation in Droysen, *Lützen*, p.20. See generally Bull, *Furie*, pp.34–5.
81. Monro, *Expedition*, p.296. For the following see F. Schiller, *Geschichte des Dreissigjährigen Krieges* (Munich, 1966: DTV edn), p.254.
82. W. Kalina, 'Die Piccolominiserie des Pieter Snayers', *Viribis Unitis. Jahresbericht des Heeresgeschichtlichen Museum* (2005), 87–116 at 94–6.
83. Seidler, *Untersuchungen*, pp.75, 82–5.
84. The movement of units from the second and third lines to join the first was misinterpreted in some Swedish accounts as the arrival of Pappenheim's infantry who were still several hours away. See Droysen, *Lützen*, p.40.
85. Droysen, *Lützen*, p.7.
86. Poyntz, *Relation*, p.73.
87. Krebs, 'Zur Beurteilung', p.327.
88. Fritsch's autobiography in K. Lohmann (ed.), *Die Zerstörung Magdeburgs von Otto von Guericke und andere Denkwürdigkeiten aus dem Dreißigjährigen Kriege* (Berlin, 1913), p.255.
89. Ibid. pp.254–5.
90. Poyntz, *Relation*, p.73.
91. Droysen, *Lützen*, pp.3–4.
92. Diodati's report in Heilmann, *Kriegswesen*, pp.388–9.
93. Poyntz, *Relation*, pp.73, 126.

Chapter 5

1. As recalled in a sermon by Lützen's Pastor Stockmann, *Lamentatio I. Luzensium, das ist Klaglied der verwüsteten Stadt Lützen* ... (Leipzig, 1635); the Swedish victory report is published on 19 November 1632 in G. Droysen (ed.), *Gedruckte Relationen über die Schlacht bei Lützen 1632* (Halle, 1885), p.14.
2. Diodati's report in J. Heilmann, *Das Kriegswesen der Kaiserlichen und Schweden zur Zeit des Dreißigjährigen Krieges* (Leipzig, 1850), p.388; Droysen, *Lützen*, pp.12, 41.
3. Heilmann, *Kriegswesen*, p.385; Droysen, *Lützen*, p.12.
4. H. J. Arendt, *Wallensteins Faktotum* (Ludwigsfelde, 2006), pp.178, 181, 204; R. Rebitsch, *Wallenstein* (Vienna, 2010), p.90.
5. For example T. N. Dupuy, *The Military Life of Gustavus Adolphus* (New York, 1969), p.147.
6. A. Stahl, '"...die Todten Cörper vf der Wahlstadt begraben". Das Amt Lützen und die Schlacht', in I. Schuberth and M. Reichel (eds), *Die blut'ge Affair' bei Lützen* (Dößel, 2012), pp.255–61 at 259–60; Droysen, *Lützen*, pp.31, 40–1.

7. Heilmann, *Kriegswesen*, p.388; Droysen, *Lützen*, pp.4–5.
8. F. Sandstedt et al. (eds), *In hoc signo vinces. A Presentation of the Swedish State Trophy Collection* (Stockholm, 2006). The imperial infantry captured at least twenty-three flags, mainly from the Yellow Brigade, while the cavalry took at least eight standards.
9. The higher figure comes from Diodati's account, while the semi-official published imperial account gives the lower total: Heilmann, *Kriegswesen*, p.388; Droysen, *Lützen*, p.12.
10. Swedish General Staff, *Sveriges Krig 1611–1632* (8 vols, Stockholm, 1936–9), VI 453, 510; R. Sennewald, *Das Kursächsische Heer im Dreissigjährigen Krieg* (Berlin, 2013), p.176.
11. P. Sielaff, *Meuchen gab dem bei Lützen gefallenen König Gustav Adolf den ersten Ruheplatz und setzte ihm das erste Denkmal* (Leipzig, 1906), p.5.
12. F. Winter (ed.), 'Mösers Aufzeichnungen über den Dreißigjährigen Krieg', *Geschichtsblätter für Stadt und Land Magdeburg*, 9 (1874), p.45; V. Buckley, *Christina Queen of Sweden* (London, 2004), pp.39–43.
13. E. Mauvillon, *Histoire de Gustave-Adolphe, Roi de Suede* (4 vols, Amsterdam, 1764), I 435.
14. *Kirchenbuch von Lützen 1627–1769* (transcribed by Jürgen Winkler). For the problems of clearing seventeenth-century battlefields, see G. Hanlon, *Italy 1636. Cemetery of Armies* (Oxford, 2016), pp.145–50.
15. M. Merian, *Topographia superioris Saxoniae* (Frankfurt, 1650), p.131.
16. General Staff, *Sveriges Krig*, VI 452. By the end of November, thirty-four imperial deserters had been caught and prosecuted as marauders in the Lützen area.
17. G. Mann, *Wallenstein* (Frankfurt, 1983), pp.745–55.
18. Droysen, *Lützen*, p.42. On the retreat, see also HA, Akt.17, General Strozzi to Hatzfeldt 22 November 1632.
19. J. Seidler, *Untersuchungen über die Schlacht bei Lützen 1632* (Memmingen, 1954), pp.93–4; K. Deuticke, *Die Schlacht bei Lützen* (Gießen, 1917), pp.84–5.
20. The pro-Swedish 1633 *Relation* admits to 100 being murdered. See Arendt, *Wallensteins Faktotum*, pp.180–1; Sennewald, *Das Kursächsische Heer*, p.179.
21. Sennewald, *Das Kursächsische Heer*, p.180; Arendt, *Wallensteins Faktotum*, p.185.
22. B. Stadler, *Pappenheim und die Zeit des Dreißigjährigen Krieges* (Winterthur, 1991), p.736.
23. F. Konze, *Die Stärke, Zusammensetzung und Verteilung der Wallensteinischen Armee während des Jahres 1633* (Bonn, 1906), pp.51–3; Arendt, *Wallensteins Faktotum*, p.185–91. Forces in Bohemia totalled 194 infantry and cavalry companies: HA, Akt.16, billeting list prepared by Holk 14 April 1633.
24. Droysen, *Lützen*, p.15.
25. Examples include: J. C. von Pfister, *Geschichte der Teutschen* (5 vols, Hamburg, 1829–35), III 534; G. Pagés, *The Thirty Years War* (London, 1970), p.145; G. Parker, *The Military Revolution* (Cambridge, 1988), p.23; R. F. Weigley,

'Auf der Suche nach der Entscheidungsschlacht. Lützen, 16 November 1632', in S. Föster, D. Walter, and M. Pöhlmann (eds), *Schlachten der Weltgeschichte* (Munich, 2004), pp.138–53; S. Crane, *Great Battles of the World* (London, 1914), pp.133–4; Dupuy, *Military Life*, p.147.

26. Daniel Defoe's *Memoirs of a Cavalier* (1720), supposedly based on a manuscript he had discovered by an English volunteer. Quotation from the 2006 edn, p.105. The text was probably based on Robert Monro.

27. A view widely held by contemporaries like Möser, 'Aufzeichnungen', p.44, and later writers like Field Marshal Montgomery, *A History of Warfare* (London, 1968), p.274.

28. M. Roberts, *Gustavus Adolphus. A History of Sweden 1611–1632* (2 vols, London, 1953–8), II 772; General Staff, *Sveriges Krig*, VI 455–9.

29. M. Junkelmann, *Gustav Adolf (1594–1632)* (Regensburg, 1993), p.461; J. P. Findeisen, *Gustav II. Adolf von Schweden* (Gernsbach, 2005), pp.291–2.

30. S. Poyntz, *The Relation of Sydnam Poyntz 1624–1636* (London, 1908), p.78.

31. R. Rebitsch, *Wallenstein* (Vienna, 2010), p.87; Arendt, *Wallensteins Faktotum*, p.182; Deuticke, *Lützen*, p.84; Seidler, *Untersuchungen*, p.91.

32. L. von Ranke, *Geschichte Wallensteins* (Berlin, 2011 edn), p.186; Mann, *Wallenstein*, pp.745–6, 748–50; Arendt, *Wallensteins Faktotum*, pp.194–7.

33. J. Pekar, *Wallenstein 1630–1634* (2 vols, Berlin, 1937), I 235–6.

34. For Holk, see Arendt, *Wallensteins Faktotum*, p.178. C. V. Wedgwood, *The Thirty Years War* (London, 1957), p.290 is wrong in believing Holk was 'the only man in the imperial army who regarded the engagement as a victory'. Others considering it a draw or stalemate include the imperial general Raimondo Montecuccoli, see T. M. Barker, *The Military Intellectual and Battle* (Albany, NY, 1975), p.160. See also Ranke, *Geschichte Wallensteins*, pp.187–8.

35. A. Gindeley, *History of the Thirty Years War* (2 vols, New York, 1892), II 147–8; H. Diwald, *Wallenstein* (Munich, 1981), p.495.

36. G. Mortimer, *Wallenstein* (Basingstoke, 2010), p.178. See also P. Englund, *Die Verwüstung Deutschlands* (Stuttgart, 1998), p.137.

37. For Saxon policy see W. Struck, *Johann Georg und Oxenstierna* (Stralsund, 1899); P. Suvanto, *Die deutsche Politik Oxenstiernas und Wallenstein* (Helsinki, 1979), pp.73–84.

38. J. Kretzschmar, *Der Heilbronner Bund 1632–1635* (3 vols, Lübeck, 1922); P. H. Wilson, *Europe's Tragedy* (London, 2009), pp.517–19.

39. R. Monro, *Monro, His Expedition with the Worthy Scots Regiment Called Mac-Keys* (Westport, CT, 1999), p.305.

40. BA III 539, 557.

41. G. Droysen, *Bernhard von Weimar* (2 vols, Leipzig, 1885), I 67–8; Pekar, *Wallenstein*, pp.236–7; Findeisen, *Gustav II*, p.295.

42. J. H. Elliott, *Count Duke Olivares* (New Haven, CT, 1986), pp.456–9; R. Bireley, *Ferdinand II, Counter-Reformation Emperor, 1578–1637* (Cambridge, 2014), p.246.

43. D. Albrecht, *Maximilian I. von Bayern 1578–1651* (Munich, 1998), pp.839–40.

44. J. Kouril et al. (eds), *Documenta Bohemica Bellum Tricennale Illustrantia* (7 vols, Prague, 1971–81), V 111. It was this letter that prompted Wallenstein to ask Holk to prepare his battle report for Christian IV: see Arendt, *Wallensteins Faktotum*, pp.193–4; G. Wittrock, 'Frya relationer om slaget vid Lützen', *Historisk Tidskrift*, 52 (1932), 307–9.

45. R. Bireley, *Religion and Politics in the Age of the Counterreformation* (Chapel Hill, NC, 1981), pp.170, 188–9; and his *Ferdinand II*, pp.246–54.

46. The best overview of this period is J. Öhman, *Der Kampf um den Frieden* (Vienna, 2005), pp.39–60.

47. HA, Akt.12, Holk to Hatzfeldt 1 January 1633; Akt.17, the General Auditor to Hatzfeldt 23 December 1633; Kouril et al., *Documenta Bohemica*, V 109–10; J. Seidler, *Das Prager Blutgericht 1633* (Memmingen, 1962), pp.9–11.

48. J. Krebs, *Aus dem Leben des kaiserlichen Feldmarschalls Grafen Melchior von Hatzfeldt 1632–1636* (Breslau, 1926), pp.185–6.

49. A view advanced by Seidler, *Untersuchungen*, pp.76, 96; Roberts, *Gustavus Adolphus*, II 768.

50. Arendt, *Wallensteins Faktotum*, p.201.

51. H. Lahrkamp, *Lothar Dietrich Freiherr von Bönninghausen (1598–1657)* (Münster, 1958), pp.272–6.

52. BA III 597; J. Seidler, *Besteht noch ein Lützenproblem?* (Memmingen, 1971), p.64.

53. For example by G. Parker, *The Military Revolution* (Cambridge, 1988), p.24; C. Jorgensen, M. F. Pavkovic, F. C. Schneid, and C. L. Scott, *Fighting Techniques of the Early Modern World* (New York, 2006), p.82.

54. Wallenstein to Gallas, Aldringen and Holk, 3 January 1633, Kouril et al., *Documenta Bohemica*, V 120.

55. P. Engerisser, *Von Kronach nach Nördlingen* (Weißenstadt, 2004), pp.460, 467; Konze, *Die Stärke*, pp.25, 32–4.

56. See Montecuccoli's assessment in Barker, *Military Intellectual*, pp.91–3.

57. Arendt, *Wallensteins Faktotum*, p.192. See also Holk's instructions to Hatzfeldt on recruiting units up to strength in HA, Akt.12 January 1633 onwards.

58. P. Hrncirík, *Spanier auf dem Albuch. Ein Beitrag zur Geschichte der Schlacht bei Nördlingen im Jahre 1634* (Aachen, 2007); Engerisser, *Von Kronach*, pp.321–50.

59. C. L. Scott, A. Turton, and E. Guber von Ani, *Edgehill. The Battle Reinterpreted* (Barnsley, 2005), pp.34–6, 50–72; K. Roberts and A. Hook, *Pike and Shot Tactics 1590–1650* (Oxford, 2010).

60. A. Hempel, *Eigentlicher Bericht so wol auch Abcontrafeyung. Eine Untersuchung der nicht-allegorischen Nachrichtenblätter zu den Schlachten und Belagerungen der schwedischen Armee unter Gustav II. Adolf (1628/30–1632)* (Frankfurt, 2001), pp.136–42.

61. Koninklijke Bibliotheek Den Haag, KB, 14/3 Eenige quartiers en slagorders onder de Princen van Oranje (1622–1643), f. 49. My thanks to Adam Marks for this reference.

62. For example, the order of battle in the Hauptstaatsarchiv Marburg, WHK 2/17.

63. B. Holl, 'Wallensteins angebliche Skizze für die Schlacht bei Lützen', in *Der Dreissigjährige Krieg* (issued by the Heeresgeschichtliches Museum, Vienna, 1976), pp.59–78 at 60–1.
64. Further discussion of the fallacy of this in P. H. Wilson, 'Meaningless Conflict? The Character of the Thirty Years War', in F. C. Schneid (ed.), *The Projection and Limitation of Imperial Powers 1618–1850* (Leiden, 2012), pp.12–33.
65. Monro, *Expedition*, p.344, with similar view expressed in the title of C. Danckaert and J. Jansson, *Historis oft waerachlich Verhael von den Gantschen toestant van Oorlooge soo die ghevoert is in Duytschlandt, door den Grootmachtichtsten en onverwinnelicksten koningh, Gustavus Adolphus* (Amsterdam, 1642). See also P. Haythornthwaite, *Invincible Generals* (Poole, 1991), and the elegies by Russell and Tooke listed in the Bibliography.
66. General Baron Gourgard, *Talks with Napoleon at St Helena* (Chicago, 1904), p.210. My thanks to Rick Schneid for drawing this quotation to my attention. For the following see *La correspondance de Napoléon Ier, publiée par ordre de l'Empereur Napoléon III* (32 vols, Paris, 1858–70), XXXI 354; J. Luvaas (ed.), *Frederick the Great on the Art of War* (New York, 1966), p.341.
67. C. G. Rößler, *Erinnerungen an Gustav Adolph König von Schweden in einer gedrängten Uebersicht der Hauptbegebenheiten des Dreißigjährigen Krieges* (Merseburg, 1832), p.55. Similar views are expressed in F. K. Wild, *Leben Gustav Adolfs des Großen, König von Schweden* (Basel, n.d.), p.53.
68. G. Rosenthal, *König Gustav Adolf von Schweden* (Bremen, 1882), p.8.
69. C. V. Clausewitz, *On War* (ed. M. Howard and P. Paret, Princeton, NJ, 1976), pp.189, 589–90, 596; A.-H. de Jomini, *The Art of War* (Philadelphia, PA, 1862), p.379.
70. H. Sack, *Der Krieg in den Köpfen* (Berlin, 2008), pp.37–9.
71. J. Bahlcke and C. Kampman (eds), *Wallensteinbilder im Widerstreit* (Vienna, 2011), p.13.
72. C. Kampmann, *Reichsrebellion und kaiserliche Acht* (Münster, 1992); Mann, *Wallenstein*, pp.731–2.
73. Count G. G. Priorato, *Historia della vita d'Alberto Valstain ducca di Fridland* (Lyons, 1643). Further discussion in K. Cramer, *The Thirty Years War and German Memory in the Nineteenth Century* (Lincoln, NE, 2007), pp.94–140; H. Mannigel, *Wallenstein in Weimar, Wien und Berlin* (Husum, 2003), S. Davies, *The Wallenstein Figure in German Literature and Historiography* (Leeds, 2010).
74. P. Paret, *The Cognitive Challenge of War. Prussia 1806* (Princeton, NJ, 2009), pp.47–55. Clausewitz discussed Wallenstein in his letters, but did not mention him or Tilly in his *On War*.
75. W. Deist, 'Hans Delbrück, Militärhistoriker und Publizist', *Militärgeschichtliche Zeitschrift*, 57 (1998), 371–84; G. A. Craig, 'Delbrück: The Military Historian', in P. Paret et al. (eds), *Makers of Modern Strategy from Machiavelli to the Nuclear Age* (Princeton, NJ, 1986), pp.326–53. Delbrück's magnum opus is translated as *History of the Art of War* (4 vols, Lincoln, NE, 1985).

76. M. Raschke, *Der politisierende Generalstab. Die friderizianischen Kriege in der amtlichen deutschen Militärgeschichtsschreibung 1890–1914* (Freiburg, 1993).

77. Sir E. Cust, *Lives of the Warriors of the Thirty Years War* (2 vols, London, 1865), I 111–222; T. A. Dodge, *Gustavus Adolphus* (2 vols, New York, 1890), I 73, 401; B. Liddell Hart, *Great Captains Unveiled* (London, 1927), pp.103–24; G. MacMunn, *Gustavus Adolphus. The Lion of the North* (New York, 1931), pp.88–93; Dupuy, *Military Life*; J. F. C. Fuller, *The Decisive Battles of the Western World and Their Influence upon History* (2 vols, London, 1970), I 471–93; Montgomery, *History of Warfare*, pp.266–70; L. H. Addington, *The Patterns of War through the Eighteenth Century* (Bloomington, IN, 1990), pp.83–6; R. F. Weigley, *The Age of Battles* (London, 1993), pp.3–8, 14–19. See also the works by Bourne, Dover, Hollings, Leak, Stevens, and Yonge listed in the Bibliography. Similar views also appeared in other languages: J. E. Oelsen, 'Gustav II. Adolf als Feldherr und Stratege', in M. Reichel and I. Schuberth (eds), *Leben und Sterben auf dem Schlachtfeld von Lützen* (Lützen, 2011), pp.73–83.

78. Jorgensen et al., *Fighting Techniques*, p.31. There is a similar view in Montgomery, *History of Warfare*, pp.270–2.

79. Weigley, *Age of Battles*, p.3.

80. General Staff, *Sveriges Krig*. An example of this is the use of Deuticke's 1917 dissertation which provided a fuller account of the imperial perspective on Lützen.

81. C. J. Rogers (ed.), *The Military Revolution Debate* (Boulder, CO, 1995).

82. Tilly is frequently but erroneously portrayed as defensively minded, e.g. Weigley, *Age of Battles*, p.20.

83. Further discussion of this point in P. H. Wilson, 'Who Won the Thirty Years War', *History Today*, 59, 8 (2009), 12–19.

84. A. Schürger, 'The Archaeology of the Battle of Lützen' (University of Glasgow PhD, 2015), pp.124–96 esp. p.157.

85. Quotation from Weigley, *Age of Battles*, p.7.

86. Jorgensen et al., *Fighting Techniques*, pp.28, 86–7.

87. *Wargames Illustrated*, no. 284 (June 2011), pp.89–90. This is despite the fact that the actual imperial battle plan was already available to English-speaking readers since B. Chapman, *The History of Gustavus Adolphus* (London, 1856), pp.371–4. Chapman was vicar of Leatherhead. His book is an impressive piece of scholarship which deserves to be better known.

88. G. H. Bachmann, M. Klamm, and A. Stahl, *Exkursion zu den Schlachtfeldern Lützen, Roßbach, Auerstadt und Großgörschen* (Halle, 2011); H. Meller and M. Schefzik (eds), *Krieg. Eine archäologische Spurensuche* (Halle, 2015); and the works by Schürger listed in the Bibliography.

89. http://www.spiegel.de/international/germany/mass-grave-from-thirty-years-war-investigated-in-luetzen-germany-a-830203.html; *Scotsman*, 16 October 2009, p.3; *Freie Presse*, 14 April 2011; S. Eickhoff and F. Schopper (eds), *1636. Ihre Letzte Schlacht* (Zossen, 2012).

Chapter 6

1. O. Chaline, *La bataille de la Montagne Blanche (8 nov.1620)* (Paris, 2000).
2. J. Burkhardt (ed.), *Krieg und Frieden in der historischen Gedächtniskultur* (Munich, 2000).
3. F. Winter (ed.), 'Mösers Aufzeichnungen über den Dreißigjährigen Krieg', *Geschichtsblätter für Stadt und Land Magdeburg*, 9 (1874), p.42.
4. Ibid. p.44; W. Harms, 'Gustav Adolf als christlicher Alexander und Judas Makkabaeus', *Wirkendes Wort*, 35 (1985), 168–83 at 174.
5. Elisabeth to the Marquis of Hamilton, 19 November 1632, in N. Akkerman (ed.), *The Correspondence of Elizabeth Stuart, Queen of Bohemia* (3 vols, Oxford, 2011–), II 145.
6. Anon., *The Great and Famous Battel of Lutzen,... here is also inserted... a Relation of the King of Bohemia's Death* (London, 1633), pp.24–7; B. C. Pursell, *The Winter King. Frederick V of the Palatinate and the Coming of the Thirty Years War* (Aldershot, 2003), p.277; A. L. Thomas, *A House Divided. Wittelsbach Confessional Court Cultures in the Holy Roman Empire, c.1550–1650* (Leiden, 2010), pp.289–90.
7. H. Braun (ed.), *Marktredwitz im 30jährigen Krieg 1628–1648* (Marktredwitz, 1961), p.27.
8. R. Großner and B. Frhr. V. Haller (eds), 'Zu kurzem Bericht umd der Nachkommen willen', *Erlanger Bausteine zur fränkischen Heimatforschung*, 40 (1992), 9–107.
9. *Kriegszüge, so ich mit Ihr Kön. Maijth, Gustavo Adolpho...* (http://www.amg-fnz.de/quellen/teitt/T-edit.htm.
10. N. Ahnlund, *Gustavus Adolphus the Great* (New York, 1999), p.198.
11. Pastor Martin Feilinger's diary entry for 30 December 1632 in J. Rullmann (ed.), 'Die Einwirkungen des 30jährigen Krieges auf die Stadt Schlüchtern und ihre Umgebung, aus Kirchenbüchern zusammengestellt', *Zeitschrift des Vereins für Hessische Geschichte und Landeskunde*, new series 6 (1877), 201–50 at 242.
12. R. Kunz and W. Lizalek (eds), *Südhessische Chroniken aus der Zeit des Dreißigjährigen Krieges* (Heppenheim, 1983), p.251.
13. B. Roeck, *Als wollt die Welt schier brechen. Eine Stadt im Zeitalter des Dreißigjährigen Krieges* (Munich, 1991), p.259.
14. G. Parker (ed.), *The Thirty Years War* (London, 1987), p.131.
15. W. Schmidt-Biggemann, 'The Apocalypse and Millenarianism in the Thirty Years War', in K. Bussmann and H. Schilling (eds), *1648: War and Peace in Europe* (3 vols, Münster, 1998), I 259–63; P. K. Monod, *The Power of Kings. Monarchy and Religion in Europe 1589–1715* (New Haven, CT, 1999), pp.96–103.
16. H. Berg, *Military Occupation under the Eyes of the Lord* (Göttingen, 2010), p.198; M. Meumann, 'The Experience of Violence and the Expectation of the End of the World in Seventeenth-Century Europe', in J. Canning, H. Lehmann, and J. Winter (eds), *Power, Violence and Mass Death in Pre-Modern and Modern Times* (Aldershot, 2004), pp.141–59 at 154–9.

17. J. R. Paas, 'The Changing Image of Gustavus Adolphus on German Broadsheets, 1630–3', *Journal of the Warburg and Courthold Institutes*, 59 (1996), 205–44.

18. S. Tschopp, *Heilsgeschichtliche Deutungsmuster in der Publizistik des Dreißigjährigen Krieges* (Frankfurt, 1991), pp.93ff.

19. Rullmann, 'Einwirkungen', pp.207, 240.

20. Quotation from H. Zschoch, 'Größe und Grenzen des "Löwen von Mitternacht". Das Bild Gustav Adolfs in der populären protestantischen Publizistik als Beispiel religiöser Situationswahrnehmung im Dreißigjährigen Krieg', *Zeitschrift für Theologie und Kirche*, 91 (1994), 25–50 at 37.

21. Tschopp, *Heilsgeschichtliche Deutungsmuster*, pp.164–82.

22. M. Roberts, *Gustavus Adolphus. A History of Sweden 1611–1632* (2 vols, London, 1953–8), II 758; Ahnlund, *Gustavus Adolphus*, p.136. One source has Gustavus saying this to Bernhard of Weimar: R. Huch, *Der Dreißigjährige Krieg* (Frankfurt, 1974), pp.645–6.

23. Quoted in G. Teske, *Bürger, Bauern, Söldner und Gesandte. Der Dreißigjährige Krieg und der Westfälische Frieden in Westfalen* (Münster, 1997), p.98. See also O. Mörke, '"Der Schwede lebet noch". Die Bildformung Gustav Adolfs in Deutschland nach der Schlacht bei Lützen', in M. Reichel and I. Schuberth (eds), *Gustav Adolf* (Dößel, 2007), pp.83–92.

24. Alexander Leslie to the Marquis of Hamilton 26 November 1632 (OS), in C. S. Terry, *The Life and Campaigns of Alexander Leslie, First Earl of Leven* (London, 1899), p.30.

25. *Monro, His Expedition with the Worthy Scots Regiment called Mac-Keys* (Westport, CT, 1999), p.299.

26. A. Schmidt, *Vaterlandsliebe und Religionskonflikt. Politische Diskurse im Alten Reich (1555–1648)* (Leiden, 2007).

27. G. Droysen (ed.), *Gedruckte Relationen über die Schlacht bei Lützen 1632* (Halle, 1885), pp.20–1, 41.

28. This 'Powder Barrel Convention' is printed in P. H. Wilson (ed.), *The Thirty Years War. A Sourcebook* (Basingstoke, 2010), pp.206–7.

29. Quoted in Harms, 'Gustav Adolf', p.175.

30. Monro, *Expedition*, p.299.

31. Philippi's recollections reported in C. H. F. Hartmann, *Der Schwedenstein. Die zweite Säcularfeier der Schlacht bei Lützen am 6. November 1632 in allen ihren An- und Nachklängen* (Leipzig, 1833), pp.62–4.

32. P. Sielaff, *Meuchen gab dem bei Lützen gefallenen König Gustav Adolf den ersten Ruheplatz und setzte ihm das erste Denkmal* (Leipzig, 1906).

33. B. Bursell, 'Die königliche Rüstkammer als Museum. Ein Vermächtnis Gustav Adolfs', in Reichel and Schuberth, *Gustav Adolf*, pp.93–104. For the following, see also F. Sandstedt et al. (eds), *In hoc signo vinces. A Presentation of the Swedish State Trophy Collection* (Stockholm, 2006), esp. pp.71–5.

34. H. Fleischer (ed.), *Das Schwarzburg Militär* (Rudolstadt, 1994), p.14.

35. H. Seitz, 'Värjan och dödsskotten', *Livrustkammaren*, 16 (1982), 22–31.
36. A claim widely accepted later: e.g. J. Le Roger sieur de Prade, *The History of Gustavus Adolphus surnamed the Great* (London, 1689), p.208; H. Diwald, *Wallenstein* (Munich, 1981), p.492.
37. H. Maué, 'Sebastian Dadlers Medaillen auf König Gustav Adolf von Schweden', and S. Ekdahl, 'Zwei unbekannte Miniaturen von Gustav Adolf und Maria Eleonora in einem zeitgenößischen Stammbuch', both in Reichel and Schuberth, *Gustav Adolf*, pp.105–14, 117–24.
38. C. Gantet, *La paix de westphalie (1648). Une histoire sociale, xviie-xviiie siècles* (Paris, 2001).
39. P. H. Wilson, *Europe's Tragedy* (London, 2009), pp.751–78, and his *The Holy Roman Empire. A Thousand Years of Europe's History* (London, 2016), esp. pp.255–92, 625–54.
40. Monod, *Power of Kings*, pp.259–70.
41. Quoted in F. G. Bengtsson, *The Life of Charles XII King of Sweden 1697–1718* (London, 1960), p.218. See also R. M. Hatton, *Charles XII of Sweden* (London, 1968), pp.212–17, 221–7.
42. C. W. Ingrao, *In Quest and Crisis. Emperor Joseph I and the Habsburg Monarchy* (West Lafayette, IN, 1979), pp.54–64; J. Vötsch, *Kursachsen, das Reich und der mitteldeutsche Raum zu Beginn des 18. Jahrhunderts* (Frankfurt, 2003), pp.38–40, 87–8.
43. G. B. Volz and F. v. Oppeln-Bronikowski (eds), *Die Werke Friedrichs des Großen* (10 vols, Berlin, 1912–14), I 41–7.
44. R. Melzer, 'Die Kraft der Erinnerung als Versicherung eigenen Handelns— König Gustav II. Adolf im Gartenreich des Fürsten Leopold III. Friedrich Franz von Anhalt-Dessau', in Reichel and Schuberth, *Gustav Adolf*, pp.125–34; M. Umbach, *Federalism and Enlightenment in Germany 1740–1806* (London, 2000).
45. W. Harte, *The History of the Life of Gustavus Adolphus, King of Sweden, Sirnamed the Great* (London, 1759), translated as *Das Leben Gustav Adolph des Großen Königs von Schweden* (2 vols, Leipzig, 1760–1); E. Mauvillon, *Histoire de Gustave-Adolphe, Roi de Suède* (4 vols, Amsterdam, 1764); A. D. de Francheville, *L'histoire des derniéres campagnes et négociations de Gustave-Adolphe en Allemagne* (Berlin, 1772).
46. A. D. de Francheville, *La mort de Gustave-Adolphe* (Breslau, 1779).
47. C. J. Jahn, *Ueber den Tod Gustav Adolphs, Königs in Schweden* (Weissenfels, 1806).
48. K. Otto (ed.), *A Companion to the Works of Grimmelshausen* (London, 2003); H. Sack, *Der Krieg in den Köpfen. Die Erinnerung an den Dreißigjährigen Krieg in der deutschen Krisenerfahrung zwischen Julirevolution und deutschen Krieg* (Berlin, 2008), pp.26–9.
49. H. Mannigel, 'Entstehung und Wandel des Wallensteinbilds Schillers in der "Geschichte des Dreißigjährigen Krieges"', in J. Bahlcke and C. Kampmann (eds), *Wallensteinbilder im Widerstreit* (Cologne, 2011), pp.107–32.
50. L. v. Ranke, *Preußische Geschichte* (Hamburg, 1934 edn), pp.148–9; J. G. Droysen, *Geschichte der Preußischen Politik* (5 vols, Leipzig, 1868–86), III part I, pp.64–86.

51. F. Schiller, *Geschichte des Dreißigjährigen Krieges* (Munich, 1966 edn), pp.261–3.
52. For an example of this view, see R. Bireley, 'The Thirty Years War as Germany's Religious War', in K. Repgen (ed.), *Krieg und Politik 1618–1648* (Munich, 1988), pp.85–106. Further discussion in P. H. Wilson, 'Dynasty, Constitution and Confession: The Role of Religion in the Thirty Years War', *International History Review*, 30 (2008), 473–514.
53. For this and the following see S. Oredsson, *Geschichtschreibung und Kult. Gustav Adolf, Schweden und der Dreißigjährigen Krieg* (Berlin, 1994).
54. K. Hagemann, *Revisiting Prussia's War against Napoleon. History, Culture and Memory* (Cambridge, 2015).
55. K. Cramer, *The Thirty Years War and German Memory in the Nineteenth Century* (Lincoln, NE, 2007); L. L. Ping, *Gustav Freytag and the Prussian Gospel. Novels, Liberalism and History* (Bern, 2006); Sack, *Der Krieg in den Köpfen*, pp.31–7.
56. F. L. v. Rango, *Gustav Adolph der Große, König von Schweden* (Leipzig, 1824).
57. e.g. in H. Vortisch, *Gustav Adolf, Christ und Held* (Potsdam, 1930). English examples include the works by Alcock, Heydernreich, Fletcher, and Trench listed in the Bibliography.
58. e.g. F. K. Wild, *Leben Gustav Adolfs des Großen, König von Schweden* (Basel, n.d.).
59. e.g. A. Thoma, *Das Leben Gustav Adolfs für deutsche Volk* (3rd edn, Heidelberg, 1932), pp.31–3, 56, 86.
60. Ping, *Gustav Freytag*, pp.262–76.
61. S. Crane, *Great Battles of the World* (London, 1914), pp.69–78, 92–3, 116, 120–4; Field Marshal Montgomery, *A History of Warfare* (London, 1968), p.265.
62. *Der Teutsche Krieg 1618–1648* (2nd edn, Berlin, 1998), esp. pp.338–41; *Gustav Adolf der Große* (Frankfurt, 1982); and with G. A. Benrath, *Gustav Adolf fromm und gerecht* (Kassel, 1993).
63. G. Seib, 'Gustav Adolf und "Der Fels der Kirche". Zur einer Populärgrafik des 19. Jahrhunderts', in Reichel and Schuberth, *Gustav Adolf*, pp.153–8.
64. e.g. Thoma, *Das Leben Gustav Adolfs*, pp.28–31, 44–7, 58–9.
65. M. Merian, *Topographia superioris Saxoniae* (Frankfurt, 1650), p.131. Riade is also referred to in the 1633 Relation: Droysen, *Lützen*, p.29, and in the anonymous pamphlet *Das Schlachtfeld bei Lützen am Tage der Monumententhüllung weiland Gustav Adolphs König von Schweden des 6. November 1837* (Leipzig, 1837), copy in SAL, Akt.9/1.
66. For example, F. L. Petrie, *Napoleon's Last Campaign in Germany 1813* (London, 1912), p.70. By contrast, only modern publications, especially those orientated towards promoting tourism, mention the other five nearby battlefields: Burgscheidungen (531), Hohenmölsen (1080), Welfesholz (1115), Lucka (1307), Dessau Bridge (1626).
67. Sielaff, *Meuchen*, p.17; Anon., *Beschreibung der zweiten Säcularfeier des Todes Gustav Adolphs* (Lützen, 1832), p.6.
68. SAL Akt.9/4 esp. 19 March 1830.

69. For the latter, see Anon., *Nürnberg-Fürth-Zirndorf. Erinnerungsfeiern im Gustav-Adolf-Jahr 1632–1932* (Nuremberg, 1932).
70. SAL Akt.9/1 and 9/6.
71. Report in the *Leipziger Tageblatt*, nr.25 (1832), pp.1514–15.
72. Sielaff, *Meuchen*, pp.11–12, 17.
73. E. G. Geiger, *Jubelfesten till den store Gustaf Adolfs Minne den 6. November 1832 in Upsala* (Uppsala, 1833); Anon., *Smulor spridde pa slagfältet wid Lützen den 6. November 1632* (Uppsala, 1833).
74. Hartmann, *Schwedenstein*, pp.65–6; the speeches are printed in Anon., *Beschreibung*.
75. H. W. Beyer, *Die Geschichte des Gustav-Adolf-Vereins in ihren kirchen- und geistesgeschichtlichen Zusammenhängen* (Göttingen, 1932), p.20; A. Rotter, 'Großmann und die Gründung der Gustav Adolf Stiftung', *EvDia*, 72 (2003), 110–30. See also the first and second GAV annual reports 1845 and 1849 in SAL 9/1. For the wider context: G. L. Mosse, *The Nationalisation of the Masses* (New York, 1975), pp.50–1.
76. Sack, *Der Krieg in den Köpfen*, pp.41–2; K. Fitschen, 'Der problematische Patron—Gustav-Adolf Erinnerung im deutschen Protestantismus des 19. Jahrhunderts', in Reichel and Schuberth, *Gustav Adolf*, pp.137–44.
77. For example, F. Blanckmeister, *Wir sind Gehilfen eurer Freude* (Leipzig, 1928).
78. *Leipziger Tageblatt*, nr.25 (1832), p.1794.
79. SAL Akt41/7. The fund had raised 8,745 talers by 1839: accounts in Akt.9/7.
80. SAL Akt.41/8, Lützen Town Council to the Merseburg regional government, 10 July 1874.
81. *Außerordentliche Beilage zu Nr.268 der Leipziger Zeitung*, 10 January 1842; F. S. Moser, *Gustav Adolph und die dankbare Nachwelt* (Zwickau, 1844), pp.77–82.
82. Dräseke's speech was published in print form to accompany the event. Copy in SAL, reference D17.
83. SAL, Akt.9/5.
84. *Lützener Heimatblatt*, 1924, nr.5; F. Hagemeyer, *Das 100jährige Gustav-Adolf-Denkmal am Schewedenstein bei Lützen* (Leipzig, 1937), pp.16–26.
85. SAL, Akt.9/1.
86. Sack, *Der Krieg in den Köpfen*, pp.76–85, 156–88, 217–19; Cramer, *German Memory*, pp.76–93.
87. SAL, Akt.9/1 esp. 8 November 1849.
88. SAL, Akt.9/5, esp. 9 December 1858.
89. SAL, Akt.41/8 19 January 1875.
90. The ceremonies were held on 15 September in 1882 because bad weather had been forecast for November. See also G. Rosenthal, *Zur Erinnerung an die Lützener Gustav-Adolf-Jubelfeier* (Halle, 1882).
91. N. E. Villstrand, 'Finnland und der Große Krieg', in Reichel and Schuberth, *Gustav Adolf*, pp.27–36.

92. Parts of Planer's collection can be accessed at http://www.museum-digital. de/san/index.php?t=sammlung&instnr=89&gesusa=682 (accessed 25 March 2016). Catalogue published as O. Planer, *Verzeichnis der Gustav Adolf Sammlung* (Leipzig, 1916).

93. SAL, Akt.41/1.

94. SAL, Akt.41/8.

95. *Lützener Volksbote*, 2 November 1905.

96. Programme in Anon., *Zur Gustav Adolf Jubelfeier in Lützen am 15. September 1882* (Lützen, 1882).

97. *Lützener Volksbote*, 2 and 4 November 1905.

98. *2.Beilage zum Leipziger Tageblatt und Anzeige*, 11 November 1897.

99. SAL, Akt.9/5 24 May 1877.

100. SAL, Akt.41/8 14 June 1895.

101. e.g. E. Lamparter, *Gustav Adolf, König von Schweden, der Befreier des evangelischen Deutschlands* (Barmen, 1982).

102. *2. Beilage zum Leipziger Tageblatt und Anzeige*, 11 November 1897. See also Sack, *Der Krieg in den Köpfen*, p.221.

103. F. Mehring, *Gustav Adolf* (2nd edn, Berlin, 1908).

104. M. Hughes, *Nationalism and Society. Germany 1800–1945* (London, 1988).

105. SAL, Akt.9/3, letter to Lützen council 8 September 1882.

106. Thoma, *Das Leben Gustav Adolfs*, p.86. See also S. Grebe, 'Todesdarstellungen König Gustavs II. Adolf in der deutschen Literatur des 18. und 19. Jahrhunderts', in Reichel and Schuberth, *Gustav Adolf*, pp.163–71 at 166–70.

107. SAL, Akt.9/5, 17 May 1894.

108. I. Schuberth, *Lützen—på spaning efter ett minne* (Stockholm, 2007), pp.238–9, 293. For the trees see *Lützener Heimatbläter*, (April–May 1933), nr.4/5. Examples of the speeches in 1. *Beilage zum Leipziger Tageblatt und Anzeige*, 8 November 1898.

109. M. Weibull, *Gustav II Adolf. Ein minnesbild* (Lund, 1883).

110. G. Jödicke, *Die Weihe des Gustav Adolf Kapelle bei Lützen am 6. November 1907* (Lützen, 1907), p.17.

111. S. Oredsson, 'Die Erinnerung an Gustav Adolf in Deutschland und Schweden', in Reichel and Schuberth, *Gustav Adolf*, pp.17–26.

112. SAL, Kasten Nr.74; I. Schubert and L. Limberg, 'Schweden und Lützen im 20. Jahrhundert. Kapelle, Reichsvereinigung und Lützenstiftung', in Reichel and Schuberth, *Gustav Adolf*, pp.159–66.

113. O. S. Lovoll, 'Preserving a Cultural Heritage across Boundaries. A Comparative Perspective on Riksföreningen Sverigekontakt and Nordmanns-Forbundet', in P. J. Anderson and O. Blanck (eds), *Norwegians and Swedes in the United States* (St Paul, MN, 2012), pp.37–54.

114. SAL, Kasten Nr.41.

115. Quoted in Schuberth, *Lützen*, p.167.

116. SAL, Akt.9/8; Schuberth, *Lützen*, pp.171–9.

117. Copy in SAL, Kasten Nr.41.
118. SAL, Kasten Nr.41 and 41a; Schuberth, *Lützen*, 195–6, 222.
119. *Leipziger Tageblatt*, 5 November 1932. See also Schuberth, *Lützen*, pp.199–214.
120. As expressed by Pastor Hagemeyer, *Gustav-Adolf-Denkmal*, p.28. See also P. Pehrsson, *Gustav Adolf. Festrede zum Schwedenkönig, der Luther-Akademie vom 9. August 1936* (Berlin, 1936), copy in SAL, C156.
121. J. Paul, *Gustav Adolf* (3 vols, Leipzig, 1932); W. Koppe, 'Gustav Adolfs Deutsche Politik', *Jomsburg. Völker und Staaten im Osten und Norden Europas*, 5 (1941), 308–31. Further discussion in B. R. Kroener, 'Ein protestantischarischer "Held aus Mitternacht". Stationen des Gustav-Adolfs-Mythos 1632 bis 1945', *Militärgeschichtliche Zeitschrift*, 59 (2000), 5–22.
122. Quoted in Schuberth, *Lützen*, p.225.
123. Ibid. pp.233–4, 241, 249.
124. Quoted ibid, p.250.
125. SAL, Kasten Nr.41, letter of 28 June 1948.
126. Schuberth, *Lützen*, p.255.
127. SAL, Kasten Nr.41, 11 May 1976. See generally A. Dorpalen, *German History in Marxist Perspective* (London, 1985), pp.129–37.
128. Copies in SAL, D325 and D536.
129. Schuberth, *Lützen*, pp.262–9, 275.
130. *Extended Session of the Presidium of the Peace Council of the GDR on 31 January 1980* (Berlin, 1980).
131. *Sächsisches Tageblatt*, 24 Oct.1981; Schuberth, *Lützen*, pp.270–2, 276.
132. For this and the following: M. Reichel and I. Schuberth (eds), *Leben und Sterben auf dem Schlachtfeld von Lützen* (Lützen, 2011), p.17; Schuberth, *Lützen*, pp.283–9.
133. O. Mörke, 'Eine Ausstellungsgästebuch und die Kraft der Erinnerung', in Reichel and Schuberth, *Leben und Sterben*, pp.15–24.

Chapter 7

1. J. Ostwald, 'The "Decisive" Battle of Ramillies, 1706: Prerequisites for Decisiveness in Early Modern Warfare', *Journal of Military History*, 64 (2000), 649–78.
2. Michael Bywater commenting on the Battle of Britain anniversary, *Independent*, 9 July 2010.
3. G. Foard, *Naseby. The Decisive Campaign* (Barnsley, 1995), pp.317–18, 343–82.
4. See http://naseby.com (accessed 2 April 2016).
5. S. Eickhoff and F. Schopper (eds), *1636. Ihre letzte Schlacht* (Zossen, 2012).

ORDERS OF BATTLE

Imperial Army

NB all units are imperial unless otherwise indicated as belonging to the Catholic League

1. Main Force

Commander	Generalissimo Albrecht Wenzel Eusebius von Wallenstein
2nd-in-command	Field Marshal Lieutenant Heinrich Holk
3rd-in-command	Major General Rudolfo Baron von Colloredo-Meis

Infantry

Regiment	Companies	Effectives	Commander
Waldstein	11	1,500	Col. Berthold von Waldstein
Alt Sachsen	8	800	Lt.Col. Bernhard Hemmerle
Colloredo	7	700	Lt.Col. Philipp Hussmann de Namedi
Kehraus*	10	1,200	Col. Andreas Matthias Kehraus
Alt Breuner	5	500	Col. Hans Gottfried von Breuner
Grana	8	1,000	Col. Francesco Grana, Marchese di Caretto
Breuner	13	900	Artillery General Hans Philipp von Breuner
Comargo	10	800	Col. Theodor Comargo (League unit)
Reinach (detachment)	1	150	(League unit)
Jung Breuner	10	500	Col. Philipp Friedrich von Breuner
Baden-Baden	6	500	Lt.Col. Stolper
	92	8,550	

* Formerly Chiesa

Cuirassiers

Regiment	Companies	Effectives	Commander
Desfours	6	300	Col. Nicolas Desfours
Götz*	9	400	Lt.Co. Moritz von Falkenberg
Holk	8	250	Lt.Col. Frantz von Uhlefeld (probably)
Lohe	5	150	Col. Von der Lohe
Alt Trčka (Terzky)	4	250	Col. Adam Erdmann Count Trčka
Bredow**	6	300	Col. Hans Rudolf von Bredow
	38	1,650	

* Col. Johann von Götz sold his regiment to Ferdinand II's nephew, Matteo de' Medici, Duke of Tuscany, late in 1632. For this reason, some contemporary accounts refer to it as the Tuscan or Florentine Regiment
** Part of Pappenheim's command, but with the main force by the start of the battle

Arquebusiers

Regiment	Companies	Effectives	Commander
Drost	5	250	Col. Wilhelm von Westfalen, Landrost von Dringenberg
Goschütz	5	250	Col. Benedikt Goschütz
Hagen	13	800	Col. Johann Nicholas Hagen von Sauwenbein
Leutersheim	6	200	Col. Johann Baron von Leutersheim
Loyers	6	200	Col. Gottfried Baron von Loyers
Piccolomini	12*	500	Col. Ottavio Piccolomini di Aragona
Westfalen (part)	3	150	Col. Heinrich Leo von Westfalen
Westrumb	3	100	Col. Johann von Westrumb
Tontinelli**	6	250	Lt.Col. Anton Tontinelli (League unit)
	59	2,700	

* Including two companies which had previously been Wallenstein's bodyguard
** Part of Pappenheim's command, but with the main force by the start of the battle

Dragoons

Regiment	Companies	Effectives	Commander
Trčka	5	100	Col. Adam Count Trčka

'Croats'

Regiment	Companies	Effectives	Commander
Isolano	5	250	General Ludwig Johann Hector Count Isolano
Beygott	5	100	Col. Daniel Beygott
Corpes	10	300	Col. Marcus Corpes
Révay	5	250	Col. Paul Baron Révay
	25	900	

Artillery: General Hans Philipp von Breuner
21 heavy guns including 9 × 24 pounders, 6 × 12 pounders, and 4 × 6 pounders
Approximately 10 regimental guns (3 pounders)

Total:
Infantry	8,550
Cavalry	5,350
	13,900

2. Pappenheim's Corps

Commander	Field Marshal Gottfried Heinrich Count von Pappenheim
2nd-in-command	Colonel Jean Count Merode-Varoux
3rd-in-command	Major General Heinrich Count Reinach

Infantry

Regiment	Companies	Effectives	Commander
Gil de Haas	6	500	Col. Gil de Haas
Goltz	10	700	Col. Martin Maximilian Baron v.d. Goltz
Moriamez-Pallant	8	500	Col. Carl Dietrich Pallant Baron de Moriamez
Pallant	10	500	Col. Rudolf Baron Pallant
Reinach	10	650	Lt.Col. Gabriel Baron Comargo (League unit)
Würzburg	remnants	75	Captain Willich (League unit)
	44	2,925	

Heavy Cavalry

Regiment	Companies	Effectives	Commander
Bönninghausen Arquebusiers	11	500	Col. Lothar von Bönninghausen
Lamboy Arquebusiers	6 or 8	250	Col. Wilhelm von Lamboy
Sparr Cuirassiers	10	300	Lt.Col. Albrecht von Hofkirchen*
Pappenheim's bodyguard	1	40	(possibly attached to his dragoons)
Merode's bodyguard	1	40	
	29 to 31	1,130	

* The formal commander, Col. Ernst Georg von Sparr, was absent, and the unit was often referred to as 'Hofkirchen'

Dragoons

Regiment	Companies	Effectives	Commander
Merode	4	120	Lt.Col. Robert Borneval d'Arlin
Pappenheim	3	100	
	7	220	

Light Cavalry

Regiment	Companies	Effectives	Commander
Batthyanyi 'Croats'	9	200	Col. Franz Count Batthyanyi
Forgacs 'Croats'	2	100	Col. Nicolas Frogacs de Gymes
Orossy 'Croats'	9	450	Col. Paulus Orossy (called Horatius)
'Polish Cossacks'	3	250	
	23	1,000	

Artillery
6 field and probably 6 regimental guns

Total:
Infantry	2,925
Cavalry	2,350
	5,275

3. Detachments

Regiment	Companies	Effectives	Commander
At Eilenburg: Col. Melchior von Hatzfeldt			
Hatzfeldt Cuirassiers*	6	600	Col. Melchior von Hatzfeldt
Mansfeld Infantry	10	500	Lt.Col. Niderun
Thun Infantry (part)**	7	600	Col. Rudolf Thun
Trčka Infantry	7	800	Lt.Col. Adrian Enckevort
At Altenberg			
Contreras Infantry	5	400	Col. Andreas von Contreras
At Zwickau	10	700	Col. Ernst Roland Baron de Suys

* Formerly Neu Sachsen
** Formerly Traun

Grand Totals

	Total	Of which present at the battle
Infantry	14,475	11,475
Cuirassiers	2,630	2,030
Arquebusiers	3,450	3,450
Dragoons	320	320
Light Cavalry	1,900	1,900
Cavalry	8,300	7,700
	22,775	19,175

4. Swedish and Allied Army

Commander	King Gustavus Adolphus of Sweden
2nd-in-command	Lieutenant General Bernhard Duke of Weimar
3rd-in-command	Major General Dodo Baron von Innhausen und zu Knyphausen

(Units listed right to left)

Regiment	Companies	Effectives	Commander

Right Wing
King Gustavus Adolphus of Sweden

First Line: Col. Torsten Stålhandske

Regiment	Companies	Effectives	Commander
Finland Horse*	8	500	Col Torsten Stålhandske
Västgöta Horse	8	400	Col. Knut Soop
Södermanland Horse	4	200	Col. Otto Sack
Uppland Horse	4	250	Lt.Col. Isaak Axelsson 'Silfversparre'
Östgöta Horse	4	100	Lt.Col. Lennart Nilsson Bååt
Småland Horse	8	400	Col. Fredrik Stenbock
Commanded musketeers			*c.*465 with 10 × 3 pounder regimental guns
Total:		1,850 cavalry and *c.*465 musketeers with 10 light guns	

* In two squadrons

Second Line: Col. Claus Conrad Zorn von Bulach

Regiment	Companies	Effectives	Commander
Duke Wilhelm Horse	12	120	(Weimar unit)
Goldstein Horse	8	150	Lt.Col. Max Conrad von Rehlinger
Bulach Horse	8	120	Col. Claus Conrad Zorn von Bulach
Beckermann Horse	4	150	Col. Eberhard Beckermann
Hessian Horse (composite formation)		380	Col. Franz Elgar von Dalwigk
Uslar Horse	8	160	Col. Georg von Uslar
Total:	1,080 cavalry		

Infantry Centre

First Line: Major General Nils Brahe, Count of Visingborg

Regiment	Companies	Effectives	Commander
Swedish Brigade	20	1,581	Lt.Col. Gabriel Kyle
Yellow (Guards) Brigade	17	1,221	Major General Nils Brahe
Old Blue Brigade	16	1,110	Col. Hans Georg aus dem Winckel
Green Brigade	40	2,036	Col. Georg Wulf von Wildenstein

Henderson's Regiment	4	228	Col. John Henderson*
Supporting Artillery: 20 heavy guns in 4 batteries			Major Joen Persson Jernlod
Total:			5,966 infantry and 20 heavy guns

* In reserve immediately behind the first line

Second Line: Major General Dodo Baron von Innhausen und zu Knyphausen

Duke Wilhelm's Brigade	24	1,726**	Col. Carl Bose
Knyphausen's Brigade	12	1,120	Maj.Gen. Knyphausen
Thurn's Brigade	48	1,832**	Col. Hans Jakob Count Thurn
Mitzlaff's Brigade	28	1,834	Col. Joachim Mitzlaff
Öhm Horse***	8	300	Col. Johann Bernhard von Öhm
Total:		5,932	infantry and 300 cavalry

** Saxon and Weimar troops
** Including 1,082 Hessians
*** In reserve immediately behind the second line

Left Wing

Lieutenant General Bernhard Duke of Weimar

First Line: Lieutenant General Bernhard Duke of Weimar

Leibregiment*	12	500	Lt.Col. Bouillon (Weimar unit)
Carberg Horse	8	220	Col. Carl Joachim Carberg
Kurland Horse	4	230	Col. Hans Wrangel
Livonian Horse	8	300	Lt.Col. Karl von Tiesenhausen
Courville Horse	5	300	Col. Nicholas de Courville
Commanded musketeers			*c.*465 with 10 × 3 pounder regimental guns
Total:			1,550 cavalry, 465 infantry and 10 light guns

* In two squadrons

Second Line: Col. Ernst Duke of Weimar

Hofkirchen Horse	12	350*	Maj.Gen. Lorentz von Hofkirchen
Anhalt Horse	8	300*	Ernst Prince of Anhalt-Bernburg
Löwenstein Horse	6	200**	

Brandenstein Horse	4	300	Col. Brandenstein
Steinbach Horse	4	200	Col. Jaroslav Wolf von Steinbach
Stechnitz Horse	4	80	Lt.Col. Georg Matthias von Stechnitz

Total: 1,430 cavalry

---

* Saxons
** Commanded by the major in the absence of Col. Georg Ludwig Count von Löwenstein

Detached Troops

Taupadel Dragoons		600*	Maj.Gen. Georg Christoph von Taupadel
Dam Vitzthum Infantry	8	270**	Col. Damien von Vitzthum-Eckstädt

---

* Guarding the lines of communications
** Saxons, posted in Naumburg with the baggage

Grand Total

	Total	Of which present at the battle
Infantry	13,098	12,828
Cavalry	6,510	5,910
	19,608	18,738

BIBLIOGRAPHY

Archival Sources

Hatzfeldt-Wildenberg Archive, Schloss Schönstein:
Akt.12
Akt.17

Hauptstaatsarchiv Marburg:
WHK 2/17

Koninklijke Bibliotheek Den Haag:
KB, 14/3 Eenige quartiers en slagorders onder de Princen van Oranje (1622–43),
  f.49.

National Archive, London:
SP81/39 part 2, fol.250–3, Colonel Dalbier's report.

Stadtarchiv Lützen:
Akt.9/1
Akt.9/2
Akt.9/3
Akt.9/4
Akt.9/5
Akt.9/6
Akt.9/7
Akt.9/8
Akt.9/9
Akt.41/7
Akt.41/8
Akt.42/1
Kasten Nr.41 and 41a; Nr.74

Contemporary Printed Sources

Akkerman, N. (ed.), *The Correspondence of Elizabeth Stuart, Queen of Bohemia* (3 vols, Oxford, 2011–).

Anon., *The Great and Famous Battel of Lutzen, . . . Here Is Also Inserted . . . a Relation of the King of Bohemia's Death* (London, 1633).

Braun, H. (ed.), *Marktredwitz im 30jährigen Krieg 1628–1648. Georg Leopolds Haus-Chronik* (Marktredwitz, 1961).

Chemnitz, B. P. von, *Königlichen Schwedischen in Teutschland geführten Kriegs* (2 vols, Stettin, 1648–53).

Danckaert, C. and J. Jansson, *Historis oft waerachlich Verhael von den Gantschen toestant van Oorlooge soo die ghevoert is in Duytschlandt, door den Grootmachtichtsten en onverwinnelicksten koningh, Gustavus Adolphus* (Amsterdam, 1642).

Droysen, G. (ed.), *Gedruckte Relationen über die Schlacht bei Lützen 1632* (Halle, 1885).

Fleetwood, G., 'Letter from George Fleetwood to His Father Giving an Account of the Battle of Lützen and the Death of Gustavus Adolphus', *The Camden Miscellany*, vol. I (London, 1847), pp.5–7.

Großner, R. and B. Frhr. V. Haller (eds), '"Zu kurzem Bericht umd der Nachkommen willen". Zeitgenössische Aufzeichnungen aus dem Dreißigjährigen Krieg in Kirchenbüchern des Erlanger Raumes', *Erlanger Bausteine zur fränkischen Heimatforschung*, 40 (1992), 9–107.

Hallwich, H. (ed.), *Brief und Akten zur Geschichte Wallensteins 1630–1634* (4 vols, Vienna, 1912).

Irmer, G. (ed.), *Die Verhandlungen Schwedens und seiner Verbündeten mit Wallenstein und dem Kaiser von 1631 bis 1634* (3 vols, Stuttgart, 1888–91).

Jessen, H. (ed.), *Der Dreißigjährige Krieg in Augenzeugenberichten* (Düsseldorf, 1963) *Kirchenbuch von Lützen 1627–1769* (transcribed by Jürgen Winkler).

Kouril, J. et al. (eds), *Documenta Bohemica Bellum Tricennale Illustrantia* (7 vols, Prague, 1971–81).

Kunz, R. and W. Lizalek (eds), *Südhessische Chroniken aus der Zeit des Dreißigjährigen Krieges* (Heppenheim, 1983).

Lohmann, K. (ed.), *Die Zerstörung Magdeburgs von Otto von Guericke und andere Denkwürdigkeiten aus dem Dreißigjährigen Kriege* (Berlin, 1913).

Lorenz, G. (ed.), *Quellen zur Geschichte Wallensteins* (Darmstadt, 1987).

Maul, J. G., *Johann Georg Mauls Diarium aus dem Dreißigjährigen Krieg* (Naumburg, 1928).

Merian, M., *Topographia superioris Saxoniae* (Frankfurt, 1650).

Monro, R., *Monro, His Expedition with the Worthy Scots Regiment Called Mac-Keys* (Westport, CT, 1999).

Poyntz, S., *The Relation of Sydnam Poyntz 1624–1636* (ed. A. T. S. Goodrick, London, 1908).

Priorato, Count G. G., *Historia della vita d'Alberto Valstain ducca di Fridland* (Lyons, 1643).

Rullmann, J. (ed.), 'Die Einwirkungen des 30 jährigen Krieges auf die Stadt Schlüchtern und ihre Umgebung, aus Kirchenbüchern zusammengestellt', *Zeitschrift des Vereins für Hessische Geschichte und Landeskunde*, new series 6 (1877), 201–50.

Russell, J., *The Two Famous Pitcht Battels of Lypsich and Lutzen* (Cambridge, 1634)

Stockmann, P., *Lamentatio I. Luzensium, das ist Klaglied der verwüsteten Stadt Lützen* (Leipzig, 1635).

Teitt, J. M., *Meine I[onas] M[ånsson] T[eitt] Kriegszüge, so ich mit Ihr Kön. Maijth, Gustavo Adolpho* (http://www.amg-fnz.de/quellen/teitt/T-edit.htm).

Ward, R., *Animadversions of Warre* (London, 1639).

Watts, W., *The Swedish Intelligencer* (3 parts, London, 1633–4).

Winter, F. (ed.), 'Mösers Aufzeichnungen über den Dreißigjährigen Krieg', *Geschichtsblätter für Stadt und Land Magdeburg*, 9 (1874), 11–69, 165–220.

Wittrock, G., 'Frya relationer om slaget vid Lützen', *Historisk Tidskrift*, 52 (1932), 307–9.

Zeeh, E. and N. Belfrage (eds), *Dagbok ford I det svenska fältkansliet, 26 maj–6 november 1632* (Stockholm, 1940).

Periodicals

Leipziger Tageblatt
Lützener Heimatblätter
Lützener Volksbote
Sächsisches Tageblatt

Secondary Sources

Addington, L. H., *The Patterns of War through the Eighteenth Century* (Bloomington, IN, 1990).

Ahnlund, N., *Gustavus Adolphus the Great* (New York, 1999).

Albrecht, D., *Maximilian I. von Bayern 1573–1651* (Munich, 1998).

Alcock, D., *The Life of Gustavus Adolphus, King of Sweden* (Bath, 1857).

Anon., *Smulor spridde pa slagfältet wid Lützen den 6. November 1632* (Uppsala, 1833).

Anon., *Das Schlachtfeld bei Lützen am Tage der Monumententhüllung weiland Gustav Adolphs König von Schweden des 6. November 1837* (Leipzig, 1837).

Anon., *Zur Gustav Adolf Jubelfeier in Lützen am 15. September 1882* (Lützen, 1882).

Anon., *Nürnberg-Fürth-Zirndorf. Erinnerungsfeiern im Gustav-Adolf-Jahr 1632–1932* (Nuremberg, 1932).

Arendt, H. J., *Wallensteins Faktotum. Der kaiserliche Feldmarschall Heinrich Holk 1599–1633* (Ludwigsfelde, 2006).

Asch, R. G., *The Thirty Years War. The Holy Roman Empire and Europe, 1618–48* (Basingstoke, 1997).

Bachmann, G. H., M. Klamm, and A. Stahl, *Exkursion zu den Schlachtfeldern Lützen, Roßbach, Auerstadt und Großgörschen* (Halle, 2011).

Bahlcke J. and C. Kampmann (eds), *Wallensteinbilder im Widerstreit* (Cologne, 2011).

Barker, T. M., *The Military Intellectual and Battle. Raimondo Montecuccoli and the Thirty Years War* (Albany, NY, 1975).

Barker, T. M., 'Generalleutenant Ottavio Fürst Piccolomini', *Österreichische Osthefte*, 22 (1980), 322–69.

Baron Dover, G. A. E., *Lives of the Most Eminent Sovereigns of Modern Europe* (London, 1833).

Barudio, G., *Gustav Adolf der Grosse* (Frankfurt, 1982).

Barudio, G., *Der Teutsche Krieg 1618–1648* (Frankfurt, 1998).

Barudio, G. and G. A. Benrath, *Gustav Adolf fromm und gerecht* (Kassel, 1993).

Bengtsson, F. G., *The Life of Charles XII King of Sweden 1697–1718* (London, 1960).

Berg, H., *Military Occupation under the Eyes of the Lord. Studies in Erfurt during the Thirty Years War* (Göttingen, 2010).

Beyer, H. W., *Die Geschichte des Gustav-Adolf-Vereins in ihren kirchen- und geistes-geschichtlichen Zusammenhängen* (Göttingen, 1932).

Bireley, R., *Religion and Politics in the Age of the Counterreformation. Emperor Ferdinand II, William Lamormani, S.J., and the Formation of Imperial Policy* (Chapel Hill, NC, 1981).

Bireley, R., 'The Thirty Years War as Germany's Religious War', in K. Repgen (ed.), *Krieg und Politik 1618–1648* (Munich, 1988), pp.85–106.

Bireley, R., *Ferdinand II, Counter-Reformation Emperor, 1578–1637* (Cambridge, 2014)

Blanckmeister, F., *Wir sind Gehilfen eurer Freude* (Leipzig, 1928).

Böttcher, D., 'Propaganda und öffentliche Meinung im protestantischen Deutschland, 1628–36', in H. U. Rudolf (ed.), *Der Dreißigjährigen Krieg* (Darmstadt, 1977), pp.325–67.

Bourne, C. E., *The Life of Gustavus Adolphus, King of Sweden* (London, 1883).

Brockmann, T., *Dynastie, Kaiseramt und Konfession. Politik und Ordnungsvorstellungen Ferdinands II. im Dreißigjährigen Krieg* (Paderborn, 2011).

Brzezinski, R. and R. Hook, *The Army of Gustavus Adolphus* (2 vols, London, 1991–3).

Buckley, V., *Christina Queen of Sweden* (London, 2004).

Bull, S., *The Furie of the Ordnance. Artillery in the English Civil Wars* (Woodbridge, 2008).

Burkhardt, J. (ed.), *Krieg und Frieden in der historischen Gedächtniskultur* (Munich, 2000).

Chaline, O., *La bataille de la Montagne Blanche (8 nov.1620). Un mystique chez les guerriers* (Paris, 2000).

Chapman, B., *The History of Gustavus Adolphus and of the Thirty Years War up to the King's Death* (London, 1856).

Chauviré, F., 'Le problème de l'allure dans les charges de cavalerie du xvie au xviiie siècle', *Revue historiques des armées*, 249 (2007) (http://rha.revues.org/index553.html).

Clodfelter, M., *Warfare and Armed Conflicts. A Statistical Reference to Casualty and Other Figures 1500–2000* (Jefferson, NC, 2001).

Craig, G. A., 'Delbrück: The Military Historian', in P. Paret et al. (eds), *Makers of Modern Strategy from Machiavelli to the Nuclear Age* (Princeton, NJ, 1986), pp.326–53.

Cramer, K., *The Thirty Years War and German Memory in the Nineteenth Century* (Lincoln, NE, 2007).

Crane, S., *Great Battles of the World* (London, 1914).

Cust, Sir E., *Lives of the Warriors of the Thirty Years War* (2 vols, London, 1865).

Davies, S., *The Wallenstein Figure in German Literature and Historiography* (Leeds, 2010).

Defoe, D., *Memoirs of a Cavalier* (London, 1720).

Deist, W., 'Hans Delbrück, Militärhistoriker und Publizist', *Militärgeschichtliche Zeitschrift*, 57 (1998), 371–84.

Delbrück, H., *History of the Art of War* (4 vols, Lincoln, NE, 1985).

Deuticke, K., *Die Schlacht bei Lützen* (Gießen, 1917).

Diemar, H., *Untersuchungen über die Schlacht bei Lützen (16. November 1632)* (Marburg, 1890).

Diemar, H., 'Der Anteil der Hessen an der Schlacht von Lützen 1632', *Zeitschrift für hessische Geschichte und Landeskunde*, new series 18 (1893), 327–53.

Diwald, H., *Wallenstein* (Munich, 1981).

Dodge, T. A., *Gustavus Adolphus. A History of the Art of War from Its Revival after the Middle Ages to the End of the Spanish Succession War* (2 vols, New York, 1890).

Dorpalen, A., *German History in Marxist Perspective. The East German Approach* (London, 1985).

Droysen, G., 'Die Schlacht bei Lützen 1632', *Forschungen zur deutsche Geschichte*, 5 (1865), 69–264.

Droysen, J. G., *Geschichte der Preußischen Politik* (5 vols, Leipzig, 1868–86).

Droysen, G., 'Das Auftreten Pappenheims in Norddeutschland nach der Schlacht bei Breitenfeld', *Zeitschrift für preussische Geschichte und Landeskunde*, 8 (1871), 410–28, 601–22.

Droysen, G., 'Der Krieg in Norddeutschland von 1632', *Zeitschrift für preussische Geschichte und Landeskunde*, 9 (1872), 245–55.

Droysen, G., *Bernhard von Weimar* (2 vols, Leipzig, 1885).

Dupuy, T. N., *The Military Life of Gustavus Adolphus, Father of Modern War* (New York, 1969).

Eickhoff, S. and F. Schopper (eds), *1636. Ihre Letzte Schlacht. Leben im Dreißigjährigen Krieg* (Zossen, 2012).

Elliott, J. H., *Count Duke Olivares* (New Haven, CT, 1986).

Elliott, J. H. and L. W. B. Brockliss (eds), *The World of the Favourite* (New Haven, CT, 1999).

Engerisser, P., *Von Kronach nach Nördlingen. Der Dreißigjährige Krieg in Franken, Schwaben und der Oberpfalz 1631–1635* (Weißenstadt, 2004).

Englund, P., *The Battle of Poltava* (London, 1992).

Englund, P., *Die Verwüstung Deutschlands. Eine Geschichte des Dreißigjährigen Krieges* (Stuttgart, 1998).

Eriksson, B., *Lützen 1632. Ett ödesdigert beslut* (Stockholm, 2006).

Ernst, A. and A. Schindling (eds), *Union und Liga 1608/09. Konfessionelle Bündnisse im Reich—Weichenstellung zum Religionskrieg?* (Stuttgart, 2010).

Field Marshal Montgomery, *A History of Warfare* (London, 1968).

Findeisen, J. P., *Gustav II. Adolf von Schweden* (Gernsbach, 2005).

Findeisen, J. P., *Axel Oxenstierna* (Gernsbach, 2007).

Fleischer, H. (ed.), *Das Schwarzburg Militär* (Rudolstadt, 1994).

Fletcher, C. R. L., *Gustavus Adolphus and the Struggle of Protestantism for Existence* (New York, 1890).

Foard, G., *Naseby. The Decisive Campaign* (Barnsley, 1995).

Francheville, A. D. de, *L'histoire des derniéres campagnes et négociations de Gustave-Adolphe en Allemagne* (Berlin, 1772).

Francheville, A. D. de, *La mort de Gustave-Adolphe* (Breslau, 1779).

Fuller, J. F. C., *The Decisive Battles of the Western World* (2 vols, St Albans, 1970).

Gantet, C., *La paix de westphalie (1648). Une histoire sociale, xviie–xviiie siècles* (Paris, 2001).

Geiger, A., *Wallensteins Astrologie* (Graz, 1983).

Geiger, E. G., *Jubelfesten till den store Gustaf Adolfs Minne den 6. November 1832 in Upsala* (Uppsala, 1833).

Gindeley, A., *History of the Thirty Years War* (2 vols, New York, 1892).

Glete, J., *Swedish Naval Administration 1521–1721* (Leiden, 2010).

Goetze, S., *Die Politik des schwedischen Reichskanzlers Axel Oxenstierna gegenüber Kaiser und Reich* (Kiel, 1971).

General Baron Gourgard, *Talks with Napoleon at St Helena* (Chicago, 1904).

Guthrie, W. P., *Battles of the Thirty Years War from White Mountain to Nordlingen, 1618–1635* (Westport, CT, 2002).

Hagemann, K., *Revisiting Prussia's War against Napoleon. History, Culture and Memory* (Cambridge, 2015).

Hagemeyer, F., *Das 100jährige Gustav-Adolf-Denkmal am Schewedenstein bei Lützen* (Leipzig, 1937).

Hamacher, T., 'Der Tod Gustav Adolfs', *Westfälische Zeitschrift*, 109 (1959), 273–81.

Hanlon, G., *Italy 1636. Cemetery of Armies* (Oxford, 2016).

Harms, W., 'Gustav Adolf als christlicher Alexander und Judas Makkabaeus', *Wirkendes Wort*, 35 (1985), 168–83.

Harte, W., *The History of the Life of Gustavus Adolphus, King of Sweden, Sirnamed the Great* (London, 1759).

Hartmann, C. H. F., *Der Schwedenstein. Die zweite Säcularfeier der Schlacht bei Lützen am 6. November 1632 in allen ihren An- und Nachklängen* (Leipzig, 1833).

Hatton, R. M., *Charles XII of Sweden* (London, 1968).

Haythornthwaite, P., *Invincible Generals: Gustavus Adolphus, Marlborough, Frederick the Great, George Washington, Wellington* (Poole, 1991).

Heilmann, J., *Das Kriegswesen der Kaiserlichen und Schweden zur Zeit des Dreißigjährigen Krieges* (Leipzig, 1850).

Hempel, A., *Eigentlicher Bericht so wol auch Abcontrafeyung. Eine Untersuchung der nicht-allegorischen Nachrichtenblätter zu den Schlachten und Belagerungen der schwedischen Armee unter Gustav II. Adolf (1628/30–1632)* (Frankfurt, 2001).

Heydenreich, L. W., *The Life of Gustavus Adolphus* (Philadelphia, PA, 1868).

Höbelt, L., *Ferdinand III. (1608–1657)* (Graz, 2008).

Holl, B., 'Wallensteins angebliche Skizze für die Schlacht bei Lützen', in *Der Dreissigjährige Krieg* (issued by the Heeresgeschichtliches Museum, Vienna, 1976), pp.59–78.

Hollings, J. F., *The Life of Gustavus Adolphus, Surnamed the Great* (London, 1838).

Hrncirík, P., *Spanier auf dem Albuch. Ein Beitrag zur Geschichte der Schlacht bei Nördlingen im Jahre 1634* (Aachen, 2007).

Huch, R., *Der Dreißigjährige Krieg* (Frankfurt, 1974; first published 1912).

Hughes, M., *Nationalism and Society. Germany 1800–1945* (London, 1988).

Ingrao, C. W., *In Quest and Crisis. Emperor Joseph I and the Habsburg Monarchy* (West Lafayette, IN, 1979).

Jahn, C. J., *Ueber den Tod Gustav Adolphs, Königs in Schweden* (Weissenfels, 1806).

Jödicke, G., *Die Weihe des Gustav Adolf Kapelle bei Lützen am 6. November 1907* (Lützen, 1907).

Jorgensen, C., M. F. Pavkovic, F. C. Schneid, and C. L. Scott, *Fighting Techniques of the Early Modern World. Equipment, Combat Skills and Tactics* (New York, 2006).

Junkelmann, M., *Gustav Adolf (1594–1632). Schwedens Aufstieg zur Großmacht* (Regensburg, 1993).

Kaiser, M., *Politik und Kriegführung. Maximilian von Bayern, Tilly und die Katholische Liga im Dreißigjährigen Krieg* (Münster, 1999).

Kalina, W., 'Die Piccoliminiserie des Pieter Snayers', *Viribis Unitis. Jahresbericht des Heeresgeschichtlichen Museum* (2005), 87–116.

Kampmann, C., *Reichsrebellion und kaiserliche Acht. Politische Strafjustiz im Dreißigjährigen Krieg und das Verfahren gegen Wallenstein 1634* (Münster, 1992).

Kitzig, B., *Rätsel um Gustav Adolfs Tod* (Stockholm, 1954).

Konfession, Krieg und Katastrophe. Madgeburgs Geschick im Dreißigjährigen Krieg (issued by the Verein für der Kirchenprovinz Sachsen, Magdeburg, 2006).

Konze, F., *Die Stärke, Zusammensetzung und Verteilung der Wallensteinischen Armee während des Jahres 1633* (Bonn, 1906).

Koppe, W., 'Gustav Adolfs Deutsche Politik', *Jomsburg. Völker und Staaten im Osten und Norden Europas*, 5 (1941), 308–31.

Krebs, J., 'Zur Beurteilung Holks und Aldringen', *Historische Vierteljahrschrift*, 3 (1900), 321–78.

Krebs, J., *Aus dem Leben des kaiserlichen Feldmarschalls Grafen Melchior von Hatzfeldt 1632–1636* (Breslau, 1926).

Kretzschmar, J., *Der Heilbronner Bund 1632–1635* (3 vols, Lübeck, 1922).

Kroener, B. R., 'Ein protestantisch-arischer "Held aus Mitternacht". Stationen des Gustav-Adolfs-Mythos 1632 bis 1945', *Militärgeschichtliche Zeitschrift*, 59 (2000), 5–22.

Lahrkamp, H., *Lothar Dietrich Freiherr von Bönninghausen (1598–1657)* (Münster, 1958).

Lamparter, E., *Gustav Adolf, König von Schweden, der Befreier des evangelischen Deutschlands* (Barmen, 1982).

Langer, H., *Stralsund 1600–1630* (Weimar, 1970).

Leak, J. J., *King and Hero. The Story of Gustavus Adolphus* (London, 1891).

Liddell Hart, B., *Great Captains Unveiled* (London, 1927).

Lockhart, P. D., *Denmark in the Thirty Years War, 1618–1648* (Selinsgrove, 1996).

Lovoll, O. S., 'Preserving a Cultural Heritage across Boundaries. A Comparative Perspective on Riksföreningen Sverigekontakt and Nordmanns-Forbundet', in P. J. Anderson and O. Blanck (eds), *Norwegians and Swedes in the United States* (St Paul, MN, 2012), pp.37–54.

Lucht, A. and J. Lucht, *Fahnen und Standarten aus der Zeit des Dreißigjährigen Krieges*, vol. II (2nd edn, Freiberg, 2015).

Luvaas, J. (ed.), *Frederick the Great on the Art of War* (New York, 1966).

MacMunn, G., *Gustavus Adolphus. The Lion of the North* (New York, 1931).

Mahr, H., 'Strategie und Logistik bei Wallensteins Blockade der Reichsstadt Nürnberg im Sommer 1632', *Fürther Heimatblätter*, new series, 50 (2000), 29–53.

Malleson, G. B., *The Battlefields of Germany from the Outbreak of the Thirty Years War to the Battle of Blenheim* (London, 1884).

Mannigel, H., *Wallenstein in Weimar, Wien und Berlin. Das Urteil über Albrecht von Wallenstein in der deutschen Historiographie von Friedrich Schiller bis Leopold von Ranke* (Husum, 2003).

Mauvillon, E., *Histoire de Gustave-Adolphe, Roi de Suède* (4 vols, Amsterdam, 1764).

Mehring, F., *Gustav Adolf. Ein Fürstenspiegel zu Lehr und Nutz der deutschen Arbeiter* (2nd edn, Berlin, 1908).

Meller, H. and M. Schefzik (eds), *Krieg. Eine archäologische Spurensuche* (Halle, 2015).

Meumann, M., 'The Experience of Violence and the Expectation of the End of the World in Seventeenth-Century Europe', in J. Canning, H. Lehmann, and J. Winter (eds), *Power, Violence and Mass Death in Pre-Modern and Modern Times* (Aldershot, 2004), pp.141–59.

Monod, P. K., *The Power of Kings. Monarchy and Religion in Europe 1589–1715* (New Haven, CT, 1999).

Mortimer, G., *Wallenstein. The Enigma of the Thirty Years War* (Basingstoke, 2010).

Mortimer, G., *The Origins of the Thirty Years War and the Revolt in Bohemia, 1618* (Basingstoke, 2015).

Moser, F. S., *Gustav Adolph und die dankbare Nachwelt* (Zwickau, 1844).

Mosse, G. L., *The Nationalisation of the Masses. Political Symbolism and Mass Movements in Germany from the Napoleonic Wars through the Third Reich* (New York, 1975).

Napoleon I., *La correspondance de Napoléon Iier, publiée par ordre de l'Empereur Napoléon III* (32 vols, Paris, 1858–70).

Öhman, J., *Der Kampf um den Frieden. Schweden und der Kaiser im Dreißigjährigen Krieg* (Vienna, 2005).

Olesen, J. E. (ed.), *Terra felix Mecklenburg. Wallenstein in Nordeuropa* (Greifswald, 2010).

Oredsson, S., *Geschichtschreibung und Kult. Gustav Adolf, Schweden und der Dreißigjährigen Krieg* (Berlin, 1994).

Ostwald, J., 'The "Decisive" Battle of Ramillies, 1706: Prerequisites for Decisiveness in Early Modern Warfare', *Journal of Military History*, 64 (2000), 649–78.

Otto, K. (ed.), *A Companion to the Works of Grimmelshausen* (London, 2003).

Paas, J. R., 'The Changing Image of Gustavus Adolphus on German Broadsheets, 1630–3', *Journal of the Warburg and Courthold Institutes*, 59 (1996), 205–44.

Pagés, G., *The Thirty Years War* (London, 1970).

Paret, P., *The Cognitive Challenge of War. Prussia 1806* (Princeton, NJ, 2009).

Parker, G. (ed.), *The Thirty Years War* (London, 1987).

Parker, G., *The Military Revolution: Military Innovation and the Rise of the West 1500–1800* (Cambridge, 1988).

Paul, J., *Gustav Adolf* (3 vols, Leipzig, 1932).

Pehrsson, P., *Gustav Adolf. Festrede zum Schwedenkönig, der Luther-Akademie vom 9. August 1936* (Berlin, 1936).

Pekar, J., *Wallenstein 1630–1634* (Berlin, 1937).

Petre, F. L., *Napoleon's Last Campaign in Germany 1813* (London, 1912).

Pfister, J. C. von, *Geschichte der Teutschen* (5 vols, Hamburg, 1829–35).

Philippi, F. E. F., *Der Tod Gustav Adolph's König von Schweden in der Schlacht bei Lützen am 6. November 1632* (Leipzig, 1832).

Ping, L. L., *Gustav Freytag and the Prussian Gospel. Novels, Liberalism and History* (Bern, 2006).

Pira, F., 'Slaget vid Breitenfeld', *Ny militär Tidskrift*, 16 (1931), 236–42.

Planer, O., *Verzeichnis der Gustav Adolf Sammlung* (Leipzig, 1916).

Polišenský, J., *Tragic Triangle. The Netherlands, Spain and Bohemia, 1617–1621* (Prague, 1991).

Polišenský, J. and J. Kollmann, *Wallenstein* (Cologne, 1997).

Puhle, M. (ed.), ' ...gantz verheeret!' Magdeburg und der Dreißigjährige Krieg (Magdeburg, 1998).

Pursell, B. C., The Winter King. Frederick V of the Palatinate and the Coming of the Thirty Years War (Aldershot, 2003).

Radler, L., Das Schweidnitzer Land im Dreißigjährigen Krieg (Lübeck, 1986).

Rango, F. L. v., Gustav Adolph der Große, König von Schweden (Leipzig, 1824).

Ranke, L. v., Preußische Geschichte (Hamburg, 1934 edn).

Ranke, L. v., Geschichte Wallensteins (Berlin, 2011 edn).

Raschke, M., Der politisierende Generalstab. Die friderizianischen Kriege in der amtlichen deutschen Militärgeschichtsschreibung 1890–1914 (Freiburg, 1993).

Rebitsch, R., Matthias Gallas (1588–1647) (Münster, 2006).

Rebitsch, R., Wallenstein (Cologne, 2010).

Reichel, M. and I. Schuberth (eds), Gustav Adolf (Dößel, 2007).

Reichel, M. and I. Schuberth (eds), Leben und Sterben auf dem Schlachtfeld von Lützen (Lützen, 2011).

Ringmar, E., Identity, Interest and Action. A Cultural Explanation of Sweden's Intervention in the Thirty Years War (Cambridge, 1996).

Roberts, K. and A. Hook, Pike and Shot Tactics 1590–1650 (Oxford, 2010).

Roberts, M., Gustavus Adolphus. A History of Sweden 1611–1632 (2 vols, London, 1953–8).

Roeck, B., Als wollt die Welt schier brechen. Eine Stadt im Zeitalter des Dreißigjährigen Krieges (Munich, 1991).

Roger sieur de Prade, J. Le, The History of Gustavus Adolphus Surnamed the Great (London, 1689).

Rogers, C. J. (ed.), The Military Revolution Debate: Readings on the Military Transformation of Early Modern Europe (Boulder, CO, 1995).

Rosenthal, G., Zur Erinnerung an die Lützener Gustav-Adolf-Jubelfeier (Halle, 1882).

Rößler, C. G., Erinnerungen an Gustav Adolph König von Schweden in einer gedrängten Uebersicht der Hauptbegebenheiten des Dreißigjährigen Krieges (Merseburg, 1832).

Rotter, A., 'Großmann und die Gründung der Gustav Adolf Stiftung', EvDia, 72 (2003), 110–30.

Rudert, O., 'Der Verrat von Leipzig', Neues Archiv für Sächsische Geschichte und Altertumskunde, 35 (1914), 68–87.

Sack, H., der Krieg in den Köpfen. Die Erinnerung an den Dreißigjährigen Krieg in der deutschen Krisenerfahrung zwischen Julirevolution und deutschen Krieg (Berlin, 2008).

Sandstedt, F. et al. (eds), In hoc signo vinces. A Presentation of the Swedish State Trophy Collection (Stockholm, 2006).

Schiller, F., Geschichte des Dreissigjährigen Krieges (Munich, 1966: DTV edn).

Schmidt, A., Vaterlandsliebe und Religionskonflikt. Politische Diskurse im Alten Reich (1555–1648) (Leiden, 2007).

Schmidt-Biggemann, W., 'The Apocalypse and Millenarianism in the Thirty Years War', in K. Bussmann and H. Schilling (eds), 1648: War and Peace in Europe (3 vols, Münster, 1998), I 259–63.

Schuberth, I., *Lützen—på spaning efter ett minne* (Stockholm, 2007).

Schuberth, I. and M. Reichel (eds), *Wallenstein. Die blut'ge Affair' bei Lützen* (Dößel, 2012).

Schürger, A., 'Die Schlacht von Lützen 1632: Archäologische Untersuchungen auf dem linken kaiserlichen Flügel', in H. Meller (ed.), *Schlachtfeldarchäologie* (Halle, 2009), pp.135–49.

Schürger, A., 'The Archaeology of the Battle of Lützen: An Examination of 17th Century Military Material Culture' (University of Glasgow PhD, 2015).

Scott, C. L., A. Turton, and E. Guber von Ani, *Edgehill. The Battle Reinterpreted* (Barnsley, 2005).

Seidler, J., *Untersuchungen über die Schlacht bei Lützen 1632* (Memmingen, 1954).

Seidler, J., *Das Prager Blutgericht 1633* (Memmingen, 1962).

Seidler, J., *Besteht noch ein Lützenproblem?* (Memmingen, 1971).

Seitz, H., 'Värjan och dödsskotten', *Livrustkammaren*, 16 (1982), 22–31.

Sennewald, R., *Das Kursächsische Heer im Dreissigjährigen Krieg* (Berlin, 2013).

Sielaff, P., *Meuchen gab dem bei Lützen gefallenen König Gustav Adolf den ersten Ruheplatz und setzte ihm das erste Denkmal* (Leipzig, 1906).

Ritter von Srbik, H., 'Zur Schlacht von Lützen und zu Gustav Adolfs Tod', *Mitteilungen des Instituts für österreichische Geschichtsforschung*, 41 (1926), 231–56.

Stadler, B., *Pappenheim und die Zeit des Dreißigjährigen Krieges* (Winterthur, 1991).

Stanford, C. S., *The Life and Campaigns of Alexander Leslie, First Earl of Leven* (London, 1899).

Stevens, J. L., *History of Gustavus Adolphus* (London, 1885).

Struck, W., *Johann Georg und Oxenstierna. Von dem Tode Gustav Adolfs (November 1632) bis zum Schluß des ersten Frankfurter Konvents (Herbst 1633)* (Stralsund, 1899).

Suvanto, P., *Die deutsche Politik Oxenstiernas und Wallenstein* (Helsinki, 1979).

Swedish General Staff, *Sveriges Krig 1611–1632* (8 vols, Stockholm, 1936–9).

Taeglichsbeck, F., *Das Treffen bei Steinau an der Oder am 11 Oktober 1633* (Berlin, 1889).

Teske, G., *Bürger, Bauern, Söldner und Gesandte. Der Dreißigjährige Krieg und der Westfälische Frieden in Westfalen* (Münster, 1997).

Thoma, A., *Das Leben Gustav Adolfs für deutsche Volk* (3rd edn, Heidelberg, 1932).

Thomas, A. L., *A House Divided. Wittelsbach Confessional Court Cultures in the Holy Roman Empire, c.1550 1650* (Leiden, 2010), pp.289–90.

T[ooke], G., *The Eagle-Trussers Elegie. A Tract Bewailing the Losse of that Incomparable Generalissimo Gustavus Adolphus* (London, 1660).

Trench, R. C., *Gustavus Adolphus* (London, 1865).

Tschopp, S., *Heilsgeschichtliche Deutungsmuster in der Publizistik des Dreißigjährigen Krieges. Pro- und antischwedische Propaganda in Deutschland 1628 bis 1635* (Frankfurt, 1991).

Umbach, M., *Federalism and Enlightenment in Germany 1740–1806* (London, 2000).

Volz, G. B. and F. v. Oppeln-Bronikowski (eds), *Die Werke Friedrichs des Großen* (10 vols, Berlin, 1912–14).

Vortisch, H., *Gustav Adolf, Christ und Held* (Potsdam, 1930).

Vötsch, J., *Kursachsen, das Reich und der mitteldeutsche Raum zu Beginn des 18. Jahrhunderts* (Frankfurt, 2003).

Watson, F., *Wallenstein. Soldier under Saturn* (London, 1938).

Wedgwood, C. V., *The Thirty Years War* (London, 1957).

Weibull, M., *Gustav II Adolf. Ein minnesbild* (Lund, 1883).

Weigel, H., 'Franken im Dreißigjährigen Krieg', *Zeitschrift für bayerische Landesgeschichte*, 5 (1932), 1–50.

Weigley, R. F., *The Age of Battles. The Quest for Decisive Warfare from Breitenfeld to Waterloo* (London, 1993).

Weigley, R. F., 'Auf der Suche nach der Entscheidungsschlacht. Lützen, 16 November 1632', in S. Föster, D. Walter, and M. Pöhlmann (eds), *Schlachten der Weltgeschichte* (Munich, 2004), pp.138–53.

Wild, F. K., *Leben Gustav Adolfs des Großen, König von Schweden. Zur Belehrung, Verehrung und Erbauung für das Volk* (Basel, n.d.).

Wilson, P. H., 'The Causes of the Thirty Years War 1618–48', *English Historical Review*, 123 (2008), 554–86.

Wilson, P. H., 'Dynasty, Constitution and Confession: The Role of Religion in the Thirty Years War', *International History Review*, 30 (2008), 473–514.

Wilson, P. H., *Europe's Tragedy. The Thirty Years War* (London, 2009).

Wilson, P. H., *The Thirty Years War. A Sourcebook* (Basingstoke, 2010).

Wilson, P. H., 'Meaningless Conflict? The Character of the Thirty Years War', in F. C. Schneid (ed.), *The Projection and Limitation of Imperial Powers 1618–1850* (Leiden, 2012), pp.12–33.

Wilson, P. H., 'Atrocities in the Thirty Years War', in M. O'Siochrú and J. Ohlmeyer (eds), *Ireland 1641. Context and Reactions* (Manchester, 2013) pp.153–75.

Wilson, P. H., *The Holy Roman Empire. A Thousand Years of Europe's History* (London, 2016).

Wilson, P. H., 'The Stuarts, the Palatinate, and the Thirty Years War', in S. Wolfson and V. Caldari (eds), *Marriage Diplomacy: Early Stuart Dynastic Politics in Their European Context, c.1604–1630* (Woodbridge, 2017).

Yonge, C. D., *Parallel Lives of Ancient and Modern Heroes* (London, 1858).

Zschoch, H., 'Größe und Grenzen des "Löwen von Mitternacht". Das Bild Gustav Adolfs in der populären protestantischen Publizistik als Beispiel religiöser Situationswahrnehmung im Dreißigjährigen Krieg', *Zeitschrift für Theologie und Kirche*, 91 (1994), 25–50.

PICTURE ACKNOWLEDGEMENTS

01. Portrait of Albrecht Wenzel Eusebius von Wallenstein, engraved by Pieter de Jode (1606-c.1678) printed by G.H., after 1625 (engraving), Dyck, Sir Anthony van (1599–1641) (after) / Deutsches Historisches Museum, Berlin, Germany / © DHM / Bridgeman Images

02. By Matthäus Merian; Foto: H.-P.Haack, Leipzig (Slg. H.-P.Haack, Leipzig) [Public domain], via Wikimedia Commons

03. Author's collection

04. Lützen Museum

05. Gustavus Adolphus praying before the battle of Lützen'/Uppsala University Library (Sweden) Ref: III 91

06. © 2015. Photo Scala, Florence/bpk, Bildagentur fuer Kunst, Kultur und Geschichte, Berlin

07. © 2015. Photo Scala, Florence/bpk, Bildagentur fuer Kunst, Kultur und Geschichte, Berlin

08. Museum of Military History, Vienna

09. Photo: Knud Petersen. © 2015. Photo Scala, Florence/bpk, Bildagentur fuer Kunst, Kultur und Geschichte, Berlin

10. Gustavus Adolphus as 'Lion of the North' 1632, Uppsala University Library (Sweden). Ref: III 20

11. Royal Armoury Stockholm (CC By-SA) 3.0 Attribution-Share Alike

12. Royal Armoury Stockholm (CC By-SA) 3.0 Attribution-Share Alike

13. © 2015. Photo Scala, Florence/bpk, Bildagentur fuer Kunst, Kultur und Geschichte, Berlin

14. Anonymous copperplate, c.1706 in the Engraving collection of the Stiftung Luthargedenkstätten, fl VIII 11090 / Luther Memorial Foundation in Saxony-Anhalt

15. National Library of Sweden

16. Author's collection

17. Lützen Museum Inv.Nr. V/K2-206

18. Author's collection
19. Author's collection
20. Dean Per Pehrssons archive (Prosten Per Pehrssons arkiv), volume 30. Kept by The Regional State Archives in Gothenburg
21. Dean Per Pehrssons archive (Prosten Per Pehrssons arkiv), volume 30. Kept by The Regional State Archives in Gothenburg

INDEX

Royalty and German princes appear in order of their first names, while all other individuals, including lesser German aristocrats, are indexed by their family name.